PRAISE FOR *SOULWISE*

"I couldn't put Phil Johnson's book down. It is a full education on the problems of the world and the roles that caring people can play to improve the lives of other members of the human family. Phil is passionate and inspiring about helping others and shows you how to do it. As an author of *Up and Out of Poverty*, I couldn't help but think that Phil Johnson is the Good Samaritan role model for the spirit and passion needed to lift countless millions out of poverty."

—Philip Kotler, Professor of International Marketing,
Northwestern University

"*Soulwise* is a rich compendium of actions needed to alleviate the world's woes, written by a wise and loving man whose life has been devoted to helping others. This book will awaken you to the possibilities of human potential."

—William E. Halal, Professor of Management,
George Washington University.

"Dr. Phil Johnson's tested seven-step guide to becoming a Soulwise Conspirator enables readers to transform the human family by the power of compassion."

—Bob Danzig, former President,
Hearst Newspapers

"That our world is seriously sick is a foregone conclusion. With timely insight, modeling, reflection and direction, Dr. Johnson points us to three things on the pathway toward healing—hope, health and harmony. *Soulwise* is a masterpiece—a must read for all who seek to make our world a better place."

—Dr. Peter Okaalet, Africa Director,
Medical Assistance Programs International

"*Soulwise* is packed with hope and possibilities for those who desire to make a difference. It offers leaders around the world a road map to significance and life-changing results."

—**Ron Tschetter, former Director,**
United States Peace Corps

"Dr. Phil Johnson is an intellectual who truly speaks from the heart. If you want to change the world and don't know where to start, this book will show you how."

—**Barbara Pietrangelo, Executive Board Member,**
Million Dollar Round Table

"Phil Johnson wants to change the world, promoting hope to counteract the cynicism of our time. He believes spiritual renewal is essential for a harmonious world."

—**Tony Campolo, Professor of Sociology,**
Eastern University

"This warm, compassionate, compelling book is a paean to hope - to its power to both inspire and save. Phil Johnson shows by his own extraordinary life what people, individually and collectively, can do to make a better world."

—**Arnold Brown, Futurist,**
coauthor of *FutureThink*

"Phil Johnson writes for the sake of action and change. Readers cannot just read, but must face up to doing, living and growing. Phil forces this confrontation: the world is not getting on so well, and you and I can do something about that."

—**Mark Fackler, Professor of Communication,**
Calvin College

OTHER BOOKS BY THE AUTHOR

Time-Out! Restoring Your Passion for Life, Love and Work
Celebrating the Seasons with Children
More Celebrating the Seasons with Children
And More Celebrating the Seasons with Children
Goodbye Mom, Goodbye
The Great Canadian Alphabet Book

SOULWISE

How to Create a Conspiracy of Hope, Health and Harmony

DR. PHIL JOHNSON

Mention of specific companies, organizations, or authorities in this book does not imply endorsement by the publisher, nor does mention of specific companies, organizations, or authorities imply that they endorse this book.

Internet addresses given in this book were accurate at the time it went to press.

For information about special discounts for bulk purchases for business or promotional use, please contact: Special Markets Department, nanohouse press, 6757 Cascade Rd. SE, PMB 132, Grand Rapids, MI 49546 or online at livesoulwisenow.com.

Printed in the United States of America

Book design by Amy Cole of a.c. studio l.l.c.

Author photograph by David DeJonge of DeJonge Studio

FIRST EDITION

Library of Congress Cataloging-in-Publication Data

Johnson, Philip Ernest, 1943-

Soulwise: how to create a conspiracy of hope, health and harmony / Philip E. Johnson—1st ed.

p. cm.

Includes bibliographical references and index.
ISBN–13   978-0-9842592-0-5   hardcover
ISBN–10   0-9842592-0-1 - hardcover
Library of Congress Control Number: 200938760

1. Self-help. 2. Spiritual life. 3. Religion. 4. Soul. 5. Johnson, Philip, 1943- .
I. Title.

Soulwise is a trademark of Philip E. Johnson used herein under license.

DEDICATED
TO
MY GRANDDAUGHTERS
ELSA MELODY BALSITIS
AND
REBEKAH GRACE HURLEY

ACKNOWLEDGEMENTS

My experiences at home and around the world forged this book and I am deeply grateful to my family, friends, colleagues, parishioners and students who have enriched my life.

I especially want to express my appreciation to my wife, Melody, who inspires me to dream and do the impossible.

I also want to thank the following for their support: The saints at New Day Church-On-The-Hill in Grand Rapids, Michigan, the members of Exodus Church in Kibera slum who faithfully coordinate Kibera Kids Kitchen, and the Rev. Professor Godfrey Nguru, Vice-Chancellor of Daystar University.

For their individual and collective contribution to my book's success, I offer my thanks to the following: Lee Dean for his conceptual assistance, Barbara McNichol for her superb editing, Amy Cole for her creative book design and production assistance, Nido Qubein for writing the Foreword, Sandy Gould and the printing team at Color House Graphics for their excellence, literary agent Michael Larsen for his encouragement, and Rotarians around the world who put service above self.

TABLE OF CONTENTS

FOREWORD

Achieving a life of success and significance, in both business and in life, does not happen without a well-thought plan. Life is all about choices. We choose to expand our horizons by learning to stretch our wings and attempt new adventures. We choose to invest our time with heroes, models, and mentors who teach us through example. We choose to become better tomorrow than we are today. These are all components of a plan to develop a path for achieving our life goals.

If any of these concepts or ideas catch your interest, you're in the right place. The book that you hold in your hands will inspire you with an energetic perspective on what it takes to build a positive and nurturing life plan that positions you for a life of hope, health and harmony.

For the timid change is frightening and for the comfortable change is threatening. But, for the confident, change is opportunity.

This book may spark in you the need to change certain aspects in your life, the need to redirect your ambitions, or the need to seek out new mentors or like-minded individuals.

By following Dr. Phil Johnson's sound advice, you will soon develop a personal power that arms you with the tools necessary to compete and cooperate in our changing world. Every improvement you experience is the result of change. And every change can lead to new and better things as long as you are focused on achieving a life of significance.

Lest you think this book is simply a spiritual, feel-good book, take note in the urgency and power behind every word. Dr. Johnson outlines

1

how our world is quickly changing, and how the need for soulful, purpose-driven leaders has never been greater. Today's successful leaders require professional drive, passionate persistence, and positive dedication to compete in a global and technology-based marketplace. I truly believe in my heart that success does not come to you, you must go to it. The path is well-traveled, but we must take the appropriate steps that will take us where we need—and want—to be.

This spiritual journey will transform your definition of living a life of significance. Study the ideas and tenets laid out before you and apply them to your personal and professional life.

Remember, life is about choices. Decide here and now that you want to make the world a better place, and build a plan that will take you there!

Dr. Nido Qubein
President, High Point University
Chairman, Great Harvest Bread Co.

INTRODUCTION

One sweltering afternoon in Kibera slum in Nairobi, Kenya, a distraught young woman ran up to me and screamed, "Help! Help my baby! He choked and stopped breathing!" Then she thrust her infant into my arms.

I put my cardiopulmonary resuscitation (CPR) training to work as I called for medical help. I laid the six month old on the ground and confirmed that he wasn't breathing. I opened his mouth to see if I could locate any obstruction and discovered a small bone lodged in his throat. With my little finger, I gently removed the bone and gave him two quick rescue breaths. He began to breathe. I sighed and gave the little boy back to his grateful mother.

In fewer than 30 seconds, I saved a child's life, thanks to my CPR course. This experience triggered a question: how many children and adults in our global family are choking—in more profound ways than this—and needing urgent care?

William Garvelink, United States ambassador to the Democratic Republic of the Congo, answered this question when he said, "On any given day in the world, there are 40 million people displaced from their homes due to civil conflict and natural disasters, another 820 million who need food aid, and another 37 million who are living in their homes but have no access to food, health care, or potable water because of conflict going on around them."

Garvelink's statement haunts me. *Almost a billion members of our global family are in critical condition and at risk of "choking" to death.* This state of emergency compelled me to write *Soulwise: How to Create a Conspiracy of Hope, Health and Harmony* and initiate a movement also called The Soulwise Conspiracy. I must reach out with compassion and breathe life and hope into my brothers and sisters.

There isn't a second to spare. Gradual action will not help, as we know from the famous frog experiment. When boiling water was poured on a frog in a beaker, it jumped out instantly. However, when the water in the beaker was gradually heated to a boil, the frog boiled to death. That's exactly how we've been adjusting to turmoil on our planet.

In contrast to my sense of urgency, American singer John Mayer insists in one of his songs that he is "Waiting for the World to Change." Here's the letter I wrote challenging John to have compassion in what he describes in another song as the "Real World."

Dear John:

Thanks for your music. You're a gifted musician and singer, and have achieved tremendous popularity and success. Congratulations.

The lyrics of your hit song, "Waiting for the World to Change," intrigue me and are burned into my internal hard drive. That's what troubles me. The message of the song as I hear it is to lull listeners into complacency. "So we keep waiting, waiting on the world to change." You repeat the word "waiting" 16 times.

What astounds me is that you encourage a "generation" that you describe as "aware and caring" to wait for some magical moment in the future to change the world. You sing with certainty, "One day our generation is gonna rule the population."

The stark reality is that your "generation" may never have the chance to "rule the population" because there may not be a civilization. We can't wait, John. Millions in our global family need people of every generation to step up to the plate. We need you to use your influence now in order to fulfill our responsibility as global citizens.

If you really do "see everything that's going wrong with the world and those who lead it," then how could you just sit back and not "rise above and beat it." How could you possibly wait until you have "the means" in a world where often the "fight ain't fair"?

John, there's no time to wait. We must act now! Through your music, you can inspire your generation to breathe hope into our global family. Instead of "waiting on the world to change," become a Soulwise Conspirator and shape the future of humankind.

Stop waiting, John. Get your rear in gear and save the world.

Cheers!

Phil

Soulwise: How to Create a Conspiracy of Hope, Health and Harmony confronts this choking crisis head on and recommends a strategy that will give hope for humanity. It's divided into the following four parts:

Part I, The Soulwise Conspiracy—offers the promise for humanity to survive and thrive.
- The Dream: One World One Family
- The Primary Principle: Interdependence

Part II, Our World Is In Critical Condition—diagnoses the health of the global family.
- Seven Inconvenient Truths
- Seven Deadly Attitudes

Part III, The Soulwise Conspirators—describes the radical nature of people who dare to confront inconvenient truths and implore others to join them in breathing life into our global family.

- The Conspirators' Core
- Radical Global Servant Leaders

Part IV, A Guide to Becoming a Soulwise Conspirator—introduces readers to the basic theory and practical skills needed to breathe hope into humanity. Each of the seven chapters in this part focuses on one of these essential steps:

- Discover Your Passion
- Define the Need
- Dream the Need Fulfilled
- Draft Your Dream Team
- Develop Your Strategy
- Declare Your Dream
- Deliver Your Dream

Journalist Norman Cousins observed, "History is a vast early warning system." And the warning signs of our global predicament are there for all to see. As another warning system, The Soulwise Conspiracy is a movement that challenges and inspires you to unleash your collective capacity to care for our human family. As a citizen of vision and courage, it calls on you to help breathe life into our suffocating world and satisfy humanity's hunger for hope.

Thank you for joining me in an urgent dialogue to shape the future of our global family. Read on to appreciate The Soulwise Conspirator's:

- Dream of One World One Family,
- Core conviction and values, and
- Role as a radical global servant leader.

Discover how you, as a Soulwise Conspirator, can:

- Serve others in the world,
- Impact the future significantly, and
- Leave a lasting legacy.

I encourage you to join The Soulwise Conspiracy. Don't delay. Read this book, which is the clarion call for The Soulwise Conspiracy movement. Then go to the website (www.livesoulwisenow.com) and join. Become an integral part of a global life-saving enterprise so that our global family—including all nations—will survive and thrive.

The mission of The Soulwise Conspiracy can be summarized in this inspiring Franciscan benediction.

May God bless you with discomfort
At easy answers, half-truths, and superficial relationships
So that you may live deep within your heart.

May God bless you with anger
At injustice, oppression, and exploitation of people
So that you may work for justice, freedom, and peace.

May God bless you with tears
To shed for those who suffer pain, rejection, hunger, and war
So that you may reach out your hand to comfort them and
To turn their pain into joy.

And may God bless you with enough foolishness
To believe that you can make a difference in the world
So that you can do what others claim cannot be done
To bring justice and kindness to all our children and the poor.
Amen.

PART I

THE SOULWISE CONSPIRACY

CHAPTER 1

THE DREAM: ONE WORLD ONE FAMILY

My dream of realizing the concept I call The Soulwise Conspiracy began while snuggling on my mother's lap when she'd spin a globe and ask, "Philip, where shall we go today?" Ah, my first taste of a lasting passion for international relations and travel. We felt free to go anywhere in the world. And we did. One day, we'd travel to Brazil, another day Greenland, and another Bolivia. But my favorite place in the whole world? The continent of Africa.

My mother, a realist, didn't spare me stories about the inequities of our human family. She explained that millions of people in the world didn't have enough food to eat, that it's the responsibility of those with plenty of food to share it. And she walked her talk by coordinating a food pantry that served 125 families every week.

My mother had planted revolutionary seeds of her world view in the fertile soil of my soul. I have both intentionally and unintentionally cultivated these seeds throughout my life, traveling to various parts of the world and meeting the people I'd only imagined as a child.

Fast forward to July 3, 2004. My wife, Melody, and I were returning to Nairobi, Kenya, after three wonderful days at the Masai Mara Game Reserve. I didn't feel well as we were leaving the hotel, but I assumed I'd feel better once we were on our way to Nairobi. As we arrived there, though, I thought I would die. And I *was* dying. I had contracted malaria and typhoid fever.

But I was lucky. I got medical treatment right away. Little Joe, a six-year-old Kenyan boy I knew, wasn't so lucky. He died of malaria in early 2005. Sadly, Little Joe was one of 3,000 children in Africa who die *every day* from malaria.

> *This life-changing experience spurred me on to create The Soulwise Conspiracy movement and write a book—the one you're holding—to help fund the prevention of malaria in children in Africa.*

Why do I use the term "conspiracy" in The Soulwise Conspiracy? After all, conspiracy refers to overthrowing a government or other authority, which is usually viewed negatively. Yet, on close examination, "conspiracy" derives from the Latin *conspirare*, to breathe together—*the very action I envision humanity taking to save our choking global family.* Thus, my dream became this: *learning to breathe together for the common good, to breathe life into a suffocating world—One World One Family.*

Chapter 1 presents the three integrated dimensions of my dream and The Soulwise Conspiracy movement: hope, health and harmony.

THE DREAM OF HOPE

Arouses Hope

"Hope," said Aristotle, "is the dream of the waking man." I believe it's the earnest desire of every human being, the capacity to believe that no matter what happens, the future will be worth living. Life *without* hope is death; life *with* hope energizes the human spirit.

Hope arouses a passion for the possible. It has, as Barack Obama maintained in his 2008 U.S. election campaign, an audacious quality. Hope may not logically persuade us that better days will come, but it can uplift our feelings so we can endure and strive for tomorrow.

Here's an example of the audacious quality of hope from my own experience. One of my parishioners in his late 70s was convinced he'd have no tomorrows due to his deteriorating physical condition. As he shared his concern, he told me he'd be seeing his doctor the following day. I asked him to call me after the appointment. At four o'clock that day, he told me his doctor gave him two options: he could confine himself to a wheelchair for the rest of his life or he could do whatever he wanted and take his chances. "Which option did you choose?" I asked. He replied, "Right now, I'm on the roof cleaning out the gutters."

The Soulwise Conspiracy represents the idea of hope declared boldly—hope that refuses to let fear immobilize anyone, anytime, anywhere. The Conspiracy frames the future as a time for seizing the day, for looking up and seeing a beautiful panorama on the horizon. It's a time for fresh beginnings, a blank page, or what the Romans called *tabula rasa*, a clean slate.

Hope throws rays of light on the darkness of our lives, living and breathing powerfully between the memory of the past and the mystery of the future. It appreciates the temporal tension that permeates our lives and enables humankind to learn from the past, live in the present, and anticipate the future.

In September, 2000, the United Nations aroused hope for our human family by setting The Millennium Goals—eight specific, quantifiable, and time-bound goals for social and economic development to be achieved by 2015. These goals are:

Goal 1   Eradicate extreme poverty and hunger
Goal 2   Achieve universal primary education
Goal 3   Promote gender equality and empower women
Goal 4   Reduce child mortality
Goal 5   Improve maternal health
Goal 6   Combat HIV/AIDS, malaria, and other diseases
Goal 7   Ensure environmental sustainability
Goal 8   Develop a global partnership for development

Together, these eight Millennium Goals convey that, as a global family, we're committed to creating a future of hope. (For a detailed description of the Millennium Goals, go to www. un.org/millenniumgoals.)

Consider The Soulwise Conspiracy an agent of hope.

Embraces Hope

How do you embrace hope? You *decide* to have it.

It's a conscious choice, an inside job. Some people hide under the dark covers of hopelessness for their entire lives. Persuaded that living in the light is not "in the cards" or that their present conditions will never change, they choose to remain in the dark. Some become addicted to the dark or its opposite, the light. Ironically, some prominent public figures—athletes, actors, executives, politicians, media personalities—hide in the light of their fame, yet still feel hopeless.

Others, however, choose to embrace hope and savor its light. As conduits for the light, they not only improve their own lives but, like a prism, radiate rays of hope to others. They accept responsibility for their futures and embrace what lies ahead with their eyes wide open. Although they recognize no guarantees in life, they take responsibility for the theater they play in as scriptwriters, directors, and producers of their own stories.

Dr. Norman Vincent Peale often told a story about a professional baseball team in San Diego. Apparently, the team secured a number of fabulous hitters who, in the early games of the season, couldn't connect with the ball. The manager decided the team needed a new beginning and a hopeful new attitude. So he threw all the bats in a wheelbarrow and took them to a self-proclaimed faith healer located a few blocks from the stadium. The manager returned with the "healed bats" and declared that a new season was about to begin. The next day, the team took to the field and hit up a storm. They won that game and went on to win the title that year.

If we're willing to embrace hope, The Soulwise Conspiracy stands ready to provide encouragement and support on the journey. And we're not alone. Soulwise Conspirators work with us to help us overcome difficulties. Theirs is not a warm, fuzzy approach; akin to tough love, it challenges us to get our rears in gear, to fish or cut bait. It's based on knowing that a little hope goes a long way to launch us into a promising future.

In 1970, I was senior pastor of a circuit of 11 churches in St. Anthony, Newfoundland. In early September, a man born and raised in Korea (who worked at the Sir Wilfred Grenfell Hospital) came to my door and told me his family had finally arrived from Korea. Could I help his children, who couldn't attend school because they couldn't speak English? He'd been told that if the children, aged seven, nine, and eleven, could show the school superintendent their competence in English within one month, they would be accepted into the system and wouldn't miss a year of school.

What an expression on this proud father's face when I agreed to teach his three children English! It exploded with hope. We started our sessions the following morning. At first, we could only smile a lot at each other, but that became the foundation of our relationship. For four weeks, we met every day, Monday through Friday, for two hours in the morning and two hours in the afternoon. The children did another hour of homework each day and also watched Sesame Street, the children's educational program, to get acquainted with Big Bird and The Count. They quickly learned to count the numbers from one to ten, forward and backward, as well as sing the songs.

In less than one month, we met with the superintendent who, resistant and incredulous at first, agreed to integrate these bright Korean kids into their appropriate classes. Although I've lost track of them now, I know all three went on to finish college—all because we embraced hope.

The one who truly lives in hope dances without the music. For hope doesn't need accompaniment; it just *is*. Hope fortifies the desire and fosters the confidence to accomplish things that may seem impossible. That's the strategic value of hope.

Hope is not wishing upon a star and waiting for success to magically appear, nor is it blind optimism that sees the world through rose-colored glasses. Rather, hope enables us to move forward with determination. Like the story of "The Little Engine that Could," hope turns the mantra of "I think I can, I think I can" into "I thought I could, I thought I could" because hope enables our success.

We live between memory and mystery—the mystery that inspires us to go boldly where angels fear to tread, the same mystery that compels us to breathe life into a hurting world.

Shares Hope

The movement we call The Soulwise Conspiracy affirms that we are all trustees of hope with a responsibility to share it with members of our global family.

In One World One Family, we share our lives as brothers and sisters with hope. As the French novelist Victor Hugo wrote, we believe that "hope is the word which God has written on the brow of every man." Every man, woman, and child deserves to be prominently and permanently tattooed with hope, for hope is the language of grace that's universally understood.

Not reserved for an arbitrarily chosen few, hope is recognized as a gift for all members of the human family. It supports every effort to close the gap between the haves and have-nots because, in theory and in practice, there's enough for everyone. *No one has to live with scarcity.* Is this a pipe dream? Never. Not when we view our abundance as a collective blessing. That's when our hearts openly share with others as a privilege of membership in our global family.

> *We can't hoard hope. If we protect it as a personal privilege, then even the hope we have will disappear and die. Hope lives and breathes and grows because it is shared. The "Hopesters," as I call them, know this principle intuitively. They appreciate the vastness of the universe and accept their relative place in it. They accept what they have and don't complain about what they don't have.*

Eric Weiner, a National Public Radio foreign correspondent, has often reported from the most desperate and war-torn places on the planet. Because of this—and the fact that he doesn't consider himself to be a happy guy—he was determined to find a contrast. So he set out to find the world's happiest places for his book *The Geography of Bliss: One Grump's Search for the Happiest Places in the World.*

The book traces Eric's travels to nine countries including Great Britain, Qatar, India, Thailand, and the Netherlands, the home of the

World Database of Happiness. What did Eric discover? He found that money can buy happiness to a certain point, but beyond it, money isn't the key factor in feeling happy. He also learned that Bhutan, with its millions of poor people, has what he calls "a tremendous sense of community." The government has even instituted a Gross National Happiness index.

Clearly, the Bhutanese enjoy the communal gift of hope.

The "Hopesters" appreciate abundance and seek opportunities to share it with other members of our global family. Their satisfaction comes in sharing with no thought of a favor returned. People vibrant with hope live with their arms wide open, eager to share their blessings for the good of all. The Bill and Melinda Gates Foundation exemplifies this attitude of generous sharing. The Foundation's website confirms the belief that every person in our global family deserves to have hope. (See details at www.gatesfoundation.org)

Similarly, the Foundation for International Community Assistance was founded on the premise that credit, not charity, provides the surest way out of poverty for poor women and their families. As the organization's brochure proclaims, "This woman doesn't need your charity.... All she needs is a chance." (Details at www.villagebanking.org)

Its promise of "Small Loans—Big Changes" is borne out in the results of its benefactors. For example, Nigerian entrepreneur Patience Okpuigie in Benin City received a $400 loan through the online micro-finance organization Kiva for her tailoring business. Since receiving the loan, her business has been booming. She repaid the loan quickly and today makes a profit of about $90 a month.

> *When we all share, we all win.*

Muhammad Yunus, 2006 winner of the Nobel Peace Prize, wrote in his book *Banker to the Poor: Micro-lending and the Battle Against World Poverty* that all human beings have an innate survival skill. The fact that poor people are *alive* is proof of that! Giving the poor access to credit allows them to use the skills they already have, produce a profit, and retain capital to rise out of poverty. I have seen this theory at work with incredible results. (Information at www.grameen-info.org)

Here's another example. In 2007, Ann Fackler from Grand Rapids, Michigan, trained 23 Maasai women at Kilgoris in rural Kenya how to make, package, market, and sell palm/coconut soap. The women named their product *Osiligi*, which means "hope" in the Kimaasai language. They market it as Osiligi: Hope Soap and package it in small bags made from brightly colored *shukas*, which are blankets worn traditionally by Maasai men. A bar of soap costs 24 cents to produce and sells to tourists for the equivalent of two dollars at three Nairobi guesthouses. The women are "cleaning up" with their sustainable business enterprise.

Soulwise Conspirators dream of One World One Family in a way that arouses, embraces, and shares hope. The Soulwise Conspiracy inspires the deep conviction that, together, there's nothing our global family can't do!

THE DREAM OF HEALTH

The first dimension of the dream of One World One Family is hope. The second is health, an essential partner with hope at every age and stage of life.

In the 21st century, global health is a shared responsibility, involving both an equitable access to essential care and a collective defense against threats. The leading organization in this effort is the World Health Organization (WHO), which directs and coordinates authority for health within the United Nations system. It's responsible for providing leadership on global health matters, shaping the health research agenda, setting norms and standards, articulating evidence-based policy options, providing technical support to countries, and monitoring and assessing health trends.

To achieve its dream of health for every member of our human family, The Soulwise Conspiracy movement aims to treat, cure, and prevent disease.

Treats Disease

"First, do no harm." This saying is part of an oath that physicians take when they enter medical practice. The original Hippocratic Oath doesn't include this exact phrase, but it does contain a similar idea and holds credibility for contemporary caregivers. One translation reads, "Declare the past, diagnose the present, foretell the future; practice these acts. As to diseases, make a habit of two things, to help, or at least to do no harm."

The Soulwise Conspiracy upholds the high ideal of doing no harm and supports the principle of helping people live and die well—a principle embodied in this World Health Organization definition of health: "a state of complete physical, mental, and social well-being and not merely the absence of disease or infirmity."

> *Genuine health honors the body, mind, and soul.*
> *Together, they contribute to our individual and*
> *collective well-being.*

Doctors Without Borders exemplifies the spirit of the dream of health. It's an international medical humanitarian organization present in more than 60 countries. Its highly skilled volunteers assist people whose survival is threatened by violence, neglect, or catastrophe. Doctors and nurses provide urgent medical care regardless of race, religion, or politics.

We know that a person's attitude toward life influences his or her perspective on health and disease. A 1993 study by A. H. Eagly and S. Chaiken provided a comprehensive view of how people's behavior influenced and determined their attitudes. The study defined attitudes as evaluations of entities, including behavior, that result in perceptions of favor or disfavor. Consequently, attitudes may predispose individuals to adopt or reject specific health-related behaviors.

Treating or preventing disease, however, involves more than simply changing one's attitude or having a positive attitude to begin with. Diseases will still occur. Those who actively adopt The Soulwise Conspiracy believe in treating people who are ill without harming them as they help minimize their pain and distress. They believe that every member of the global family should have access to health care.

Technological advances have enabled medicine to dramatically improve diagnosis. Already, clinics and hospitals are beginning to store medical histories in far different forms than piles of paper. Many physicians can now access electronic medical records on a computer screen, and soon they will be able to view an onscreen avatar that's a walking, talking, three-dimensional representation of a patient's body.

By a single click on a body part or organ, a doctor and patient will be able to see an MRI or other image, laboratory results, and all your physician's text entries. Then the computer will automatically compare test results to millions of similar patient records, enabling the doctor to precisely diagnose and treat the patient. Although advanced technology like this is gradually becoming available to the developing world, its widespread use will require major investments of money and education. The dream of The Soulwise Conspiracy is that these technologies will be available in Kenya and Kabul as well as Kentucky.

Coupled with the technological advances are the discoveries of drugs that can treat diseases more effectively. For example, substantial breakthroughs have been achieved in drugs to treat persons afflicted with one of the big three diseases in the world: HIV/AIDS, malaria, and tuberculosis. Other drugs have contributed to treating diseases such as diabetes, cancer, heart disease, Alzheimer's, and arthritis. Intensive research continues to drive the development of drugs that will alleviate pain and extend life.

Cures Disease

As The Soulwise Conspiracy addresses disease, its proponents actively seek to discover cures for diseases.

Polio is one example. Although efforts to eradicate polio began in the 1960s, an intensive campaign started in 1988 and continues today with amazing results. Before this campaign began, this debilitating disease paralyzed about 1,000 children a day or 350,000 a year. Today, polio is still endemic to only four countries and cases of polio paralysis are about 1,000 a year. This dramatic decrease in the number of polio cases marks the most critical period of potential eradication and requires dedication and considerable resources to achieve the ultimate goal.

Some have called stem cells "biological blank checks" because they can be converted into any kind of cells in the body. Scientists believe that stem cells could produce cures or powerful new treatments for a wide range of dread diseases including diabetes, Parkinson's, and Alzheimer's as well as spinal chord injuries. This technique is especially promising because stem cells obtained from a patient's own tissues wouldn't be rejected by the person's immune system.

The effort to cure the "big three" is intensifying. In June 2007, the Group of 8—representatives from industrialized nations—pledged to commit $60 billion to fight AIDS, malaria, and tuberculosis. That's a considerable sum, but hardly enough to meet the need to provide treatment, care, and preventive services for even one of these diseases over the next few years.

Progress is being made. Also in June 2007, Dr. Pedro Alonso, the University of Barcelona professor who leads clinical trials for Glaxo-SmithKline, indicated that a new malaria vaccine worked in infants under one year old. The vaccine is made by fusing a bit of outer protein of the deadly *falciparum* strain of the malaria parasite with a bit of hepatitis B virus and a chemical booster. The latter two are added to provoke a stronger immune reaction. At least nine other malaria vaccines are in development.

> *In January 2008, the Bill and Melinda Gates Foundation, "dedicated to the idea that all people deserve to live a healthy and productive life," generously awarded The Rotary Foundation a challenge grant of $100 million for this global campaign to eradicate polio.*
> *The challenge has been accepted enthusiastically. The Rotary Foundation plans to match the grant dollar-for-dollar through fundraising over several years. In 2009, the Gates Foundation contributed an additional $225 million. Truly eradicating this crippling disease would represent a landmark public health achievement.*

Jeffrey Sachs, the Columbia University economist and author of *The End of Poverty*, put out a plan for eradicating malaria called the $10 solution. This $10 represents the cost to manufacture, ship, and distribute insecticide-treated bed nets designed to last up to five years. He estimated that spending $2 to $3 billion on malaria might save more than one million lives a year, making it "the best bargain on the planet." For the billion people living in high-income parts of the world, that amounts to $3 a person or one Starbucks coffee a year.

Sachs also recommended mobilizing Red Cross volunteers to distribute the bed nets and provide training in tens of thousands of villages across Africa. In a pilot project, the Red Cross distributed nets to more than half the residents of Togo in 2004 and Niger in 2005 with encouraging results. Two other organizations doing tremendous work in this area are Malaria No More (www.malarianomore.org) and Nothing But Nets (www.nothingbutnets.net).

Prevents Disease

The Soulwise Conspiracy movement is dedicated to the proverbial wisdom that an ounce of prevention is worth a pound of cure. This is particularly true in medicine. Anticipating disease enables us to nip it early so it doesn't cause injury, suffering, or death. Projecting the probability of epidemics enables us to prepare to reduce, if not eliminate, their devastating effects. The focus is on prevention, early diagnosis, and treatment.

Across the world, access to immunization varies greatly. For example, a child in a developing country is 10 times more likely to die of a vaccine-preventable disease than a child from an industrialized one. Immunization, however, is among the most cost-effective interventions. Since the 1980s, medicine has made considerable progress in immunization against measles, polio, pertussis, diphtheria, tetanus, and tuberculosis.

Granted, preventing disease takes an enormous amount of energy and resources. Warren E. Buffett's $31 billion gift to the Bill and Melinda Gates Foundation will help the Foundation pursue its longstanding goal of curing the globe's most fatal diseases. This enormous gift will do much more, including finding vaccines for AIDS and malaria. Melinda Gates said that her "fondest dream" is an AIDS vaccine, something that scientists have been pursuing for three decades but could take another two decades to realize. Bill Gates stated he wants to use improved global health as a base upon which to build what he called "the virtuous cycle" of longer lifetimes, jobs, markets, infrastructure, tax bases, and all other steps that lift poor countries out of poverty.

> *The Soulwise Conspiracy movement fosters and sustains a healthy climate and environment, respecting the abundance of all creation and honoring practices of responsible environmental stewardship. It understands the need to be dependable trustees of all the resources of the natural world and recognizes that future generations depend on it. Indeed, they will hold us accountable.*

The international communities must work together to protect our planet. Such a commitment was evident at the United Nations Intergovernmental Panel on Climate Change Conference held in Bali, Indonesia, in December 2007. There, 187 countries laid the groundwork for forging an agreement to cut emissions of carbon dioxide and other greenhouses gases, with the intent to replace the Kyoto Protocol when it expires in 2012.

THE DREAM OF HARMONY

The concept of a culture of peace was first elaborated for the United Nations Educational Scientific and Cultural Organization (UNESCO) at the International Congress on Peace held at Yamoussoukro, Cote d'Ivoire, in 1989. The Yamoussoukro Declaration called on UNESCO to "construct a new vision of peace by developing a peace culture based on the universal values of respect for life, liberty, justice, solidarity, tolerance, human rights and equality between women and men."

The United Nations declared the year 2000 the International Year for the Culture of Peace and 2001 to 2010 the International Decade for a Culture of Peace and Non-Violence for the Children of the World.

The UN's declaration of an International Year of Peace aligns with its peace role guidelines that bring clarity to the nature of international harmony. These guidelines include four major stages of conflict resolution and support for peace:

1. Conflict prevention—preventing and resolving conflict before it results in violence
2. Peace making—using diplomatic measures to negotiate a cease fire
3. Peace keeping—overseeing the preservation of peace agreements
4. Peace building—establishing a climate of tolerance and respect to rebuild society after conflict.

I have adapted these stages to reflect The Soulwise Conspiracy's commitment to a human family that *seeks* peace, *makes* peace, and *keeps* peace.

Seeks Peace

Be assured that if you're alive, you will experience conflict. Guaranteed. Next to death and taxes, you can count on conflict being around. Even in my reasonably well-adjusted family, we have conflict over what items to put on our pizza! "A healthy organization—whether a marriage, a family or a business corporation—is not one with an absence of problems," advised psychiatrist Dr. M. Scott Peck, "but one that is actively and effectively addressing or healing its problems."[1]

The Soulwise Conspiracy's primary emphasis is on seeking peace, including preventing conflict. It reflects a dream of peaceful coexistence, not just absence of war. Clearly, the only thing humans can control in war is the first shot taken. Conflict that leads to war and destruction wastes valuable time, energy, and human life. As Jeanette Rankin, the first woman elected to the United States House of Representatives and first female member of Congress in 1916, observed, "You can no more win a war than you can win an earthquake."

Preventing conflict is complex, which could be why so few serious national and international conflicts get resolved. It may seem easier to duke it out than work things out in a painstaking but non-violent way. Conflict resolution is hard work, yet its payoff outweighs the alternatives by far.

The Soulwise Conspiracy dream focuses heavily on education for peace and conflict resolution. Why? Because educating people is a less expensive and more effective way to attack the root causes of unrest before they explode into violence, and because winning a war is only a precondition to winning the peace.

Education for peace may provide a solid foundation on which to build lasting peace in the world. Part of this education requires learning the language of peace in the tongues of members of the global family. Living in harmony requires an appreciation of the words other members of the human family use to talk about harmony and the meanings those words convey.

Learning the languages of peace enables us to talk to each other and establish bonds of trust—so essential in preventing a conflict that could go out of control. Inevitably, history shows that conflict prevention boils down to trust. Even a quick review of our collective history can instruct and liberate us to work with each other no matter how different we are. Regrettably, people who don't know their own history (or others') tend to repeat it. War, as I said, is the antithesis of trust.

Seeking peace requires the three interrelated dimensions of:
- knowledge (self-awareness, recognition of prejudice, theories of conflict analysis, prevention, and resolution),
- skills (communication, active listening, patience, and self-control), and
- attitudes (tolerance, self-respect, and social responsibility).

> *Reviewing history informs and empowers people to intentionally create a culture of peace locally and internationally.*

As a peace-seeking influence, sport provides a universal avenue for promoting education, health, development, and peace. As the Olympic

Creed states, "The most important thing at the Olympic Games is not to win but to take part, just as the most important thing in life is not the triumph but the struggle. The essential thing is not to have conquered but to have fought well." The second sentence of the creed reflects the irony of the tradition of the Olympic Truce where warring factions would suspend fighting during the Games.

In July 2000, the International Olympic Committee (IOC) launched the International Olympic Truce Foundation and the International Olympic Truce Center (IOTC) as instruments to create a culture of peace in our times. The Olympic Truce Center (www.olympictruce. org) once again calls on humanity to lay down its weapons and work toward building the foundations of mutual respect, understanding, and reconciliation. An International Forum on Sport for Peace and the Olympic Truce (www.olympicspirit.org/press_070521_peacefo-rum.php) took place May 19-21, 2009, in Olympia, Greece, the cradle of the Olympic movement. This Forum was organized by the Greek government, IOTC, International Olympic Academy, and Greek National Olympic Committee.

IOC president, Jacques Rogge, who welcomed the participants as the president of the International Olympic Truce Foundation (IOTF), said at the opening of the International Forum, "The IOC was founded on the belief that sport, especially in an Olympic context, can bring benefits beyond those simply related to physical activity. Sport is a global language. It does not matter where you come from—every-one, given the chance, can speak 'Sport'! Sport fosters understanding between individuals, facilitates dialogue between divergent communi-ties and breeds tolerance between nations."

When the IOC revived the ancient concept of the Olympic Truce in 1992, the committee relayed it to the United Nations to garner a higher impact. Since 1993, the UN General Assembly has repeatedly expressed its support for the IOC by unanimously adopting, one year before each edition of the Olympic Games, a Resolution titled "Building a peaceful and better world through sport and the Olympic ideal." Through this symbolic Resolution, the UN invites its member countries to observe the Olympic Truce individually and collectively and, conforming with the goals and principles of the UN Charter, seek to settle all interna-tional conflicts through peaceful and diplomatic means.

Peace-seeking skills such as listening and compromise, coupled with attitudes of tolerance and respect, combine to keep disputing parties connected so they can resolve their differences amenably. In my experience as a mediator and arbitrator, negotiations break down when individuals lack these fundamental skills and attitudes.

Here's an example. A few years ago, I mediated a divorce in which the only contentious issue between the couple was custody of their eight-year-old boy. Naturally both parties wanted the best for their son. Because they lived on opposite coasts, they believed that sole custody would be the most beneficial solution for their child. After discussing the issues reasonably, they reached a compromise that everyone could live with.

> *To seek peace is to live peace day in and day out.*
> *It demands a commitment to start in the hearts*
> *and minds of individuals and then spread to our*
> *collective spirit and will.*

Makes Peace

Supporters of The Soulwise Conspiracy dream of a world that makes peace. They accept the reality that conflicts can and will arise, yet they have a responsibility to foster open dialogue that enables conflict resolution. They actively encourage diplomatic measures to negotiate ceasefires and establish terms of peace agreements that include the reconstruction of society. They echo this challenge from ordained priest and novelist James Carroll: "We must reclaim peace as possible." Carroll truly speaks in character; the word for "priest" originally meant "bridge-builder."

Diana Butler Bass, a scholar and author, posed this interesting question on October 11, 2006, after the Amish school shooting: "What if the Amish were in charge of the war on terror?" (www.beliefnet.com/blogs/godspolitics/2006) The Amish have an incredibly powerful practice of forgiveness demonstrated so poignantly after the tragic school shooting in Lancaster, Pennsylvania. More than 30 members of the Amish community attended the funeral of the man who killed five of their beloved children. We can learn a lot from their peacemaking attitude and actions.

Why not put the Amish in charge of the U.S. Department of Homeland Security? What would they have fashioned out of the 24 tons of molten scrap steel from the World Trade Center? I have a hunch it wouldn't have been the USS New York, a new class of warship designed for missions that include special operations against terrorists. The USS New York will carry a crew of 360 sailors and 700 combat-ready marines to be delivered ashore by helicopters and assault craft. Ironically, the ship's motto is "Never Forget."

The distinctions between war, civil unrest, terrorism, and crime have become increasingly blurred and conventional industrial-age force less effective. According to the 2006 State of the Future report, at least 75% of those killed or wounded in armed conflicts are noncombatants. The Conspiracy's desire to shift from *cross fire* to *cease-fire* protects combatants and innocent bystanders as well.

Building the peace is a twofold process that requires clearing away the structures of violence and creating the structures of peace. The failure to build new structures often sabotages peacekeeping efforts. According to the 2006 State of the Future report, one study found that 44% of countries affected by conflict return to war within five years of a cease-fire. Thus, peace, development, and democracy form an interactive, mutually reinforcing triangle.

Courageous examples of peace building abound. The 2007 book *Three Cups of Tea* by Greg Mortensen and journalist David Oliver Relin described how Mortensen, an American mountaineer, began building schools for peace. After a failed attempt to climb the K2 peak on Pakistan's border, the former U.S. Army medic met village children who didn't have paper or pencils. He promised to build them a school. He did build that school, then founded a nonprofit foundation called Central Asia Institute (www.ikat.org) and built more. By May 2009, he and his team had constructed 78 schools in Afghanistan and Pakistan. Mortensen operates from the belief that "education can overcome the despot leaders, dictators, and clergy who use illiteracy to control an impoverished society."

In another example of making peace, I think of Amani ya Juu. Whenever I go to Nairobi, Kenya, I visit Amani ya Juu, a sewing and reconciliation project for marginalized women in Africa. Amani ya Juu means "higher peace" in Swahili. The women involved in the project are learning to work together through a faith in God who provides a higher peace that transcends ethnic differences. The group itself displays a unique picture of diversity, with its members from Rwanda, Burundi, Congo, Uganda, Sudan, Kenya, Ethiopia, and Somalia as well as other African countries.

I met these remarkable survivors of atrocities; I listened to their personal testimonies and songs of reconciliation that inspired me to the depths of my soul. Instead of seeking revenge, they are dedicated to the practice of peace. The 500+ products they make range from colorful women's bags to soft toys to tie-dyed or wax-print place-mats and tablecloths. The intriguing piece that caught my eye was a beautifully crafted "Unity Quilt" that consists of 12 panels depicting how conflicts are resolved in 11 African countries. (You can view this "Unity Quilt" at www.amaniafrica.org/quilt.php)

One of the women, Veronica Godlaya, described to me how conflict is typically resolved in Sudan. After it's been decided that a dispute between two families needs to be settled, family members sit together with the elders and talk about the problem. Once the problem has been sorted out, each member involved spits into a pot, beginning from the youngest to the oldest. To spit into the *same* pot signifies nothing comes between them any longer. Then some of this spit is poured on the doors of conflicting parties' houses. The remaining spit is thrown in the direction of the setting sun to represent that the problem is disappearing. The light blue panel features three Sudanese dressed in bright colors seated on small stools around a large decorated pot. Each of the persons is spitting into the pot.

Keeps Peace

Soulwise Conspirators dream of a world of harmony that also seeks to keep peace.

Keeping the peace helps parties resolve a dispute and live by the terms of their peace agreement in a state of shared freedom. They're urged to be open to altering the terms of their agreements as needs change.

> *As Albert Einstein once observed,*
> *"Peace cannot be kept by force. It can only*
> *be achieved by understanding." That's why compro-*
> *mise may be the best medicine for keeping the peace.*
> *This point is reflected in my favorite line from the*
> *1984 movie Rhinestone Cowboy: "There'll be a lot of*
> *compromisin' on the way*
> *to my horizon."*

The *2006 State of the Future* report noted that peacekeeping is the second largest deployed military presence in the world, directly affecting the lives of 200 million people. In 2008, according to United Nations reports, 88,000 uniformed personnel and 17,000 civilians from 107 countries were serving in 20 UN peacekeeping operations. Peacekeeping professionals engage in dangerous work; the estimated number of United Nations staff members including peacekeepers who paid the ultimate price with their lives was 22 in 2006 and 42 in 2007.

Most often, people view conflict as a negative. However, conflict can be a positive influence in keeping the spirit of an agreement. John Dewey, an American psychologist, philosopher, educator, social critic, and political activist, described the benefits of conflict this way: "Conflict is the gadfly of thought. It stirs us to observation and memory. It instigates us to invention. It shocks us out of sheep-like passivity, and sets us at noting and contriving."[2]

For example, the bloody aftermath of the December 2007 presidential elections in Kenya revealed underlying conflicts that needed to be addressed. After 40 years of relative stability, Kenyans must now deal openly and creatively with their systemic difficulties to lead their country into a more positive future.

One of the best resources on peacekeeping is the Stanley Foundation, founded by Max Stanley, a wealthy businessman from Muscatine, Iowa. This Foundation brings fresh voices and original ideas to debates on global and regional problems. Its mandate seeks a secure peace based on world citizenship and effective global governance with freedom and justice built in. Its initiatives include actively supporting proposals for UN renewal put forward by the High-level Panel on Threats,

Challenges, and Change. The Foundation explores in depth the global security role that the United States could and should play in the 21st century. It also promotes avenues toward national and global security in light of continuing proliferation of nuclear weapons and increasing demand for energy alternatives.

Another major peacekeeping resource is the Carnegie Endowment for International Peace, a private nonprofit organization that advances cooperation among nations and promotes international engagement by the United States. Founded in 1910, its nonpartisan work seeks to achieve practical results. For example, in 2007, Carnegie Endowment launched its new vision, transforming itself from a private think tank on international issues to the first multinational global think tank addressing globalization, nonproliferation, and security affairs. The Endowment offers programs with leading experts on international affairs, particularly in Russia and Eurasia, China, the Indian subcontinent, and South Asia.

In his book, *Crucial Questions About the Future*, futurist Allen Tough offered an insightful summary of our predicament as a civilization. He wrote, "Human civilization today is vibrant, powerful, flourishing, rapidly changing, deeply concerned. Developed over thousands of years, it has now spread to every region of our planet, and occasionally to other bodies in our solar system. Human civilization includes a remarkable diversity of cultures, organizations, beliefs, worldviews, values, music, architecture, environments, capacities, and life-styles. It simultaneously encompasses altruism and selfishness, joy and misery, wealth and hunger, love and revenge, compassion and terrorism, peace and war, highly positive potentials and extraordinary dangers, penetrating insight and foolish shortsightedness.

"If we look ahead a few decades, we note that our civilization has enormous potential not only to flourish happily, but also to deteriorate appallingly. In fact, humanity literally has the capacity to exterminate itself, thus joining the many other species that have become extinct. However, our civilization also has the capacity to avoid the worst dangers and to flourish peacefully for thousands of years. At this peculiar moment in human history, our extreme potentials (for destroying everything and for achieving a highly positive future) may both be vaster than at any time during the past 10,000 years."[3]

What an exciting time to be alive! We stand at a crossroads for our civilization. One road leads to life in all its fullness, the other to extinction. Which path will we take?

Supporters of The Soulwise Conspiracy dream of One World One Family—an integrated dream of hope, health, and harmony. This dream can powerfully compel us to work tirelessly for a future of promise. I invite you to join Soulwise Conspirators around the globe in making this dream come true.

Soulwise Conspirators honor peace, negotiate and build peace, and maintain peace. They feel inspired by the meaning of this Chinese proverb that beautifully describes how peace moves from the individual soul to being embraced by the collective soul:

If there is light in the soul,
There will be beauty in the person.
If there is beauty in the person,
There will be harmony in the house.
If there is harmony in the house,
There will be order in the nation.
If there is order in the nation,
There will be peace in the world.

TAKE FIVE FOR REFLECTION

1. What would have to happen for the dream of One World One Family to be realized?

2. How have you been involved in achieving The Millennium Goals?

   Goal 1 – Eradicate extreme poverty and hunger

   Goal 2 – Achieve universal primary education

   Goal 3 – Promote gender equality and empower women

   Goal 4 – Reduce child mortality

   Goal 5 – Improve maternal health

   Goal 6 – Combat HIV/AIDS, malaria, and other diseases

   Goal 7 – Ensure environmental sustainability

   Goal 8 – Develop a global partnership for development

3. What signs of hope have you seen in the world? Where have they been?

4. Name three things you consider to be serious threats to the health of our earth.

   •

   •

   •

5. Name at least three steps global leaders can take to secure peace. What three steps can you take to make your own life more peaceful?

   •

   •

   •

CHAPTER 2

THE PRIMARY PRINCIPLE: INTERDEPENDENCE

N o one is an island. People may assert that they can live by themselves, but the stark reality is we need each other to live productive and prosperous lives. Indeed, the future of civilization depends on a reciprocal relationship between all the members of our human family.

The primary principle of The Soulwise Conspiracy is interdependence. Let's begin by exploring its premise.

THE PREMISE

We're All Related

In his final speech as secretary-general of the United Nations in January, 2007, Kofi Annan summarized the five lessons or principles he'd learned for conducting international relations during his 44 years at the United Nations. These principles include:

- collective responsibility,
- global solidarity,
- the rule of law,
- mutual accountability, and
- multilateralism.

Annan's first lesson is that "in today's world, the security of every one of us is linked to that of everyone else." Marin Luther King Jr.

echoed Annan's lesson in a convincing letter King wrote from jail on April 16, 1963. It read, "Moreover, I am cognizant of the interrelatedness of all communities and states. I cannot sit idly by in Atlanta and not be concerned about what happens in Birmingham. Injustice anywhere is a threat to justice everywhere. We are caught in an inescapable network of mutuality, tied in a single garment of destiny. Whatever affects one directly, affects all indirectly. Never again can we afford to live with the narrow, provincial 'outside agitator' idea. Anyone who lives inside the United States can never be considered an outsider anywhere within its bounds."[4]

My mother had pointed out to me that the lines on our family globe dividing countries identified special parts of the human family. As far as I could tell, everybody in the world was related. We were all members of one very large human family. When she and I talked about the people of various countries—what they looked like, how they dressed, how they worshipped, what they ate, what music they played, and what they did for fun—I realized they were different, but I always considered them family.

Although we're becoming increasingly interdependent, our world continues to be divided by economic, religious, and cultural differences. Former vice president of the United States Al Gore put our relatedness in perspective when he said, "And just as the false assumption that we are not connected to the earth has led to the ecological crisis, so the equally false assumption that we are not connected to each other has led to our social crisis."[5]

We're All Responsible

The second lesson Kofi Annan noted is that "we are not only all responsible for each other's security. We are also, in some measure, responsible for each other's welfare. Global solidarity is both necessary and possible."

An African proverb advises,
"It takes a village to raise a child."

The Declaration of Independence that the founding fathers of America's 13 original states unanimously signed in 1776, not only declared the independence of the United States of America but honored the individual and the importance of self-reliance.

The Declaration lifts up the ideal of individuals bonded together for a "more perfect union." Members of this union are responsible not only for themselves but also for each other. The principles of independence and interdependence are not mutually exclusive. On the contrary, like two sides of a coin, they are complementary.

Healthy independent people act interdependently. The old saying that "we may have come on different ships but we're all in the same boat now" is true. When one suffers, all suffer to some degree. When one rejoices, all can legitimately rejoice.

Anil Hira, an associate professor of political science, specializes in international political economy at Simon Fraser University in British Columbia, Canada. He has proposed systemic reform of global institutions as a way to create security in a world he believes has gone mad. As Hira pointed out, "What is good for us as individuals and as nations is in many ways directly tied in with the welfare of others."[6] Likewise, what is not good for us.

For example, we're all affected by global warming no matter where we live. We all feel the impact of market fluctuations on Wall Street and in other financial centers. And when I asked a convention audience of 1,500 how many had been affected directly or indirectly by cancer, every hand in the room went up.

We all have the privilege and responsibility to take care of each other and the universe—not only for ourselves but for those who will come after us. The Earth Charter is a statement of our shared values and principles. Initially conceived in 1987 at a United Nations Environment and Development Conference, the Charter was originally attempted at Rio Earth Summit in 1992 and subsequently launched at The Hague Peace Palace in June 2000.

> *The Earth Charter's values and principles became formulated and refined through sustained dialogue involving representatives of the world's cultural and spiritual traditions. The Earth Charter states: "We must join together to bring forth a sustainable global society founded on respect for nature, universal human rights, economic justice, and a culture of peace. Toward this end, it is imperative that we, the peoples of Earth, declare our responsibility to one another, to the greater community of life, and to future generations." The Earth Charter initiative continues to promote the transition to sustainable ways of living and a global society. It's founded on a shared ethical framework that includes respect and care for all life and ecological integrity.*

Leitourgia is the Greek word for liturgy, which literally means "the work of the people." Faith communities often refer to their worship as liturgy, the work of the people offered to honor and praise their Creator. As global citizens we're all related, and our "work of the people" is to care for and be responsible for one another. The Soulwise Conspiracy accepts its responsibility to breathe life into the world.

Now let's consider how we're all accountable to each other.

We're All Accountable

Secretary-General Annan's final speech at the United Nations concluded with these important lessons he'd learned about global accountability: "My third lesson is that both security and development depend on respect for human rights and the rule of law. My fourth lesson is that governments must be accountable for their actions in the international arena, as well as in the domestic one. My fifth lesson is that we can only do all these things by working together through a multilateral system, and by making the best possible use of the unique instrument bequeathed to us by Harry Truman and his contemporaries, namely the United Nations."

What goes around comes around. Living together on Planet Earth requires us to be responsible for each other and accountable to each other. The Roman philosopher Seneca described our mutual accountability this way: "We are members of one great body. Nature planted in us a mutual love, and fitted us for a social life. We must consider that we were born for the good of the whole."

Yes, we share a common public life that will determine our destiny. It's essential for our survival as a species to take seriously our accountability for all humankind and strive to form a community of citizens who look out for one another. If we don't care for each other, we'll never experience the richness of our human family.

> It's as if we're actors in an unfolding international
> family drama—each with his or her critical role
> to play on the world stage. Having passion for
> our individual parts isn't enough; we're expected as
> members of the human family to put our
> passion into action.

In Allen Tough's *Crucial Questions About the Future*, the futurist commented on what we might call global theater by saying, "Each of us can play a significant positive role in this extraordinary drama. Each of us can vigorously join the worldwide effort to improve humanity's prospects, even to change the course of human history. Each of us can choose this effort as our exhilarating mission in life, our highest purpose, our supreme challenge—our opportunities to participate in the ultimate human adventure!"[7]

Let the adventure continue as we address the promise of The Soulwise Conspiracy.

THE PROMISE

The primary principle of interdependence promises members of the global family freedom with its benefits as well as its responsibilities. In this section, I refer to Articles from the Universal Declaration of Human

Rights adopted and proclaimed by the General Assembly of the United Nations on December 10, 1948.

The Articles of the Declaration highlight three intersecting elements at the heart of interdependence: the freedom to be, the freedom to belong, and the freedom to become.

Freedom to Be

Interdependence declares that you have the freedom to be you.

Being is an art. Unfortunately, for many, the complexity and speed of contemporary living gives "doing" the edge over "being." I must confess that for most of my life I've been one of the "doers." When I announced to my family that I was writing a book about taking time off, they laughed. However, I learned by writing *Time-Out! Restoring Your Passion for Life, Love and Work* that "being" and "doing" are two dimensions of life, and that balancing them is critical to health and satisfaction.

Article 2 of the Declaration clearly sets out your right with these words: "Everyone is entitled to all the rights and freedoms set forth in this Declaration, without distinction of any kind, such as race, color, sex, language, religion, political or other opinion, national or social origin, property, birth or other status. Furthermore, no distinction shall be made on the basis of the political, jurisdictional or international status of the country or territory to which a person belongs, whether it be independent, trust, non-self-governing or under any other limitation of sovereignty."

But who *am* I? That's a question we ask our whole lives—an excellent question particularly because we only scratch the surface of our identity, which grows as we discover our real selves. The human search for meaning constantly changes. We experience a deep hunger to be just who we are in the world—with our idiosyncrasies, strengths and weaknesses, successes and failures, and hopes and fears.

Article 2 in its genius gives us permission to be ourselves today and tomorrow. The solid foundation of interdependence makes it possible to express our unique gifts and graces to the world. With a clear sense of our own being, we can accept our incredible creation and relate to other members of the human family with authenticity. Article 2 defines our right to be persons of worth. It encourages us to say "yes" to life in all its fullness, accept the creative power of our being, and affirm ourselves as self-determining.

Article 3 of the Universal Declaration of Human Rights states, "Everyone has the right to life, liberty and security of person." Interdependence assures us of the opportunity to find the distinctiveness of our "being," to communicate that distinctiveness to others, and to feel safe in doing so.

National Public Radio host Diane Rehm didn't feel safe being herself in her own family. Her book *Finding My Voice* explains how important it was for her to find and express her unique gifts. She describes how she endured physical and emotional abuse from her Turkish immigrant parents, especially the cruel treatment from her mother. At age 37, her career in broadcasting was spurred by the urging of her women's group.

In 1998, doctors diagnosed Rehm with spasmodic dysphonia, a rare neurological disorder that causes hoarseness and vocal tremors. This complicated her life, especially because her voice was key to her livelihood. Although she's found her voice professionally with a noteworthy career in broadcasting, Rehm still wrestles with what she considers personal inadequacy as she engages in finding her voice—both figuratively and literally. She continues to conduct insightful interviews on radio even though her voice is shaky.

It takes courage to live so that our being and the expression of our being are congruent. It's a challenge to walk the talk. Without courage, however, it's almost impossible to stand alone. Interdependence allows us to stand alone, openly and without fear of persecution, and to be respected for doing so. When one feels supported to be oneself by family (or by friends as Diane found in her women's group), one can have the inner confidence to fully be independent as well as interdependent.

Freedom to Belong

Interdependence declares that you have the human right to belong.

As human beings, we have an insatiable hunger to belong. We have a strong need for union with others and a deep desire for acceptance. At root, we want to feel secure in our relationships so we can live without fear of rejection in an atmosphere of mutual respect and unconditional love. That's a tall order.

> *Combining the freedom to "be" with the freedom to*
> *"belong" produces a significant tension.*
> *The first describes our individual being, and the*
> *second describes our human connection to other*
> *members of the global family. Whether we like it or*
> *not, we're irrevocably connected.*

When we strike a balance between our individuality and our collective spirit, we realize we're stronger together than apart. Only then can we fulfill our collective potential. As American psychologist William James reflected, "The community stagnates without the impulse of the individual. The impulse dies away without the sympathy of the community." (www.williamjamesassociation.org)

Freedom to belong begins with birth into a specific family of origin, which defines our national lineage and identity. Ancient wisdom says that home is where the heart is. To deny someone this identity strikes at the heart. Article 15 of the Universal Declaration of Human Rights confirms the importance of this national identity, stating, "Everyone has the right to a nationality.... No one shall be arbitrarily deprived of his nationality nor denied the right to change his nationality."

As we relate to the wider world, national identity is especially important. Parents or guardians who foster in their children a healthy foundation of individual identity plus national pride enable them to accept persons belonging to other nationalities. Each of us shares a common bond with every other human being on the planet. When we recognize that we're all part of one magnificently diverse family, our differences seem slight by comparison.

I am immensely proud of my Canadian heritage and still retain my Canadian citizenship even though I've lived in the United States with a green card for several years. When I served as a pastor in the late '70s in St. Anthony, a small fishing community of 2,500 in the north of Newfoundland, I'd often hear people say, "You can take the boy out of the Bay, but you can't take the Bay out of the boy." A significant part of me will always be Canadian, eh!

Interdependence declares that we have a right to belong to the global family, and moreover, that right comes with the responsibility to contribute to the family's common good. Article 1 of the Universal Declaration of Human Rights states, "All human beings are born free and equal in dignity and rights. They are endowed with reason and conscience and should act towards one another in a spirit of brotherhood."

As legitimate members of the human family, it's not enough for us to rest on our laurels. The global community expects its citizens to contribute to the common good, to our "commonwealth," a term that dates from the 15th century and literally meant "common well-being." The writers of the American Constitution captured this spirit of citizenship by adopting "commonwealth" to mean sharing the wealth and good fortune of the community.

When we recognize we belong to each other, we'll feel secure to work together in an atmosphere of mutual respect. Then we can understand the wisdom of psychologist Rollo May when he declared, "Our enemy is as necessary for us as is our friend. Both together are part of authentic community." Respecting our enemies with whom we strongly disagree constitutes the most challenging dimension of practicing interdependence. However, respect rather than alienation offers the possibility of forging a truly compassionate global community.

Mahatma Gandhi, the former political and spiritual leader of India, reflected on the interrelation of the freedom to be and the freedom to belong this way: "Interdependence is and ought to be as much the ideal of man as self-sufficiency. Man is a social being. Without interrelation with society he cannot realize his oneness with the universe or suppress his egotism. His social interdependence enables him to test his faith and to prove himself on the touchstone of reality."[8]

To feel at home in the world, we need to have the freedom to be, the freedom to belong, and the freedom to become. Let's turn our attention to the third freedom.

Freedom to Become

Interdependence declares that we have the freedom to become, promising a future we can actively create with other members of the human family.

Article 29 of the Universal Declaration of Human Rights indicates that every global citizen has the opportunity, and indeed the responsibility, to work with others to create a future of promise. "Everyone has duties to the community in which alone the free and full development of his personality is possible.... In the exercise of his rights and freedoms, everyone shall be subject only to such limitations as are determined by law solely for the purpose of securing due recognition and respect for the rights and freedoms of others and of meeting the just requirements of morality, public order and the general welfare in a democratic society."

To create the future, we need to accept that we're inseparably connected as human beings in this adventure we call life. The fulfillment of our dreams requires us to engage one another in the development of humankind. Together, we have the freedom to embrace a creative spirit to realize our potential and take pleasure in our creation. We hold an unlimited future in our hands.

> *Accepting each other in this grand adventure requires us to risk and support one another in both failure and success on the journey. None of us knows what the future may bring.*

Certainly St. Irenaeus of Lyons held this vision when he described humanity at its best this way: "The glory of God is man fully alive." Going forward together "fully alive" requires courage, sacrifice, and forgiveness. "A man's errors," commented writer James Joyce, "are his portals of discovery."

Without a solid foundation of trust, the transformation of society would be impossible. Trust enables the human family to progress—develop and mature—together in an environment characterized by stability, safety, and security. Although contemporary society yearns for this kind of basic trust, in many ways it's reluctant to take the risk. Our leaders bear an awesome responsibility to set the tone for trust, especially as the world "shrinks" with advanced technology and instant news.

Interdependence promises the freedom to be, the freedom to belong, and the freedom to become. It requires us to be bold adventurers in discovering the future. French novelist Marcel Proust said, "The real voyage of discovery consists not in seeing new lands, but in having new eyes." Humanity must be able to envision bold new possibilities for reality.

We've now considered the premise and promise of The Soulwise

Conspiracy's primary principle—interdependence. Next, let's turn to the program that brings this principle to life—a program to foster, practice, and declare it.

THE PROGRAM

Foster Interdependence

"For each one of us there is a moral imperative to increase the probability, by however little, of a better world," said Kenneth Boulding, economist, peace activist, devoted Quaker, and co-founder of General Systems Theory. "The more people accept this moral responsibility, the greater the probability of a better world will become."

The United Nations projects the most visible and active presence of interdependence in the world. Although the UN has come under fire—sometimes intense—UN officials readily admit its shortcomings and are working to shape the institution for its role in contemporary society.

Timothy Wirth, president of the United Nations Foundation and the Better World Fund, reported these findings from a 2006 poll that revealed how Americans view the UN: "It is clear that a majority of Americans recognize the value of the United Nations, believe in its mandate to provide a more peaceful and cooperative global society and value the UN as a vehicle for sharing the risks and costs of global security." (www.betterworldcampaign.org/newsroom/press_releases/2006/UN_poll_10230b.asp)

Other key findings from the poll were that—

- 78% of Americans believe "it is in America's best interest to continue to actively support the UN."
- 76% of Americans believe "recent events prove we need to make the United Nations stronger so it can do more to address problems like terrorism and weapons of mass destruction."

Additionally, in 2007, an international poll by The Chicago Council on Global Affairs showed that Americans are not only supportive of working through the United Nations to resolve international crises, but out of 18 countries and the Palestinian Territories polled, they're among those most in favor of giving the world body dramatic new powers. Three out of five Americans (60%) believe their country should make decisions through the United Nations even if that means it "will have to go along with a policy that is not its first choice." Four out of five Americans (79%) consider strengthening the United Nations to be an important foreign policy goal, including 40% who think it's "very important." (www.thechicagocouncil.org)

To better understand and appreciate the UN, it helps to put a face on this large complex institution. For me, this face is that of Gillian Sorensen, who offers not only a wealth of knowledge about the UN but a passion for its peacemaking role. She's held a variety of UN posts, including six years as assistant secretary-general for external relations under former UN Secretary-General Kofi Annan. *The New York Times* called her the "diplomats' diplomat." Sorensen currently serves as senior adviser at the UN Foundation and as vice-chair of UNA-USA's National Council (United Nations Association of the United States of America). Her primary responsibility is to educate, inspire, and mobilize Americans, especially university students, concerning the work of the United Nations.

I had the pleasure of meeting Gillian and hearing her speak persuasively about the mission of the UN at a special event in conjunction with dedicating a monument honoring Michigan Senator Arthur Vandenberg's contribution to the formation of the UN. I witnessed her "diplomatic magic" as she responded to questions from a highly critical and moderately hostile audience. Gillian possesses a humble but powerful presence.

Audience members asked Sorensen specifically about the UN's faults, its mismanagement of the Oil-for-Food Program, its reform progress, and its dealings with situations like Rwanda's violence. She received their questions like gifts and opened them carefully, sincerely answering their concerns with the underlying premise that we need each other in the world and must join forces for the benefit of humankind. Sorensen said, "I am a teacher and an advocate, but I am a debater and defender. I am also a realist. I address the UN's flaws and failures and put them in perspective."

Just as youth are a major focus for Sorensen's work, youth are considered the critical "transition generation" by James Martin, the founder of the James Martin Institute for Science and Civilization at Oxford University. In his latest book, *The Meaning of the Future*, he presented the 17 great challenges of this century that together constitute the 21st-century transition. He pointed out the crucial role young people must play in addressing those challenges.

"Generation X has been described as apathetic, but what I see are young people involved with AmeriCorps and other programs," asserted U.S. Secretary of State Hillary Rodham Clinton at a 2004 gala honoring congressional leaders for their support of youth initiatives. "They should be called 'Generation X-tra': extra-committed, extra-caring, extra-concerned." Each year, AmeriCorps offers 75,000 opportunities for youth and adults of all ages and backgrounds to serve through a network of partnerships with local and national nonprofit groups. 70% are youth between the ages of 18 to 25. (www.americorps.gov and www.nationalservice.gov)

The American Recovery and Reinvestment Act of 2009 (Recovery Act), signed into law by President Barack Obama on February 17th, 2009, includes $201 million in funding for the Corporation for National and Community Service to support an expansion of AmeriCorps State and National and AmeriCorps VISTA programs. AmeriCorps VISTA is the national service program designed specifically to fight poverty, one of the critical challenges of the future.

How will the youth of today face such critical challenges? The seeds of interdependence need to be sown early so they can securely take root. As these seeds grow and mature, young people will come into adulthood with confidence that they can address the challenges together.

College youth are grasping the concept of interdependence in a variety of ways, including study abroad programs. In Grand Rapids, Michigan, for example, Calvin College's Study Abroad Program has ranked fourth in the U.S. for its size, according to a report from the Institute of International Education whose mission is "Opening Minds to the World." The evaluation criteria include the college's academic excellence, its adequacy of funding, and its global perspective.

Calvin sent 527 students abroad in the 2004-5 school year in the college's eight Study Abroad Programs. Students gain access to countries such as Britain, China, France, Ghana, Honduras, Hungary, Kenya and Spain. In 2007, 550 students at Calvin participated in three-week, short-term programs during the school's January interim. Funding came primarily from students with additional funding from the college. A key to its success is a strong commitment to strengthening civil society, democracy, human rights, and academic freedom.

From my experience with hundreds of university students, I know they're becoming more informed about interdependence and are enthused about going out to make a difference as well as make a living. They anticipate the time when they will lead the world.

Practice Interdependence

The Soulwise Conspiracy practices interdependence mainly in two ways: philanthropy and service.

Philanthropy reflects the commitment of individuals and organizations who have resources to share for noble purposes. These trustees of abundance believe that to whom much is given, much is expected. For example, when representatives of the Brann Family Foundation of Grand Rapids, Michigan, heard me speak of the desperate hunger of children in Kibera, a slum in Kenya, they responded immediately and generously by contributing funds to establish a feeding program.

Philanthropy is not just for the wealthy. It represents an opportunity for all global citizens to contribute what they can to the welfare of fellow members of the human family. Examples abound. A $10 contribution to the United Nations Foundation can give a malaria-preventing bed net to a child in Mali. A $25 gift can reconnect 10 families displaced by conflict in Darfur. A $75 contribution can support UN peacekeeping missions around the world. A $100 contribution can vaccinate 100 children.

Together, our gifts, no matter how large or small, make a world of difference. Pennies add up. Like the widow's mite in the biblical story, sacrificial giving can produce wonderful results. Philosophically, it's not about the amount of the gift but about the heart of selfless motivation that prompts us to give.

Here's a wonderful example. Hundreds of thousands of New York City students from more than 800 schools went door to door collecting pennies to donate to organizations of their choice. Common Cents' 17th annual Penny Harvest resulted in Penny Harvest Field, a display of an estimated 100 million pennies in an area 30 feet by 165 feet—as long as a city block.

Although many small gifts add value and significance, the reality is that some philanthropists have more resources than others. Their large investments can produce incredible results.

On June 26, 2006, Warren Buffett pledged to donate the bulk of his estimated $44 billion fortune—$31 billion—to the Bill and Melinda Gates Foundation. It was an historic moment that affirmed the power of the primary principle of interdependence. Their trend-setting philanthropic partnership as the world's biggest charitable foundation has one goal—to make the world a better place, especially for the poorest.

Americans generously give billions to charity. In 2006, they contributed the following (in billions) to these nonprofits: United Way of America, $4.1; The Red Cross, $3; Salvation Army, $1.6; American Cancer Society, $1. Of all the countries in the world, the following contribute the highest percentage of aid for development assistance around the world (according to World Bank reports): USA, 22.8%; Japan, 15.9%; France, 9.4%; Germany, 9.1%; United Kingdom, 8.5%; Netherlands, 5.7%.

Ten million people volunteered to support the immunization of 550 million children as part of the Global Polio Eradication Initiative in 2000. The total value of this support was estimated at $10 billion.

Soulwise Conspirators practice interdependence by serving others with their time, talent, and energy as well as giving money. By their unselfish acts, they unleash the power of love on the global family, perform miracles, and establish relationships that can last for a lifetime.

Specifially, Conspirators volunteer in a variety of places and ways and for different durations. Fred and Lavonne Grunewald volunteer right where they live by serving a meal once a month at Renucci Hospitality House, which provides lodging for families of Spectrum Hospital patients in Grand Rapids, Michigan. Patti Radzik travels regularly thousands of miles from her home in the U.S. to work with orphans in Swaziland.

Todd and Tamara Rasmuson have served others for long periods, including eight years as missionaries in Tanzania. Mary-Ellen Connolly, a part-time accountant, left her husband and their children in Chelsea, Quebec, to volunteer for two weeks in Cambodia on what has become known as a "volunteer vacation." She has volunteered at home teaching the visually impaired to ski but wanted to give back. "I'm so sick off going to typical tourist attractions," she said, "and doing the same old tourist thing."

College students are volunteering more than ever. About 3.3 million college students volunteered in 2005, up more than 20% from 2002 (2.7 million). That's 30% of all college students, representing more than double the increase reported for volunteers of all ages, according to a study by the federal Corporation for National and Community Service. Tutoring and mentoring are the most common activities.

In 2005, 65 million people volunteered in the United States. Volunteers worked through many types of organizations, including religious organizations, 35%; education or youth services, 26%; social or community services, 13%; hospital or other health services, 8%; civic, political, professional, or international organizations, 6%; and other organizations or services, 12%.

According to the numbers, we're experiencing a boom in volunteering. In 2006, the Peace Corps inducted 7,810 volunteers, the largest number in 30 years, up more than 20% over the year 2000. Applications for Teach for America, which recruits college graduates for underserved urban and rural areas, hit almost 19,000 in 2006, nearly triple the organization's number of volunteers in 2000.

Another outlet for volunteer service is Habitat for Humanity, founded in 1976 by Millard Fuller and his wife, Linda. This nonprofit ecumenical Christian housing organization builds simple, decent, affordable housing in partnership with people in need. Its network of 3,300 affiliates has built 225,000 houses around the world for more than 1 million people in more than 3,000 communities. Habitat has a presence in more than 90 countries, including all 50 states of the U.S., the District of Columbia, Guam, and Puerto Rico.

Clearly, many avenues exist for practicing interdependence. Soulwise Conspirators need only look around and choose ways to give or serve that are appropriate for them and warm their hearts.

Declare Interdependence

Whenever individuals or groups of persons want to identify their public support or opposition, they make a declaration. For example, citizens declare their candidacy for elected office, activists declare their outrage at abuse of women and children, countries declare war on another country, and couples declare their commitment to one another in the marriage ceremony. On July 4, 1776, the United States Congress issued the Declaration of Independence, a critical statement of its desire to live independently as a nation.

Officially declaring *inter*dependence means that as members of the global family we promise to live according to the primary principle of interdependence. Such a statement doesn't rule out our declaration of *in*dependence. In fact, declarations of independence and interdependence complement one another, especially in today's globalized reality. The Soulwise Conspiracy's Declaration of Interdependence articulates our promise to accept responsibility for being our brother and sister's keeper.

The idea of declaring interdependence isn't new. Writer, philosopher, and historian Will Durant, who won the Pulitzer Prize and Medal of Freedom, proposed the first major Declaration of Interdependence on April 4, 1944. Durant, Meyer David, and Christine Richard wrote it and launched a movement for its support on March 22, 1945. Their document was introduced into the Congressional Record later that year on October 1, 1945.

In 1976, the Global Interdependence Center (www.interdependence. org/index.php) was launched during Philadelphia's Bicentennial Celebration and included a Declaration of Interdependence crafted by the historian, educator, and author Henry Steele Commager. The declaration called on global citizens to "declare interdependence with the people of all nations, and to embrace those principles and build those institutions which will enable mankind to survive and civilization to flourish."

Many other organizations have proposed declarations of interdependence. One is the nonprofit organization We, The World, which invited internationally concerned activist groups to support a tradition of celebrating interdependence, starting September 1, 2002. Endorsing this declaration were notable people such as Daniel Elsberg, former American military analyst, Hazel Henderson, world-renowned futurist and evolutionary economist, and Ervin Laszlo, Hungarian philosopher of science and systems theorist.

The Soulwise Conspiracy's primary principle is interdependence. It urges the international community to deliver an articulate and contagious Declaration of Interdependence. It's unclear why earlier good formulations of such a declaration haven't gained traction for debate and acceptance.

In any case, I'm persuaded that the timing is right to introduce another declaration, and that by making full use of the Internet, the movement can initiate a grassroots buzz that can't be ignored.

> *The Soulwise Conspiracy proposes that we*
> *not only make a Declaration of Interdependence,*
> *but that we celebrate a Global Interdependence Day*
> *as a reminder of our connectedness in*
> *the human family.*

Why establish yet another day to observe, you may ask? We already observe a zillion international days and years and decades in our crowded calendar. There's World Food Day, World Health Day, International Day for Eradication of Poverty, World Day for Water, International Day of Peace, World Understanding Month, and the UN Decade of Education for Sustainable Development (2005-2015).

We establish another day so we don't forget who we are as a global family—so we don't forget we're all related, we're all responsible for each other, and we're all accountable to one another.

A six-year-old girl asked her mother to tell her what the mom did at the university where she went every day. Her mother replied, "I'm in the art department. I teach people how to draw and paint." Astonished, the young girl inquired, "You mean they forget?"

Yes, sometimes we forget things we're supposed to know.

Let's celebrate Global Interdependence Day in conjunction with a day that's already recognized, such as United Nations Day (October 24—the anniversary of the establishment of the UN Charter on October 24, 1945), the International Day of Peace (September 21, which calls for a day of peace and a ceasefire throughout the world), or World Community Day, observed every year on New Year's Day (January 1). Another option is to celebrate Interdependence Day with *all* of these days.

The world awaits. Let the members of the global family join together to create our own Declaration of Interdependence. As anthropologist Margaret Mead said, "Never doubt that a small group of thoughtful, committed citizens can change the world. Indeed it is the only thing that ever has."

TAKE FIVE FOR REFLECTION

1. Name three areas in which you've observed the need for interdependence in your home, community, and beyond.

    •

    •

    •

2. Name at least three organizations that foster global interdependence.

    •

    •

    •

3. Who are three contemporary people who model interdependence?

    •

    •

    •

4. Describe ways you can live more interdependently with others in your family. In your community. In your nation. Around the world.

5. When do you recommend we celebrate Global Interdependence Day? Would you like to see it happen more than once during the year?

If we could shrink the Earth's population to a village of 100 with all human ratios remaining the same, it would look something like this:
There would be 59 Asians, 12 Europeans,
14 Americans (North, Central, and South), and 15 Africans.
70 would be non-white, 30 white.
70 would be non-Christian, 30 would be Christian.
50% of the entire world's wealth would be in the hands of
six people, and all six would be citizens of the United States.
70 of us would be unable to read and write.
50 would suffer from some degree of malnutrition.
80 would be homeless or live in substandard housing.
One of us would have a college education.[9]

PART II

OUR WORLD IS IN CRITICAL CONDITION

CHAPTER 3

SEVEN INCONVENIENT TRUTHS

O ur world is in critical condition. But are you aware of its life-threatening severity?

Take a look at this Quick Quiz on the State of the World:

1. How many people are living on less than $1 a day? (Note: $ indicates U.S.$ throughout the book.)
2. How many children die every year from causes related to malnutrition?
3. What are the three most numerous diseases in the world?
4. What percentage of all armed conflicts involve children 18 and under?
5. What percentage of the world's population cannot read or write?
6. How many slaves are there in the world today?
7. How many of the hottest years on record occurred during the last 14 years?

(You'll read the answers to this quiz throughout this chapter, and they're also consolidated at the end of the chapter.)

Our global family is choking to death. We're...
Gasping with poverty,
Fainting with hunger,
Choking with disease,
Strangling with violence,

Asphyxiating with illiteracy,
Groaning with injustice, and
Wheezing with pollution.
Let's examine each of these seven.

GASPING WITH POVERTY

Slum-Dunked

I thought I knew what poverty was. I had intellectually formed accurate definitions of poverty. I knew a mountain of statistics about poverty. As a well-meaning, short-term missionary tourist, I knew poverty from a safe distance. I also knew I would be returning to my American home in a few weeks.

However, in the summer of 2004, I encountered poverty up close and personal in Kibera, a slum of more than a million people in Nairobi, Kenya. I met gracious "slummers" as they call themselves who were gasping with poverty, unable to take even a shallow breath. I felt slum-dunked.

After one Sunday morning worship at Exodus Church, I visited a single mother whose husband had died a year earlier because of AIDS. She was ill and her eight-year-old daughter was taking care of her three younger siblings aged six, four, and two. The mother cried as she told me she had no money for food or medicine or rent on her 8-foot by 8-foot shed with its tin roof and dirt floor. The shed had no running water, no refrigeration, no toilet, no electricity, and no beds. The children slept in between stacking tables. She pointed to the back of the shed and asked if I would pronounce a blessing on her two children buried there. She couldn't afford to report their deaths to the authorities. My heart broke.

The people of Kibera are among the over 3.3 billion people of the world who live in urban environments. The number anticipated for the world's urban population will rise to 5 billion by 2030. They are also part of the 924 million people living in slums worldwide in 2001; at present growth rates of urbanization, about 2 billion people will be living in slums in 2030.[10]

What does it mean to be poor? The World Bank called poverty "multidimensional" in its 2000 in-depth report "Voices of the Poor: Can Anyone Hear Us?" That means in addition to lacking necessary resources for basic well-being—especially food, but also shelter, clothes, and other basics—poverty means:

- Lack of physical, human, social, and environmental assets, which leaves people vulnerable to natural and man-made disasters.
- Limited or no access to basic infrastructure, particularly roads, transport, water, and sanitation.
- Inadequate access to services such as health care and education.
- Lack of voice, power, and independence, which subjects poor people to exploitation.
- Inability to maintain a cultural identity and fully participate in community life.

The report also revealed that 2.5 billion people, or 40% of the world's population, live on $2 a day (or less).

Capital Chasm

Looking at the urgency from another angle, here's the capital chasm in a nutshell: 80% of the world's population earns only 20% of existing global income.

According to the *2007 State of the Future* report, a publication of The Millennium Project (see Chapter 2), 2% of the world's richest people own more than 50% of the world's wealth, while the poorest 50% own 1% of its wealth. The income of the 225 richest people in the world is equal to that of the poorest 2.7 billion, or 40% of the world's population. Approximately 4 billion people have an annual income that's less than $1,500.

The proportion of people in developing countries living in extreme poverty has fallen from 28% in 1990 to 19% in 2002. But, while the number of people living on $1 a day (or less) has fallen, the number living on between $1 and $2 a day has risen. That means more than 1 billion people live on less than a dollar a day; so do more than half of those living in Africa.

As you can see, the numbers stagger the imagination, for even though global income exceeds $31 trillion a year, 1.2 billion people still earn less than $1 a day in our global family.

Inflation and War

As of research done in 2008, international efforts to relieve the debt burden of the world's poorest countries appear to be succeeding. However, we still face tremendous challenges, one of which is inflation in many areas. For example, during the first six months of 2007, the official rate of inflation in Zimbabwe rose to 7,634%, while unofficial estimates come closer to 20,000%. That's a significant problem for a country where 5 million men, women, and children lack adequate shelter.

The research shows that on average, a war between nations, civil war, or insurgency shrinks an African economy by 15 percent a year. In total, this continent loses an average of $18 billion a year due to armed conflict.[11]

Poverty is inextricably linked with hunger. The United Nations Food and Agricultural Organization (FAO) has estimated that the direct and indirect costs of hunger in terms of medical care and lost productivity fall between $500 billion and $1 trillion, numbers that reflect gross domestic product losses.

People who are gasping with poverty are often fainting with hunger, the next inconvenient truth.

FAINTING WITH HUNGER

Seven Days Without Food Makes One Weak

Every Saturday morning in Kibera, the humanitarian group called Compassion invites children aged four through seven to participate in a program of games followed by a light lunch. About 15 minutes after wolfing down their simple meal of beans and bread, I noticed many children quietly going to a corner of the field near where we had set up the program. I asked my pastoral colleague what they were doing. "They're vomiting," he explained. "Their stomachs have shriveled and they aren't able to retain the food." He then told me the meal they'd just eaten was probably the only one they'd had that week.

Seven days without food makes one weak!

According to the United Nations World Food Program, one in seven people is chronically hungry and doesn't get the food needed to lead a healthy, active life.

Most of the world's hungry people are found in the developing world while 34 million are in the developed world. Among the hardest-hit areas is sub-Saharan Africa, where 30.5 million people need food while 36 million have only enough to prevent starvation.

In 1996, the World Food Summit upheld the basic human right to have food and said that food security exists when all people, at all times, have physical and economic access to enough safe and nutritious food to meet their dietary needs and food preferences for an active, healthy lifestyle. A culture that's considered "food secure" has food that's available, affordable, and used. "If you have enough food," advised a Chinese proverb, "you can have many problems. If you have no food, you have only one problem."

Vulnerable to Malnutrition

Malnutrition is implicated in more than half of all child deaths worldwide. It weakens children's health and reduces their resistance to disease.

Malnutrition, an invisible condition in which the body receives too few of the nutrients it needs, affects close to 800 million people worldwide, particularly the poor. Young children are especially vulnerable to malnutrition. Those surviving may suffer ongoing disease and disability, affecting their ability to learn and develop to their full potential.

More than one-third of all children in the world are malnourished and 6 million children a year die of causes related to malnutrition. Hunger and malnutrition claim more than 10 million lives each year worldwide. That's more than AIDS, malaria, and tuberculosis combined.[12]

"There are people in the world so hungry," commented Mahatma Gandhi, "that God cannot appear to them except in the form of bread." They're not only starved for attention, they're starved for food.

The World Bank classifies countries according to their average income, also called their gross national income per capita. Countries with average incomes of less than $10,725 in 2005 are classified as developing or low- and middle-income economies, and countries with incomes of $10,726 or more are classified as developed or high-income economies.

In low-income countries today, 1 child in 8 dies before his or her fifth birthday, compared with 1 in 143 in high-income countries. Of all child deaths, 53% can be attributed to being underweight.

The rural poor make up an estimated 80% of the world's 800 million hungry people. A large proportion of the hungry are concentrated in areas that are vulnerable to environmental degradation and climate change.

Distribution Disaster

The tragedy is that even though there's enough food in the world for everyone to have enough to eat, it's unevenly distributed. According to the United Nations Food and Agriculture Organization (FAO), enough food was produced in 2001 to provide every person in the world with 2,807 food calories per day, an amount more than the FAO's recommended intake of 2,000 calories per day.

> *In her article "Why Millions Still Go Hungry," Barbara Crossette, consulting editor for the United Nations Association of the USA, wrote, "Even in the midst of available food, millions of people are malnourished or sometimes starving around the world because of government social policies, income inequalities, inefficient farming, post-traumatic stress following civil wars, and a low status and educational level of women—the mothers who have to feed their families."[13]*

CHOKING WITH DISEASE

The human family is choking with "diseases of poverty" plus the "diseases of wealth."

The former include the "Big Three"—HIV/AIDS, malaria, and tuberculosis (TB)—that kill more than 6 million people each year. An estimated 99% of these deaths occur in developing countries, which explains why they are called the diseases of poverty.

Every year, more than 10 million children (that's 30,000 a day) die of these preventable diseases. Five diseases—pneumonia, diarrhea, malaria, measles, and HIV/AIDS—account for half of all the deaths in children under five. By comparison, more children died of diarrheal disease during the 1990s than all people who were lost in conflict in World War II.

The United Nations Children's Fund (UNICEF) reported that 9.7 million children around the world died before reaching age five in 2006, the vast majority from causes preventable through a combination of good care, nutrition, and simple medical treatment. Child mortality is therefore closely linked to poverty, with child malnutrition implicated in more than half the deaths worldwide.

A Save the Children report on global newborn mortality indicated that 2 million babies die in the first 24 hours of life, while 4 million babies around the world die in their first month of life. Most deaths result from some type of infection, such as pneumonia or diarrhea, or complications related to premature births. Africa's infant mortality rate is nearly 15 times that of the developed world.

Let's look briefly at each of "The Big Three" diseases, beginning with HIV/AIDS.

HIV/AIDS Epidemic

HIV/AIDS, the worst epidemic in the world's history, is the leading cause of infectious disease death. The *2007 State of the Future* reports that the disease is the fourth leading cause of deaths in the world. Approximately 25 million have died from it, with 3.16 million deaths in 2005. Another 65 million people are living with HIV/AIDS, a number that increased by 4.9 million in 2005, the largest one-year increase.

Dr. Peter Okaalet, senior director of the health and HIV/AIDS policy for Africa's Medical Assistance Programs (MAP International) based in Nairobi, Kenya, knows firsthand how life expectancy in Africa is falling due to HIV/AIDS. He reported that life expectancy in Botswana before HIV/AIDS was 74.4 years. In 2006, it dropped to 26.7 years.

Children in sub-Saharan African countries such as Botswana, Swaziland, and South Africa are hardest hit by HIV/AIDS. It's estimated that child mortality more than doubled as a result of this disease. In 2008, 14 million HIV/AIDS orphans lived in sub-Saharan Africa. Adolescent girls and young women are especially vulnerable to the disease and account for 60% of the 10 million HIV-positive youths (aged between 15 and 24).

Fortunately, the conspiracy of silence about HIV/AIDS has been broken. But if the tens of billions of dollars needed to provide care, treatment, and preventative services aren't invested over the next five years, the consequences will be even more horrific.

Malaria Misery

In preparation for my initial trip to Africa in June 2004, I took all the required precautions including my daily medication to prevent malaria. In spite of my diligence, a tick bit me and I contracted malaria. I shook uncontrollably for seven hours with severe alternating chills and fever. I fainted while lying down in bed.

Of the four strains of malaria, I got the one that comes with a lifetime guarantee. That means for a couple of hours every month, I feel like I have the flu and my temperature sometimes reaches 105 degrees.

According to the World Health Organization, malaria threatens 2 to 3 billion people, or roughly 40% of the world's population. It causes at least 300 million cases of acute illness and two million deaths each year (90% of which are in Africa) at a cost of $12 billion annually. Approximately 60% of all deaths from malaria occur among the poorest 20% of the world's population.

Malaria, the leading cause of deaths in young children, is particularly dangerous for pregnant women, causing severe anemia, miscarriages, stillbirths, low birth weight, and maternal death. A prediction that malaria deaths could double in the next 20 years should spur us on to find effective treatments and a cure. It's a big part of why I'm passionate about preventing malaria in children. It has hit close to home for me.

Tuberculosis Prognosis

The World Health Organization has reported that Tuberculosis (TB), the third disease of the "Big Three," is the main cause of death from a single infectious agent among adults aged 15 to 45. Two million people die of TB every year and nearly 9 million new active cases are diagnosed.

Overall, one-third of the world's population is currently infected with the TB bacillus. In fact, someone in the world gets newly infected with tuberculosis bacilli every second.

In 2007, an estimated 1.3 million deaths resulted from TB, with 95% of cases and 98% of deaths occurring in the developing world. In sub-Saharan Africa, the incidence per capita is nearly 400 cases per 100,000 population. Left untreated, each person with active TB disease will infect between 10 and 15 people every year.

> *What's the prognosis for tuberculosis?*
> *Unless immediate action is taken, tuberculosis could be an even bigger killer in the future than it is today. Part of the problem is that HIV/AIDS and TB have combined to make an explosive and deadly combination, with each disease speeding the other's progress.*

TB is the leading cause of death for those infected with HIV and is implicated in up to one-half of all AIDS deaths. Because HIV compromises the immune system, HIV-positive people are 50 times more likely to develop TB than those who are HIV-negative.

In some regions of Africa where the number of new TB cases has more than quadrupled since 1990, 75% of TB patients are HIV-infected. Although the global co-infection rate is only 0.35%, in eight African countries, the prevalence rate exceeds 5%.

STRANGLING WITH VIOLENCE

Death

As a pastor, I deal with death regularly. But when the morning television news showed the burned bodies of Americans suspended from a bridge over the Euphrates River in Falluja, Iraq, I broke into tears. I feared that the ones hanging lifelessly were soldiers from families I know personally. Wouldn't you agree that death takes on particular poignancy when your family and friends are involved?

While Iraqis chanted anti-American slogans in the background, in my mind, I heard Bruce Springsteen singing over and over: "War. What is it good for? Absolutely nothing." The lyrics of "War" held a new meaning for me that morning.

War is something that I despise
For it means destruction of innocent lives
For it means tears in thousands of mothers' eyes
When their sons go out to fight to give their lives[14]

War is a deadly enterprise, with World Wars I and II taking more than 100 million lives. In only one decade—from 1990 to 2000—war claimed the lives of 5 million worldwide. (www.globaleducation.edna. edu.au) The United Nations Assistance Mission to Iraq's Human Rights Office reported that 34,452 Iraq civilians were killed in 2006.

Since 1980, almost one-half of the world's largest developed countries have suffered from a major conflict. In recent times, more than 90% of wars take place *within* states rather than *between* them. In Rwanda, for example, Hutu death squads massacred 800,000 people in 100 days. The conflict in Darfur has claimed the lives of over 200,000 and it continues, with starvation being used as a weapon of war.

> *It's ironic that, in this International Decade*
> *(2001-2010) for the Culture of Peace and*
> *Non-violence for the Children of the World, we should*
> *have so much death and destruction.*
> *In fact, at the beginning of the new millennium,*
> *regional, local, ethnic, terrorism, and religious and*
> *civil conflicts proliferated around the world.*
> *The United Nations General Assembly strived to*
> *draw attention to the challenges of creating a culture*
> *of peace, and to encourage international action to*
> *make the transition from a culture of*
> *war to a culture of peace globally.*

An excellent book by P.W. Singer, *Children at War*, noted that three-quarters of all armed conflicts in the world involve children 18 and under.

The number of children under the age of 18 who have been coerced or induced to take up arms is thought to be around 300,000.[15]

Clearly, war is expensive, both monetarily and personally. The Associated Press estimated that the U.S. government spent $170 billion on the wars in Iraq and Afghanistan in 2008 alone. James Glanz reported in an article, "The Economic Cost of War," in *The New York Times* that the war in Iraq will cost United States taxpayers an estimated $860 billion. The cost of overseas conflicts looks like this: $144 billion in the fiscal year 2009, $130 billion in 2010, and $50 billion for 2011 and beyond.[16] The Congressional Research Service estimated that in 2006 (the latest available figures), it cost $390,000 a year to sustain each American trooper overseas. In a *Washington Post* article, "The Iraq War Will Cost Us $3 Trillion, and Much More," Linda Bilmes and Joseph Stiglitz noted how the significant cost of the war limits our ability to fund programs at home for health-care, education, and infrastructure, and to help others in need around the world.[17]

Distress

Some days I think this bumper sticker's message accurately depicts our inclination: "We're making enemies faster than we can kill them." Yes, our world is strangling from violence and its accompanying distress.

Listen to the tone of excerpts from letters to his parents from 19-year-old Marine Pfc. Moises A. Langhorst of Moose Lake, Minnesota, who was killed by small-arms fire in Iraq's Al Anbar Province on April 6, 2007. "March 13. As far as my psychological health, we look out for each other pretty well on that… I've been praying a lot and hope you're praying for the Dirty 3rd Platoon, because there is no doubt that we are in the Valley of the Shadow of Death." Many, like Pfc. Langhorst, never return home from war. Their fractured and fragmented families are forced to face the realities of loss and emotional exhaustion.

For increasing numbers who return from the battlefield after the fighting ends, another war begins in part due to advanced battlefield medicine. According to the Department of Veterans Affairs, 179,713 Vietnam War veterans are currently being compensated for Post Traumatic Stress Disorder (PTSD). Nearly 16,000 veterans of Operation Iraqi Freedom and Operation Endurance Freedom have been seen at Veterans Affairs medical centers for the disorder. We can expect to see more cases of PTSD as global conflicts wear on.

Danger

The *2007 State of the Future* report began with this dichotomy: "People around the world are becoming healthier, wealthier, better educated, more peaceful, and increasingly connected and they are living longer, but at the same time the world is more corrupt, congested, warmer, and increasingly dangerous."

A poll conducted in 2008 by Public Agenda in partnership with *Foreign Affairs* magazine found that four out of five U.S. residents think the world is becoming increasingly dangerous for the United States. The survey indicated 69% believed the U.S. government is doing only a "fair" or "poor" job in helping create a more peaceful and prosperous world, and 58% believed that U.S. foreign policy was on the "wrong track." This evidence supports the assertion that we live in an age of anxiety.

The danger is real. Massively destructive powers are available to individuals willing to blow themselves up for their cause, thus inflicting death and destruction on purpose. Although the Cold War has ended, 27,600 nuclear weapons still exist in the world in 2009 according to the Carnegie Endowment for International Peace (www.ProliferationNews.org).

Recent reports indicate that terrorist events will become more common and more deadly.

"Increasingly terrorists see no limitations to their violence," said Jessica Stern, a lecturer at Harvard University who studies terrorism. The message behind televised beheadings is loud and clear. As Gabriel Weimann, an expert on Islam at the Washington-based U.S. Institute of Peace, said, "These beheadings are an example of the 'theater of terror.' There is a set script, players, even props... an escalation of horror."

Global trends analyst and defense adviser Marvin J. Cetron doesn't see any immediate relief from the clear and present danger. He asked futurists about potential terrorist scenarios and concluded that terrorist events will become more common and bloodier in the years ahead. They will largely be initiated by Islamic extremists and backed by an expanding al-Qaeda. Jihadists, or Muslim extremists, he predicted, will acquire nuclear weapons in the next decade, if they don't possess them already. He contended that the war on terror will drag on for decades; changing its course represents the biggest challenge the West faces.

ASPHYXIATING WITH ILLITERACY

Can't Read

Twenty years ago, a Fortune 500 company engaged me to consult with its executive team. One of my responsibilities was to offer quarterly leadership seminars to stretch the team's critical thinking skills. During one of these seminars, I noticed that whenever I handed out reading material, one vice-president would always leave the room so his secretary could read the material and then brief him on its contents.

He couldn't read. And he's not alone; 70% of the world's population can't read or write, amounting to millions of illiterate people in the world. According to United Nations Educational, Scientific and Cultural Organization (UNESCO), in 1970, about 37% of all people over the age of 15 were illiterate. That number has fallen to less than 18% in 2008, with the remaining 52% 15 and under and with 98% of all non-literates living in developing countries. About two-thirds of the adults who lack minimum literacy skills are women. Worldwide, 88 adult women are considered literate for every 100 literate men.

We're a long way from the ideal of education for all, and to the improved prosperity, health, and security it would bring. Worldwide, about 100 million primary school-age children remain out of school; 132 million people without literacy are at or between ages 15 and 24. This is particularly disturbing because the digital and information revolution has changed the way the world learns, communicates, does business, and treats illnesses. For example, in 2002, 364 people per 1,000 in high-income countries were using the Internet, while only 10 per 1,000 in low-income countries were using this tool.

Can't Write

Millions of people in the world are handicapped because they can neither read nor write, thus they face short- and long-term ramifications that can be devastating. Reading and writing go hand-in-hand. They reinforce each other to promote self-sufficiency and to connect people around the corner and around the world.

When I was first ordained and on the mission field in the Canadian north (where the average winter temperature was 43 degrees below zero), two people in my congregation knew only one letter: "X." They couldn't even write their names. Occasionally, I would verify their identities when they were "signing" a legal document such as hospital admission papers. They had never had the opportunity to learn how to write. Hymn-singing, for example, presented some difficulties. They would look at their open hymnbook and sing from memory with great gusto. The introduction of a new hymn prompted a quick trip to the restroom to quietly get help!

"Will Africa ever catch up economically with the rest of the world?" my MBA students at Daystar University in Nairobi have repeatedly asked. They wondered if I thought they had a reasonable chance to bring prosperity to Africa. It's a relevant question in a continent that has a literacy rate of less than 60%, so if people can't read or write, it would seem that the chances of catching up, let alone leading the world, are out of the question. My safe answer became "it all depends."

> *The 2007 State of the World report indicated the troubling state of global education this way: "The great paradox of our age is that while more and more people enjoy the benefits of technological and economic growth, growing numbers of people are poor and unhealthy, and nearly the same percentage of the population has lacked access to education over the last 30 years."*

Can't Count

Did you know that 70% of the world's population can't read, write... or count!

They haven't learned to do basic mathematical operations: addition, subtraction, multiplication, and division of whole numbers. That puts them at a distinct disadvantage, especially economically. Without numeracy—the knowledge and skills required to manage the mathematical demands of diverse situations—they can never conduct business effectively or profitably.

In combination, reading, writing, and counting are essential for every aspect of life. These skills increase our capacity to solve problems and find solutions, to figure out what's important, and then to synthesize, understand, prioritize, and use everything we have to deal with on a daily basis.

Unfortunately, the world has a shortage of teachers. To achieve universal primary education by 2015, the United Nations Educational and Cultural Organization has estimated that an extra 15 to 35 million more teachers will be required—right now!

GROANING WITH INJUSTICE

"Just Us" Justice

"Just us" justice that applies to a select group is no justice at all. Human rights are considered universal, indivisible, and fundamental for development and democracy. *All people must have access to all rights for the world to be a safe and secure place.*

Yet refugees totaled 8.4 million at the end of 2005, the lowest level since 1980, accounting for 4% of the migrants in the world. A refugee is defined as a person who, owing to a well-founded fear of being persecuted for political opinion or for reasons of race, religion, nationality, or membership of a particular social group lives outside the country of his or her nationality. These people are unable, or unwilling due to fear, to avail themselves of the protection of that country.

At the beginning of 2004, the number of people "of concern" to the United Nations Office of the High Commissioner for Refugees (UNHCR) was 17.1 million. This number included 9.7 million refugees (57%), 985,500 asylum seekers (6%), 1.1 million returned refugees (6%), 4.4 million internally displaced persons (26%), and 912,200 others of concern (5%).

The Population Reference Bureau reported that, in 2005, at least 25 million people in 40 countries worldwide have been forcibly displaced within their own countries by violent conflict or environmental disasters such as hurricanes or earthquakes.

71

The Christian Science Monitor of September 1, 2004 declared an ugly truth in its article "Slavery Is Not Dead, Just Less Recognizable." The article by Susan Llewelyn Leach stated that "... 27 million people throughout the world are enslaved, more than at the height of the transatlantic slave trade. Although banned in every country, slavery has boomed in the last 50 years as the global population has exploded. A billion people scrape by on a $1 a day." (http://www.csmonitor.com/2004/0901/ p16s01-wogi.html)

Human trafficking is flourishing in 137 countries. Annually, the income from forced prostitution or labor is $22 billion. The majority of exploited victims are women and girls forced into the sex trade. Tragically, 1.2 million children are trafficked every year and 2 million children work in the commercial sex industry.

Women and Children Last

Dead last. Millions of women and children have died as victims of violence. The *2007 State of the Future* report indicated that violence against women by men continues to cause more casualties than wars.

Women and children make up 80% of the world's refugees. Two-thirds of the world's illiterate people are age 15 and older and female, and in no region of the developing world do women have equal access to social services and productive resources. Women's participation in politics and government also remains limited, making it difficult for them to influence policy. Women hold fewer than 20% of seats in national parliaments in much of the world, including more developed countries.

> *And children fare no better, even though nearly all countries in the world have signed the Convention on the Rights of the Child (CRC) and committed themselves to promoting, protecting, and fulfilling the rights of children. An estimated 250 million children aged 5 to 14 are working around the world, and close to 2 million children have been killed in armed conflicts in the past decade.*

It hurts to be a woman. It hurts like hell. An estimated one-quarter to one-half of all women have suffered physical abuse. The United Nations Development Fund for Women noted that one in three women will suffer some form of violence in her lifetime. In addition, the World Health Organization (WHO) reported that "after diseases and hunger, violence against women is the greatest cause of death among women."

The WHO also noted that one in five women will be a victim of rape or attempted rape in her lifetime and that, depending on the country, 10-69% of women reported being physically assaulted by an intimate male partner at some point in their lives. Amnesty International has estimated this figure to be about 33% worldwide.

If that isn't sad enough, it's believed that 2 million children, mostly girls, are sex slaves in the multibillion-dollar sex industry, also according to the United Nations Development Fund for Women. About 80% of the 600,000 to 800,000 individuals trafficked per year are female, making it the "largest slave trade in history" and one of the fastest-growing areas of organized crime.

Human Wrongs

Discrimination in any form—race, color or creed—is an ugly human wrong that can be blatant or subtle. I admit it. I have been guilty of racism. Let me explain.

Early one summer morning when I was in Atlanta to speak at a convention, I needed exercise. I'd been warned not to run alone at night, but it was broad daylight. So I left my valuables at my downtown hotel's front desk, stretched, and started running.

About five minutes after I left the hotel, I was conscious of someone running behind me. When I turned a corner, I saw three young muscular black men getting closer and closer to me. The faster I moved, the faster they moved, too.

When I turned another corner, the three had multiplied to ten—and the group was gaining on me. I panicked. I pulled away as fast as I could, but to no avail; they were right on my tail. I could see my hotel a short distance away and ran hard. In my younger days, I had been a champion sprinter and hurdler, and hoped I could run fast enough to avert a pending tragedy.

I burst through the front doors of the hotel and stopped to catch my breath. The "black" group, to my amazement, had followed me into the hotel lobby. As one of them came near me, he politely asked, "Who are you?" Puzzled, I responded, "Who are *you*?" That's when they all laughed and said, "We're on the U.S. track team."

Rampant Corruption

Another form of human wrong is rampant corruption, with illicit trade estimated to exceed $1 trillion a year. McAfee, an Internet security company, has indicated that cybercrime may be as high as $105 billion. These figures don't include extortion or organized crime's part of the $1 trillion in bribes that the World Bank estimates are paid annually. Nor does it include organized crime's part of the estimated $1.5 to $6.5 trillion annually in laundered money. The total illicit income could exceed $2 trillion—about twice all the nations' military budgets worldwide.

> *The World Bank has estimated that more than $1 trillion is paid each year in political bribes, of which $20 to $40 billion lines the pockets of public officials from developing and transition countries, and $60 to $80 billion in more developed countries.*

Personally, I've seen corruption prevail at the highest and lowest levels of society. On a trip to Africa, for example, a representative from the university where I was to teach picked me up in a private bus at the airport at night. On our way to the hotel, the police stopped and searched us and our luggage, then demanded a fee. When I asked others about the fee, they told me the police needed to meet their month-end fee obligations.

WHEEZING WITH POLLUTION

Planet in Peril

"We are witnessing," said 2007 Nobel Peace Prize winner Al Gore, "a collision between our civilization and the earth."

The former U.S. vice president's Academy Award-winning movie *An Inconvenient Truth* issued a wake-up call for humanity. It's probably the most publicized inconvenient truth that's ever existed, sparking heated discussions about climate change among ordinary citizens and scientists around the world.

For many, the subject of global warming is the political hot potato of our time. "There are good people who are in politics in both parties who hold this at arms' length," said Gore, "because if they acknowledge and recognize it, then the moral imperative to make big changes is inescapable."

Kofi Annan, former secretary-general of the United Nations, takes a radically different stance. In an opening address to the United Nations Climate Change Conference in Nairobi, Kenya, on November 15, 2006, he called climate change the "defining issue of our era." Annan concluded his remarks by challenging the conference delegates with these words: "The question is not whether climate change is happening or not, but whether, in the face of this emergency, we ourselves can change fast enough."

Has our civilization reached an environmental tipping point? How can we return our planet to an ecological equilibrium? Or do we face the decline and eventual collapse of our planetary structures and focus on damage control?

In my opinion, the biggest burning question is this: *Do we have the will to practice environmental stewardship?*

The Heat is On

The heat is on, full blast. Like Elphaba, the Wicked Witch of the West in the play *Wicked*, we're melting at an unprecedented rate. Some think we might die from the heat.

Of the 12 hottest years on record, 11 have occurred since 1995, with the hottest being 2005. Temperatures have risen by 0.74 degrees Celsius over the past century—an unbelievable increase in a short period. Why? Because the difference in temperature between the ice ages and the 21st century is about 5 degrees Celsius, making this temperature increase the most significant in thousands of years. If it's sustained for even a brief time, it will contribute to a dramatic and perhaps catastrophic rise in sea levels.

A report from the Intergovernmental Panel on Climate Change has predicted that by 2100, temperatures will have risen somewhere between 1.1 and 6.4 degrees from 2008. As a result, sea levels will rise by 18 to 59 centimeters. That means that by the end of the 21st century, sea levels could rise 2 feet, swamping coastal areas worldwide. In addition, the global rate of ice melt has more than doubled since 1988 and could raise sea levels approximately 27 centimeters by 2100. That means arctic ice could completely disappear during summers by the year 2100.

Again, we need to ask this question: *Do we have the will to practice environmental stewardship?*

Running Dry

The planet is in peril, the heat is on, and we're also running dry. Our water—a basic element in life along with earth, air, and fire—is steadily and quickly evaporating.

> *As of 2008, more than 670 million people live in countries that face chronic, widespread water short-ages. By 2025, 1.8 billion people could be living in water-scarce areas that have become desperate enough to spark mass migrations.*

I suspect water will be to the 21st century what oil was to the 20th century as an essential, scarce, and precious commodity for commerce and living in general. As the global population grows, water will continue to increase in value and help determine the wealth of nations. Also increasing will be competition for access to water, especially for use in agriculture.

The trend has begun. The United Nations reported in March, 2007, that 4 billion people don't have access to clean water and more than 1 billion people lack access to an adequately protected source of water within 1 kilometer of their dwelling, mostly in rural areas. Worldwide, nearly one-third of rural residents lack access to safe drinking water.

On top of that, around 2.6 billion people have no access to improved sanitation, resulting in 80% of the world's diseases being water-related. As a result, high rates of diarrhea are recorded and 6,000 children die every day from water-borne contaminants.

To sum it up, *every 15 seconds a child dies from diseases caused by contaminated water.*

These seven inconvenient truths face our civilization, whether we like it or not. Chapter 4 addresses seven deadly attitudes that are primarily responsible for this massive global dilemma.

TAKE FIVE FOR REFLECTION

How have you encountered the following Seven Inconvenient Truths in your life? Write down *your* experiences, and include how you felt and what you learned from them.

1. Poverty

2. Hunger

3. Disease

4. Violence

5. Illiteracy

6. Injustice

7. Pollution

Answers to the Quick Quiz on the State of the World

1. 2.5 billion people are living on less than $1 a day.

2. 2.6 million children die every year from causes related to malnutrition.

3. AIDS, malaria, and tuberculosis are the three most numerous diseases in the world.

4. 75% of all armed conflicts involve children 18 and under.

5. 70% of the world's population cannot read, write, or count.

6. 27 million slaves exist in today's world.

7. 10 of the hottest years on record have occurred during the past two decades.

CHAPTER 4

SEVEN DEADLY ATTITUDES

Everybody has attitude; some have more than others. An attitude is a state of mind, a feeling, a disposition. Attitude is essential to survive and thrive.

Attitude can be positive or negative. The *2006 State of the Future* report published by The Millennium Project concluded by indicating the report "can help decision-makers and educators who fight against hopeless despair, blind confidence, and ignorant indifference—attitudes that too often have blocked efforts to improve the prospects for humanity." (www.acunu.org/millennium/sof2006.html)

This chapter discusses seven attitudes of the deadly variety. It's not coincidental that each of these deadly attitudes begins with the letter "I," for it's the "I" that most often gets in the way of approaching life in a positive and beneficial way.

You'll see that fear is invariably at the root of these attitudes. What kind of fear? It could be a fear of self, a fear of others, a fear of failure, or most notably, a fear of success that can play a significant role.

The seven deadly attitudes are:

- Indifference,
- Inhumanity,
- Insensitivity,
- Insolence,
- Insularity,

- Intolerance, and
- Invincibility.

Let's discover how each of these attitudes has the potential to be deadly to our global family.

INDIFFERENCE

"Whatever"

Have you noticed? The watchword for those who approach life with indifference is "whatever." This one word speaks volumes. Whatever the topic or concern—race, refugees, women, children, trafficking, environmental responsibility, the poor, the hungry—their profoundly simplistic response is accompanied by a shrug of the shoulders and "whatever." I call them the wind people because they'll go wherever the wind blows.

Indifference originally meant "not differentiating or discriminating." Now it means: "having no particular interest in or concern for oneself or others." Those who habitually use it epitomize *Merriam Webster's* 2006 word of the year, "truthiness," coined by TV personality Stephen Colbert. He described "truthiness" as an inclination to believe in ideas without regard to logic or evidence.

Indifferent people are not active or involved with the world; they're disengaged, out of gear, in neutral. And they're not alone. A recent Gallup poll found that fewer than 30% of American workers are fully engaged at work, 55% are not engaged, and 19% are actively disengaged. The cost of this disengagement adds up to trillions of dollars.

Indifference can mask a sincere fear of the future. The apparent indifference, disengagement, or boredom exhibited by young people in particular most often reveals their earnest attempt to make sense of the world and their place in it. To some extent, everyone attempts this essential endeavor at every age and stage of life. Unfortunately, some never escape from the "indifference trap"; they go through life merely showing up, regardless of the consequences.

Indifference curtails civic involvement on every level: local, state, national, and international. For example, in the 2004 U.S. presidential election, more than one-third of the electorate, and more than one-half of those between 18 and 24, didn't cast a vote. By contrast, millions voted for their favorite entertainer on the television show *American*

Idol. Harvard professor Robert Putnam argued in his book *Bowling Alone* that this attests to a trend *away* from all kinds of civic involvement. One shining exception is the extensive grassroots involvement of voters during the 2008 presidential election.

Perhaps a change of heart has been stirred for good. Only time will tell.

Numb and Number

Recently I watched a television newscast showing a man in his late 80s being beaten by a gang of young men in the mall parking lot of a major city. A surveillance camera caught shoppers watching the entire spectacle from a safe distance. Not a single person responded to the man's desperate calls for help; they stood numb.

> *Indifference, like an anesthetic, numbs a person's heart and soul. Over time, people get numb and number until they take no responsibility for anything that happens. They choose to do nothing; they're couch potatoes watching life go by.*

According to the A.C. Nielsen Co., the average person in the U.S. watches more than four hours of television a day, which translates into 28 hours a week or two months a year. A 65-year-old person will have spent nine years glued to the tube. In these statistics, the United Kingdom is tied with the U.S., and Italy isn't far behind with 27 hours watching TV every week. People in Ireland, France, and Germany have clocked in at 23 hours a week, and those in Australia, Finland, Norway, and Sweden averaging 18 hours a week.

It's worth noting that by the time an average child finishes elementary school in the U.S., he or she has seen 8,000 murders on television.

Indifference has the effect of lowering expectations. On his website www.despair.com, Dr. E.L. Kersten, founder and chief operating officer of despair.com, offers demotivators intended to increase success by lowering expectations. For example, inscribed at the bottom of one of his posters of the Egyptian pyramids are these words: "Achievement: You can do anything you set your mind to when you have vision, determination, and an endless supply of expendable labor." Another warns: "Potential: Not everyone gets to be an astronaut when they grow up."

Dr. Ray Bennett has written the consummate handbook for the indifferent—*The Underachiever's Manifesto: The Guide to Accomplishing Little and Feeling Great*. Through it, he urges readers to lower the bar a notch. Dr. Bennett consciously walks his talk; in his book, the page titled "Other Books by The Author" is blank.

Indifference stifles the human spirit, blocks out reality, and restricts purposeful living. It perpetuates unconscious drifting and encourages comatose behavior. As Winston Churchill remarked, "The tragedy in life is that people stumble over the truth and then get up and go on as if nothing happened." To which the indifferent person would predictably reply "whatever."

INHUMANITY

"Take That!"

A "Maxine" comic catches the essence of the deadly attitude of inhumanity this way: "A stray, rabid dog bit my neighbor. I went to see how he was and found him writing frantically on a piece of paper. I told him rabies could be treated, and he didn't have to worry about a will. He said, 'Will? What will? I'm making a list of the people I want to bite.'"

The attitude of inhumanity means lacking pity or compassion, or acting with cruel intent to cause pain and suffering. Inhumanity causes interaction and confrontation that is overtly abusive, even deadly. Consider this bumper sticker that invites a violent response: "Take your Ex out tonight. It only takes a bullet."

Inhumanity is a cancer of hatred that will eat away every aspect of our existence as a human family and will eventually destroy civilization. Simply hearing the names of Auschwitz, Rwanda, Abu Ghraib, Darfur, Columbine, Kent State, Virginia Tech, and others evokes vivid images of humankind's cruelty to one another.

Maybe it's human to have a dark side. In his book *The Lucifer Effect: Understanding How Good People Turn Evil*, psychologist Philip Zimbardo reported that nearly everyone would treat others viciously or look the other way at abuse under certain conditions. He also found that when family and normal routines are absent, one's inner character seldom survives. Some, it seems, get hooked on horror.

Mean-Streakers

In one of my undergraduate university communications classes, we were discussing the attacks of 9/11 when a student suddenly became agitated and shouted, "Kill the bastards! Kill them all! Wipe them off the face of the earth! They're getting what they deserve. Serves them right."

The class sat for a few moments in stunned silence. Then one student calmly voiced his disbelief at his classmate's violent expression and asked, "Who the hell do you think you are?" "How could you be so mean and callous?" asked another. The student answered by saying, "Don't you know that the Bible says 'an eye for an eye and a tooth for a tooth'? I say, kill them before they kill you."

It wasn't surprising to learn that this strident student had been abused as a child. Abusers often live out unresolved painful experiences and inflict hurt on others. Abusive spouses have admitted being abused as children in our counseling sessions and because they were once victims, they believe somebody else should have a taste of what abuse means. It's as if they feel entitled to seek revenge and cause suffering.

I view terrorists as mean-streakers who act fanatically to inflict maximum suffering and destruction. Their intent is clear: obliterate the enemy at any cost. I recall seeing a crowd of people in another part of the world cheering with delight at the destruction of the World Trade Center's Twin Towers in New York on 9/11.

The mean-streakers' callous disregard for human life is unthinkable, especially when one considers they often act in the name of a religion or other ideology. Hell bent to kill for what they consider their just and divine cause, they're like contemporary pirates who follow the pirate's creed to the letter: "Take what you can. Give nothing back."

INSENSITIVITY

"So What"

A middle-aged man's sweatshirt said it all: "I can only be nice to one person a day, and today is not your day. Tomorrow doesn't look too good either."

85

> *A disturbing smugness can reside in those who exude the attitude of insensitivity. They reek of an inability to care about the feelings or circumstances of others, as if they switched their automatic attitude pilot to "unfeeling." Their response to others' pain and suffering is simple apathy. Incapable of emoting, they're not only indifferent; from the core of their being, they are unmerciful toward others.*

Insensitive people possess a distinct poverty of spirit. Those who are dedicated in principle to care for our global family can become apathetic, even if the needs are revealed right in front of them. I recall going to an interview for a position as senior pastor at a church in Manhattan. On the way into the church, I had to step over five people huddled near a vent to keep warm. I asked those in the church's selection committee how they were helping these men. Their surprising answer was "we've got our own troubles." It's like saying, "So what."

Bishop Desmond Tutu has conveyed a different view. "If you are neutral in situations of injustice, you have chosen the side of the oppressor," he reflected. "If an elephant has its foot on the tail of a mouse and you say that you are neutral, the mouse will not appreciate your neutrality."

Perhaps insensitivity erupts from a lack of respect for oneself, and this discomfort in one's own skin causes a lack of respect for anyone else. Rather than dealing with their responsibility as members of our human family, people shut down. As a result, they feel no remorse, which stifles any inner urge to help someone in distress.

Concrete Hearts

Some people's hearts are like concrete, all mixed up, permanently set, and hardened to the plight or circumstances of others. In sleep mode, their hearts still beat but only for themselves.

It reminds me of the 2005 movie *The Constant Gardener* in which a drug company demonstrated its concrete corporate heart. The company never thought about the consequences of testing its new medications on unsuspecting African citizens as displayed in this movie.

Fortunately, all drug manufacturers aren't cut from the same cloth.

Many care passionately about their customers' health and take every precaution to ensure that no harm is done during their research and product testing.

It's often painful to care for others, so some protect themselves from feeling the pain of suffering by letting apathy control their hearts. They sail through life without hearing the cries of their brothers and sisters in distress. For example, they're unable to deal with the genocide in Darfur, refusing to consider putting concern about thousands being murdered on their agenda. It's not their problem.

For them, it wouldn't matter if an issue like genocide was halfway around the world or just around the corner—the situation wouldn't have anything to do with them. The suffering of our global family simply isn't detected by their antennae, and if it is, they quickly tune it out.

Concrete hearts don't possess the supple quality so necessary for life in all its fullness. And their personal protection plans prevent their hardened hearts from ever being broken. One can only hope that the concrete-hearted might hear the Nickelback song of challenge and hope "If Everyone Cared," from their five-time platinum album, *All the Right Reasons*.

If everyone cared and nobody cried
If everyone loved and nobody lied
If everyone shared and swallowed their pride
Then we'd see the day when nobody died.

INSOLENCE

"Me, Me, Me"

I was discussing a pending wedding ceremony with a couple in their mid-20s. When it came to their vows, they said they didn't want the words "for better or worse" in the ceremony; they were only interested in the "for better" part. I hate to say I told you so, but their marriage lasted less than a year. It's as if they were singing a scale and it got stuck: "Do Re ME, ME, ME, ME..."

Insolence rears its ugly head in arrogance and presumptuous behavior. It doesn't take a rocket scientist to identify egomaniacs. They're self-absorbed and look out only for numero uno.

Persons afflicted with insolence ask only one question: "What's in it for me?" They're greedy and selfish. They're conceited and rude. They believe they deserve what they have, and it's their right and responsibility to enjoy the fruits of their labors without interference. "It's mine, all mine, and nobody can take it away from me."

They cast an air of entitlement and a belief that they owe no one anything. This self-centeredness assumes they can do as they please regardless of the needs of others in the community. Preoccupied and obsessed, they have no time or concern for anyone else as they project an isolation that sometimes marks independence.

Regrettably, "ME" people are determined to let you know they have a special divine quality that deserves everyone's attention. Humility can't be found in their repertoire. Quite the opposite; they despise others who they regard to be "beneath them."

The Arrogance Dance

Benjamin Franklin once stated, "A man wrapped up in himself is a small bundle."

Like peacocks, self-centered persons proudly strut through life in the arrogance dance. They draw attention to their undisputable magnificence, their colorful feathers extended, their heads tilted beyond contradiction, and their big beady eyes focused on themselves.

The arrogance dance epitomizes the deadly sin of pride. Traditionally, St. Gregory the Great in the sixth century compiled a list of the seven deadly sins. They are pride, avarice, lust, anger, sloth, gluttony, and envy. The list is not one of prohibited actions like the Ten Commandments, but rather poisonous states of mind. Pride—an excessive belief in one's own strength—is considered the worst of the seven deadly sins because it's the gateway to the other six.

When one is focused exclusively on oneself, complacency creeps in and lulls human sensibility about the rest of the world. Pride does go before a fall. And the old adage is true: the higher they climb, the farther they fall. I know executives who have climbed the corporate ladder of success without regard for anyone but themselves. They suffer rude awakenings when they're forced to come down that self-created ladder of importance.

The arrogance dance of power exists to gain fame and fortune. It's popular because our Western celebrity culture emphasizes independence and individualism. Arrogant dancers stop at nothing to get what they desire.

An example of arrogance is displayed in the following fictitious transcript of a radio conversation between a U.S. naval ship and Canadian authorities off the coast of Newfoundland.

Canadians: Please divert your course fifteen degrees to the south to avoid a collision.

Americans: Recommend you divert your course fifteen degrees to the north.

Canadians: Negative. You will have to divert your course fifteen degrees to the south to avoid a collision.

Americans: This is the captain of a U.S. Navy ship. I say again, divert YOUR course.

Canadians: No. I say again, you divert YOUR course.

Americans: This is the aircraft carrier USS Lincoln, the second largest ship in the United States Atlantic Fleet. Three destroyers, three cruisers, and numerous support vessels accompany us. I demand that you change your course fifteen degrees north. I say again, that's one-five degrees north. I say again, that's one-five degrees north, or counter measures will be undertaken to ensure the safety of this ship.

Canadians: This is the Ferryland Head Lighthouse. Your call.

INSULARITY

"Don't Tell Me"

As French novelist Victor Hugo once reflected, "He does not weep who does not see."

People afflicted with insularity don't want to see the harsh realities of the world. They detach themselves from our human family and isolate themselves from the rigors of responsible citizenship. They put their blinders on so that nothing and no one disturbs their comfortable life behind high thick walls.

I respect people who are legitimately unaware and can appreciate someone who honestly says, "I didn't know that." However, I have little respect for those who consciously choose to be ignorant, whose thoughts are narrow and provincial. Irresponsible blindness, the curse of our time, is a perverse approach to life rooted in a fundamental misunderstanding of our place on the planet. We live in a profoundly interdependent world that requires interdependent thinking, feeling, and action. Therefore, shutting out the world doesn't protect anyone.

On the contrary, insularity endangers us. Deliberately unaware people think that what they don't know won't hurt them. They've been persuaded that if they don't know, then they won't be expected to respond. Some even refuse to watch television or read a newspaper. "The news is just too disturbing," someone complained to me. "Don't tell me."

The "insulars" clothe themselves in bubble-wrap to cushion themselves against what William Shakespeare called the "slings and arrows of outrageous fortune." They protect themselves from the sudden bumps and jolts of ordinary life. The Feb. 8, 2006 issue of *USA Today* indicated that most people aren't concerned about increasing globalization. In answer to the question "How would you rate the risks related to globalization?" 41% said moderate, 35% said low and 24% said high.

Monkey Business

Like the three monkeys, some succumb to the deadly attitude of insularity and "see no evil, hear no evil, and speak no evil." It's a common phrase used to describe people who don't want to get involved or turn a blind eye to the immorality of life around them. Sometimes, a fourth component "do no evil" is added to the phrase.

"Monkey business" people surround themselves with barbed-wire walls to preserve their privacy, and more importantly, to keep the world at a safe and invisible distance. They perceive the world to be so dangerous that the only way to be protected is to build an impenetrable fortress around themselves.

More than that, they desire isolation at home and in the global community. In 2007, the Pew Research Center released a report called "The Pew Global Attitudes Project," which showed that people "broadly embrace key tenets of economic globalization but fear the disruptions and downsides of participating in the global economy." People apparently worry about losing their traditional culture and national identities, believing their way of life needs protection against what the report calls "foreign influences."

Simply put, they fear immigration and might state their attitude this way: "We'd love you to visit but prefer you not stay."

Yet this deadly attitude of insularity betrays the fact that we share a common membership in the global family. Still, millions prefer to live alone on their little islands with no view of contemporary society and no connection to the fullness of life.

INTOLERANCE

"Do Not Touch!"

The deadly attitude of intolerance refers to an unwillingness to tolerate differences of opinions or beliefs. In *The Passionate State of Mind*, Eric Hoffer described intolerance using this revealing image: "Intolerance is the 'Do Not Touch' sign on something we cannot bear touching. We do not mind having our hair ruffled, but we will not tolerate any familiarity with the toupee that covers our baldness."[18]

In the movie *Pleasantville*, the citizens of the town can't tolerate change of any kind in any form by anyone. In Pleasantville, everything must remain pleasant. Ironically, at a town meeting, the mayor declared that any deviation from standards set by the Council would not be tolerated. So when basic colors got introduced into this "black and white" town, civil disobedience broke out.

Intolerance begins with ignorance and has far-reaching implications. As Helen Keller said, "No loss by flood and lightning, no destruction of cities and temples by the hostile forces of nature has deprived man of so many noble lives and impulses as those which his intolerance has destroyed." Intolerance knows no boundaries, spreading like a contagious virus, eating us from the inside out. It permeates our lives as a global family and prevents us from fulfilling our calling as a human race. It may even cause our global family's demise.

I'm acquainted with a narrow-necked-know-it-all who is a senior minister of a large Protestant church and believes he's God's only perfect gift to the world. He expresses his messiah complex by preaching with authority—his own authority—and by stating his opinion about everything from baseball to ballistic missile defense systems. Completely unable to listen, he interrupts people in mid-sentence to correct their faulty thinking and mistakes.

I know firsthand that he feels threatened when challenged. Once, at a meeting with him and five of our colleagues, I asked him a question that triggered an instant outburst, a verbal tirade, and a pounding on the table. He stormed out of the meeting and never came back. Even though I subsequently reached out to him, he still refuses to speak to me. His "Do Not Touch" message came through loud and clear.

Diversity Adversity

Intolerance shows up in diversity adversity, which is the unwillingness to be open to others different from us. It's the "they're different from me so I don't like them" syndrome that curses humankind. In my experience, it's one of the deadliest of the seven attitudes because it causes agonizing pain, and may, in the end, contribute to the collapse of civilization.

Another way of describing diversity adversity is prejudice. "Prejudice," wrote Ambrose Bierce in *The Devil's Dictionary* "is a vagrant opinion without visible means of support."[19] It's an adverse opinion formed beforehand or without knowledge or examination of the facts, a preconceived preference confirming the notion that "ignorance is bliss." People often act this way because they have little or no respect for themselves. As a result, they judge others from their own narrow viewpoints.

Years ago on my elementary school playground, I remember hearing this taunting chorus aimed at a bully in my fifth grade class: "Sticks and stones may break my bones, but names will never hurt me." I don't know who first said that, but whoever it was, they didn't get it right. Names *do* hurt. They sting. They cause pain far worse than a bloody nose or a bruised jaw. They penetrate deep into the human psyche and can cause irreparable damage. "Nigger." In our culture, that single word hurled at African Americans speaks volumes about fear, hate, and prejudice.

Here's a poignant example. A British primary school teacher, Gillian Gibbons, was teaching her class of second-graders in Sudan about voting by letting the children choose a name for the class mascot, a teddy bear. The kids chose Mohammed, a common name in this majority-Muslim country. However, in December, 2007, Gibbons was arrested on suspicion of blasphemy. She faced a possible sentence of 40 lashes and as many as six months in jail. Why? Because the naming of the teddy bear was considered an insult to the Prophet Mohammed. After diplomatic intervention, Gibbons served only a few days in jail, but was still found guilty of blasphemy and ordered to be deported. Prejudice at work.

INVINCIBILITY

"Above 'Em All"

The parish priest in a small country church said this to his congregation: "One day, everyone in this parish is going to die." A man in the back pew started to laugh. The priest, a little surprised, decided that the gentleman didn't hear him, so he repeated it loudly and clearly. "One day, everyone in this parish is going to die." The man continued to laugh. In frustration, the priest looked directly at him and repeated his statement. "One day, EVERYONE in this parish is going to DIE." The man kept laughing. "What's your problem, mister?" the priest finally asked. The man replied, "I'm not from this parish."

Invincibility is the close sibling of the deadly attitude we've already discussed, insolence.

Theses two attitudes walk through life hand-in-hand, believing that together as invincibility insurgents, they have life by the tail. They are absolutely certain they can overcome or defeat anything or anyone. Unconquerable. Invincible.

Writer Mark Twain pointed out the obvious danger of being ignorant and confident when he said this: "What gets us into trouble is not what we don't know. It's what we know for sure that just ain't so."

Consider, for example, the case of Jacob Zuma, age 64, deputy leader of the ruling African National Congress and former deputy president in South Africa. He was accused of raping a 31-year-old HIV-positive woman. At his trial, he admitted having unprotected sex with his accuser but said he "took a shower" afterward to diminish the risk of infection. He added insult to injury when he said he felt obliged to have sex with his accuser for "cultural" reasons—that is, the woman wore a skirt indicating she wanted sex and Zulu tradition dictated that he oblige. Regrettably, the judge acquitted Zuma.

Persons who suffer from the deadly attitude of invincibility have no knowledge or respect for lessons from the past. History informs us of the fragility of life and that having security—past, present, future— is an illusion. Feeling superior in a world of uncertainty is not only foolish but recklessly irresponsible. We ignore history at our peril.

The Grand Illusion

The 2002 movie *Catch Me If You Can* came out with the astute tag line "The true story of a real fake." It's about Frank Abagnale Jr. who, before his 19th birthday, successfully passed more than four million dollars of bad checks in 26 countries as a pilot, doctor, professor, and attorney. Abagnale avoided capture for a long time. Finally, police tracked him down and caught the young con artist in France where he was extradited, tried, and jailed.

Abagnale had buried himself under the illusion that he would never get caught. Eventually, reality hit. The deadly attitude of invincibility tricks people into believing they're untouchable, that nothing can penetrate their protective bubble. What were the Enron executives thinking? Why are those who engage in unprotected sex surprised when they're diagnosed with HIV/AIDS? Why do white supremacists think they have a monopoly on human worth?

Having confidence is one thing, but feeling superior begs trouble. "That will never happen to me. Never." On what planet are people who think like this living? On this earth, we can protect ourselves to the best of our ability, but we still have to realize that worst case scenarios do happen. Forget any illusion that implies we can be absolutely safe and secure.

Ironically, our contemporary society is so addicted to security, we've actually become more vulnerable as the so-called "war on terror" has pointed out perfectly. Security technologist Bruce Schneier, the author of *Beyond Fear: Thinking Sensibly about Security in an Uncertain*

World and called a "security guru" by *The Economist,* has been quoted as saying, "Exactly two things have made airline travel safer since 9/11: reinforcement of cockpit doors, and passengers who now know that they may have to fight back. Everything else… is security theater."[20]

While we're trying desperately to identify the good guys from the bad guys, fake identification and impersonators are commonplace. As much as we might like to legislate a safe environment for all to grow and prosper, we know intuitively we won't reach that state of trust unless we embrace the concept of the interdependence of the global family. And what's more dangerous than the clash of ideologies is the false sense of security that many maintain in the spirit of invincibility.

This chapter has addressed seven deadly attitudes that contribute to the seven inconvenient truths discussed in Chapter 3. This concludes Part II, which spelled out the choking condition of the global family. Here comes the good news. Part III, The Soulwise Conspirators, looks at how Soulwise Conspirators offer hope for improving the health of our global family.

TAKE FIVE FOR REFLECTION

How have you experienced these seven deadly attitudes? Write down incidents when you've observed or participated in ways each one has played out. Doing so will sharpen your antenna when you see others' behavior and sensitize your own in the future.

1. Indifference

2. Inhumanity

3. Insensitivity

4. Insolence

5. Insularity

6. Intolerance

7. Invincibility

PART III

THE SOULWISE CONSPIRATORS

CHAPTER 5

THE CONSPIRATORS' CORE

B ecause I travel a lot domestically and internationally, I have the opportunity to spend hours, sometimes days and nights, watching fellow travelers in airports and hotels. I try to guess their occupations and accomplishments, their disappointments and dreams. But most of all, I want to discern who they are underneath the trappings I see. I want to discover who they are at their core. What matters most to them? What do they believe?

This chapter explores the Soulwise Conspirators' core conviction and values to discover who they really are.

THEIR CORE CONVICTION

In 1964, at 13 years of age, John Arnold was on a Boy Scout National Jamboree trip to Valley Forge. On the way, his bus stopped in New York City. From the bus window, he saw an old woman ravenously eating garbage from a garbage can. She was somebody's grandmother, he thought. And she was so hungry! The movie-like scene "freaked me out," he said.

John's compassion for this starving old woman sparked a personal passion for addressing hunger. He discovered that hunger and poverty are close companions. Today, he's the executive director of the Second Harvest Gleaners Food Bank in Grand Rapids, Michigan, that in 2008 distributed 22 million pounds of food through 1,200 agencies to

400,000 people in West Michigan. John anticipates that the Food Bank will distribute 24.5 million pounds of food in 2009.

A Widening Circle

As noted previously, the primary principle of The Soulwise Conspiracy is interdependence, which claims we're all related and we're all responsible for and accountable to each other in the human family. Integral to the primary principle is compassion, the core conviction of Soulwise Conspirators.

Interdependence provides the universal relationship of the members of the human family, and compassion provides the energy to realize the family's full potential.

Compassion, derived from the Latin *compassio*, to suffer with, is the deep awareness of the suffering of another coupled with the wish to relieve it. Compassion is at the very heart of every Conspirator; it's the humble yet compelling feeling that determines and directs individual and collective values, visions, missions, strategies, and action.

The mission of The Soulwise Conspiracy is to breathe together with compassion, to enrich life, especially for society's less fortunate. The Hebrew Scriptures described the Conspiracy's mission as *tikkum olam*, accepting the challenge to "repair our world."

The expression of compassion, like throwing a pebble in a pond, creates a ripple effect and a widening circle of care and concern. Compassion provides the common ground on which to build a just and vigorous society.

Two *USA Today* columnists agree on this, if not much else. Cal Thomas, author and conservative syndicated political columnist, and Bob Beckel, liberal political consultant and former diplomat, have different opinions on almost every subject imaginable. Their weekly column, "Common Ground," demonstrates how Americans can build bridges between differences and find points of agreement. I heard them speak at the Economic Club of Grand Rapids on March 19, 2007, when they declared, "We need a more compassionate country." They want to open doors for civil discourse that's rooted in compassion.

The Soulwise Conspiracy is a prophetic voice in the wilderness of 21st-century humankind. The idea of living with compassion in the world is certainly not new. The Old Testament prophet Isaiah said, "Spend yourselves on behalf of the hungry and satisfy the needs of the oppressed, then your light will rise in the darkness." (Isaiah 58:10) He urged the faithful to be "a refuge for the poor, a refuge for the needy in distress, a shelter from the storm and a shade from the heat." (Isaiah 25:4) A more modern prophet, U.S. President Franklin D. Roosevelt, put compassion in perspective this way: "The test of our progress is not whether we add more to the abundance of those who have much; it is whether we provide enough for those who have too little."

Compassion compels us to respond from the heart, cutting through to the center of our lives so we can be ambassadors of hope. To many, it makes no sense. To Soulwise Conspirators, however, it makes perfect sense. For example, Dr. Paul Farmer, a graduate of Harvard Medical School, had every opportunity to practice in the United States with all its benefits and comforts. But Farmer chose to devote his life to fighting AIDS and tuberculosis in destitute places around the world. He currently lives in Haiti where he heads up Partners in Health.

> *Compassion creates a widening circle because our small, simple acts of love inspire others to offer their own acts of love.*

Small and Simple

Mother Teresa, an Albanian Catholic nun who founded the Missionaries of Charity, received the Nobel Prize for Peace in 1979 for her work among the poverty-stricken people of Calcutta. She observed, "We can do no great things, only small things with great love."

Acts of compassion are small, simple gifts to others—like a fresh orange juice commercial says, "simply unfooled around with." Although compassion on some level may be complex, it always comes down to acting in simple magical ways that often defy logic. "Kindness," said Mark Twain, "is the language that the deaf can hear and the blind can see."

A couple of years ago, I met a five-year-old child in a Maasai village in Kenya. Fascinated by my pencil, she asked if she could hold it. Without hesitation, I gave her the pencil and told her to keep it. I also gave her a small pad of paper. Her eyes lit up as if I had given her the world. She wrapped her arms around my leg and wouldn't let go.

Compassion, by its very nature, offers help to others without any expectation of return. Ironically, those who make compassionate investments receive substantial dividends anyway. As an example, a few months after returning to the States, I received in the mail a poem written in Swahili in pencil from that little girl I had met in Kenya. I will treasure that poem forever.

Sources of Inspiration for Compassion

President John F. Kennedy concluded his inaugural address on Friday, January 20, 1961, with these inspirational words: "Finally, whether you are citizens of America or citizens of the world, ask of us the same high standards of strength and sacrifice which we ask of you. With a good conscience our only sure reward, with history the final judge of our deeds, let us go forth to lead the land we love, asking His blessing and His help, but knowing that here on earth God's work must truly be our own."

For many including President Kennedy, the inspiration for compassion comes from God. In the world, a wide variety of religious belief systems advocate a life of compassion. But the religious community doesn't hold a monopoly on living compassionately; this mode has many legitimate sources.

My personal responsibility to act with compassion comes because I am a passionate follower of Jesus. I respect those who arrive at acting compassionately in other ways, but for me, the model of compassion in Jesus is exemplary and spiritually fulfilling. I share Jesus's core conviction of compassion and his direction to "love one another." (John 15:12).

This book, *Soulwise: How to Create a Conspiracy of Hope, Health and Harmony*, most commonly prompts the question, "Is it religious?" For people of faith, it probably is. Because the book deals with things that are eternal and unseen, it may be considered religious and/or spiritual. Certainly the idea of breathing life into our broken world has a spiritual foundation. However, I know many people who claim no religious or spiritual connection who perform selfless acts of compassion.

For those who follow a religious tradition, religions have far more in common than we usually consider. One of the difficulties in our cosmopolitan world is not knowing enough about our own faith, let alone the faith and practice of other religions.

Stephen Prothero, chair of the religion department at Boston University and author of *Religious Literacy: What Every American Needs to Know—and Doesn't*, argued that everyone needs to grasp the core beliefs, stories, symbols, and heroes of other faiths. He's claimed that religious illiteracy runs rampant in the United States, and that such ignorance is perilous because religion "is the most volatile constituent of culture" and often "one of the greatest forces for evil" in the world.[21] Prothero's research indicated that most Americans, even Christians, can't name even one of the four Gospels. Consequently, the professor would give Americans a failing grade in religion.

Sir Jonathan Sacks, chief rabbi of the United Hebrew Congregations of the British Commonwealth, has reminded us of the need to remain confident in our faith while being open to the journey of faith others may be taking. He said, "Those who are confident of their faith are not threatened but enlarged by the different faiths of others. ...There are, surely, many ways of arriving at this generosity of spirit and each faith may need to find its own."[22]

How Different Religions View the Golden Rule

This brief survey of world religions demonstrates how—at the core of their beliefs—they hold the message of compassion contained in the Golden Rule in common.

Buddhism
"A state that is not pleasant or delightful to me must be so for him also; and a state which is not pleasant or delightful for me, how could I inflict that on another?"
Samyutta Nikaya V. 353.35-354.2

Chinese Religion
"Do not do to others what you do not want them to do to you."
Confucius, Analects 15.23

Christianity
"In everything do unto others as you would have them do to you."
Matthew 7:12

Hinduism
"This is the sum of duty: do nothing to others that would cause you pain if done to you."
Mahabharata XIII. 114.8

Islam

"No one of you is a believer until he desires for his brother that which he desires for himself."
40 Hadith (sayings of Mohammad) of an-Nawawi 13

Jainism

"A person should treat all creatures as he himself would be treated."
Sutrakritanga 1.11.33

Judaism

"Do not do unto others what you would not want them to do to you."
Rabbi Hillel, Shabbat 31a

Shortly after Sept. 11, 2001, in an environment of increasing suspicion and hostility, Dr. Akbar S. Ahmed (a committed Muslim) and J. Douglas Holladay (a committed Christian) met and built a bridge of friendship. Dr. Ahmed holds the Ibn Khaldun Chair of Islamic Studies at American University in Washington, D.C., and Ambassador Holladay is a partner at Park Avenue Equity Partners and a chair of the Buxton Initiative, which facilitates interfaith dialogue.

Ahmed and Holladay agreed that "consciously or not, the world is in search of authentic models that engender hope and where genuine faith breeds civility and trust." They opened what they called their "bank account of goodwill and respect" and regularly made deposits. As trust in each other grew, they widened their circle to include CEOs, ambassadors, policy-makers, senators, military leaders, and journalists.

Ahmed and Holladay observed, "What we are learning is profound in its simplicity. *We are all more alike than different.* At the heart of most faith traditions is the desire to seek peace and to love one's neighbor. Caring and attempting to understand another's faith journey and perspective are not compromises but rather love in action. Differences need not be threatening; mutual understanding in an increasingly violent world needs to be rediscovered.

"In many parts of the world today, people are fighting over differences. We have decided instead to delight in our differences, concluding that on this small planet, a sustainable model of hope and civility might serve as a light in the midst of so much darkness." (www.buxtoninitiative.org/about/news_text.php)

Ahmed and Holladay's bank account of good will and respect keeps growing today with active Christian-Muslim dialogue and friendship on Capitol Hill. For example, an event sponsored by the Berkley Center for Religion, Peace, and World Affairs and the Interfaith Council of Georgetown University in Washington, D.C. will celebrate the efforts of Georgetown students to advance religious understanding on campus— an excellent display of the Golden Rule in action.

THEIR CORE VALUES

Values have a long history in the development of the world; they form a foundation for determining moral and ethical behavior. Benjamin Franklin, for example, sought to live by what he called 13 virtues: temperance, silence, order, resolution, frugality, industry, sincerity, justice, moderation, cleanliness, tranquility, chastity, and humility. Every week he would focus on one of the values, using it to help him evaluate his decision-making and behavior.

The United Nations Millennium Declaration adopted by the General Assembly of the United Nations on September 8, 2000, indicates the importance of the values of human dignity, equality, and equity at the global level. "As leaders we have a duty therefore to all the world's people, especially to the most vulnerable, and, in particular, the children of the world, to whom the future belongs...," states the Declaration. "We believe that the central challenge we face today is to ensure that globalization becomes a positive force for all the world's people." (www.un-documents.net/a55r2.htm)

The Declaration's six fundamental values believed to be essential to international relations in the 21st century are:

Freedom. Men and women have the right to live their lives and raise their children in dignity, free from hunger and from the fear of violence, oppression or injustice.

Equality. No individual and no nation must be denied the opportunity to benefit from development.

Solidarity. Global challenges must be managed in a way that distributes the costs and burdens fairly in accordance with basic principles of equity and social justice.

Tolerance. Human beings must respect one another, in all their diversity of belief, culture and language. Differences within and between societies should neither be feared nor repressed, but cherished as a precious asset of humanity.

Respect for nature. Prudence must be shown in the management of all living species and natural resources, in accordance with the precepts of sustainable development. Only in this way can the immeasurable riches provided to us by nature be preserved and passed on to our descendants.

Shared responsibility. Responsibility for managing worldwide economic and social development, as well as threats to international peace and security, must be shared among the nations of the world and should be exercised multilaterally.

The core conviction of compassion inspires six core values that direct the attitudes and behavior of Soulwise Conspirators. These six values closely mirror the values contained in the United Nations Millennium Declaration. The acronym GROWTH makes them easy to remember:

Generosity

Respect

Openness

Wisdom

Trust

Honesty

Generosity

Soulwise Conspirators give from the heart with no expectation of return. They live with a spirit of thanksgiving, appreciating their own blessings, and, in turn, sharing their abundance with others in need. They don't have to be persuaded to give; they only have to be made aware of the need.

Joy Lawrence, a member of my congregation several years ago, exemplifies a Soulwise Conspirator. On a Sunday morning, she'd heard me say in a sermon I was eager to enter doctoral studies but didn't have the necessary resources. She had also learned I wanted to purchase a specific book for my library. One day, she handed me a wrapped present that not only contained the book I'd mentioned, but five crisp $1,000 bills as bookmarks.

*I'm convinced that most people do want to
share but don't know how. Children who grow
up in homes where generosity is modeled usually
follow the tradition of generosity in their lives
and pass it on to their own children. After church
one Sunday, I met a distraught child in my congregation. Through her sobs and tears, she told me she'd
lost her offering. "It was a shiny one," she said. "It's for
the hungry kids." We searched everywhere and finally
found the lost coin—a brand new shiny penny.*

A Soulwise Conspirator doesn't have to be wealthy to be generous. According to a study by the NewTithing Group, a San Francisco philanthropic organization that analyzed IRS data to measure the percentage of income given to charity, the super-rich are not the most generous. We give what we can in the currency of our lives—our time, talent, and resources. The most some people can afford to do is be present with others in their time of need.

In his book, *Giving: How Each of Us Can Change the World*, President Bill Clinton encouraged people to move from *getting* to *giving*. "We all have the capacity to do great things," said President Clinton. "My hope is that the people and stories in this book will lift spirits, touch hearts, and demonstrate that citizen activism and service can be a powerful agent of change in the world." He urges each of us, regardless of income, available time, age, and skills to give people the opportunity to live out their dreams.[23]

Susan Arnold, president of Procter and Gamble's Global Business Units and recipient of the United Nations Association of the USA's 2007 Global Leadership Award, epitomizes corporate generosity. Proctor and Gamble (P&G) invests in corporate social responsibility through its Live, Learn & Thrive program dedicated to improving life for children in need. Each year P&G reaches roughly 50 million children through the program. Another initiative, Children's Safe Drinking Water, provided 2 billion liters of water to avert 80 million days of diarrhea and save 10,000 lives in 2007.[24]

Respect

The second value inspired by the core conviction of compassion is respect.

Soulwise Conspirators consider themselves trustees of their own lives as well as the lives of every other member of the human family. They also consider themselves trustees of all creation and its four basic elements of earth, air, fire, and water. They conduct their lives with a keen sensitivity to all living creatures and the environment.

They are impartial in their dealings with other human beings. They celebrate the diversity of humanity and nature, and take seriously personal and environmental stewardship. For them, this sense of responsibility is not relegated to a program to sustain the environment. Rather, it's a philosophy they hold and practice in their everyday lives.

Soulwise Conspirators are tolerant of all people. Others are never seen as strange, simply different. They treat all human beings the same regardless of their status, wealth, or position, their gender or age, their race, color, or creed. I especially admire the approach the Episcopal Church takes regarding funerals. Whether the deceased was a prince, a princess, or a pauper, each soul receives the same words of honor and comfort in burial rituals.

The American poet and essayist Walt Whitman described respect this way:

> *This is what you should do: Love the earth*
> *and sun and animals,*
> *despise riches, give alms to everyone that asks,*
> *stand up for the stupid and crazy,*
> *devote your income and labor to others, hate tyrants,*
> *argue not concerning God,*
> *have patience and indulgence toward the people...*
> *reexamine all you have been told in school or*
> *church or in any book,*
> *dismiss what insults your very soul,*
> *and your flesh shall become a great poem.*[25]

I've been blessed with many people in my life whose lives were "great poems," models worthy of my respect. Although they're very different, the common thread that connects them is their respect-ability.

One of these people I deeply respect is Edith Lucas, a Baptist deaconess I came to know at Junior Church, a lively Christian education program she coordinated for 10 to 12 year olds for an hour on Sunday morning. "Aunt Edie," as we affectionately called her, was consistent. When she spoke, we listened and respected her judgment. One day she announced I'd be preaching at the morning service of the whole church. Aunt Edie didn't ask if I felt comfortable with the idea; she just declared I would do it and she'd be proud of me. Because she took me under her wing, I preached my first sermon when I was 10 years old. Thanks to Aunt Edie, I have preached thousands of sermons since.

Openness

The third value inspired by the core conviction of compassion is openness, the capacity to be receptive to new and different ideas or opinions of others. Soulwise Conspirators are willing to think with an open mind about the views of others no matter how wild or wacky those ideas may be. They are confident and comfortable enough in their own skin to welcome up-close-and-personal conversations.

Soulwise Conspirators make friends with change and feel invigorated by its presence. They aren't afraid to grapple with any issue, even contentious ones, from several vantage points at the same time. They openly evaluate new evidence and see things from a wide variety of perspectives. And, after rigorous assessment, they're willing to change their minds.

Soulwise Conspirators have a particular openness to what's next. They perceive their role to be creators of the future so they leave the world better than when they found it. They consider themselves trustees of their own lives as well as the lives of others in the global family.

> *What others may consider setbacks, Conspirators see as possibilities or opportunities. As Tour de France champion cyclist Lance Armstrong reflected, "The most interesting thing about cancer is that it can be one of the most positive, life-affirming, incredible experiences ever."*[26]

In an age when so many appear to be close-minded and rigid in their perceptions, Soulwise Conspirators want to dialogue with anyone anywhere in the world who will enter into serious conversation. They'd agree with former Soviet leader Mikhail Gorbachev, who said this in a speech to the United Nations, December 7, 1988: "Freedom of choice is a universal principle to which there should be no exceptions."

When I was in seminary, I had the rare opportunity to have a professor who personified openness. I got to know Dr. Gay Albaugh well because I took his classes for three years and completed my master's thesis under his direction. I am grateful for his remarkable quiet openness to the wide variety of religious experiences and for his unwavering commitment to creative substantive dialogue. Like a Soulwise Conspirator, Albaugh believed one must look up to see the horizon.

Wisdom

Common sense makes common practice. That's the singular purpose of wisdom inspired by the core conviction of compassion. Soulwise Conspirators seek wisdom in order to accurately and sensitively address the needs of the global family, and then they develop strategies to fulfill those needs.

Wisdom is the power to understand what's true, right, or lasting and integrate it into everyday living. It demands an internal process of discernment, a quality of being able to grasp and comprehend what is obscure, and then translate that obscurity into practical clues for living fully in the 21st century.

Wisdom is the skill of applying knowledge with insight, of carefully weighing various influencing factors, making sense of complicated and often conflicted situations, and thus providing guidance for the road ahead.

Who has contributed wisdom to enrich your life? I was fortunate to grow up with "wisdom personified." My mother, Mary Anne Sawyer Johnson, who died before her time at 48 (when I was 10 years old), modeled a calm wisdom that continues to inspire me. Her favorite phrase was "the future is as bright as the promises of God." My father, Lamont Webster Johnson, brought a different kind of wisdom to our family. He loved music and played a sweet saxophone with big band leader Guy Lombardo and the Royal Canadians. For him, life was like a musical score that we write and perform one song at a time.

Soulwise Conspirators draw on the power of collective wisdom. The thesis of *New Yorker* business columnist James Surowiecki's book *The Wisdom of Crowds: Why the Masses Are Smarter Than the Few and How Collective Wisdom Shapes Business, Economies, Societies, and Nations* is that "under the right circumstances, groups are remarkably intelligent, and are often smarter than the smartest people in them."[27]

It may sound counterintuitive, but the numbers show it's true if Surowiecki's three key criteria—independence, diversity, and decentralization—are satisfied. If you ask a large enough group to make a prediction, their errors will cancel one another out. For example, an analysis of the TV studio audience of "Who Wants to Be a Millionaire" found that the audience guessed the right answer to questions 91% of the time, while "experts" guessed the right answer only 65% of the time.[28]

Given the "wisdom of crowds," Soulwise Conspirators from time to time feel as if they're all alone and can't reach the world with their wisdom. But they must be willing to dare, to be so confident in the wisdom of their cause that they don't even consider following the crowd.

> *Lebanese-American poet Kahlil Gibran put the daring conspiratorial component of wisdom in perspective this way: "There are seasons in human affairs, of inward and outward revolution when new depths seem to be broken up in the soul, when new wants are unfolded in multitudes and a new undefined good is thirsted for. These are periods when to dare is the highest wisdom."*

Of all the values Soulwise Conspirators live by, wisdom is key.

Trust

I had the privilege of being in Boy Scouts and attained the honor of Queen's Scout, the Canadian equivalent to the American Eagle Scout designation. The most valuable lesson I learned (beyond not eating too many wild raspberries or little green apples) was how to earn and maintain trust, the foundation of all human interaction. Trust wasn't just a good philosophical idea, it was practical, especially when we were shooting the rapids or staying warm camping in the northern Ontario winter.

Others who've been involved with the Scouting movement confirm this essential benefit of learning to trust. That trust imbedded in our psyches has had a ripple effect on people around the world. Scouts have taken on a variety of leadership roles in society and fulfilled this Scout Oath: "On my honor I will do my best to do my duty to God and country and obey the Scout Law; to help other people at all times; to keep myself physically strong, mentally awake, and morally straight." (www.scouting.org/boyscouts.aspx)

Here are examples of the ripple effect. In 2003, of the 100 U.S. senators serving in Washington, 53 were Scouts, 8 of whom were Eagles. NASA's astronaut list includes 108 former Scouts and 37 Eagles. Every man who died on the space shuttle Columbia had been a Boy Scout.

Trust may even play a part in longevity. Why do residents of Okinawa, Japan, and Sardinia, Italy, and Loma Linda, California, live longer and have healthier lives than anyone else on earth? Dan Buettner sought to find out their common secrets to long life despite their many differences in backgrounds and beliefs. In an article in *National Geographic*, "New Wrinkles on Aging," Buettner summarized these super seniors' secrets with these actions: honor family, stay active, find purpose, keep friends, eat vegetables, have faith, take time off, and celebrate life.[29] Note how all of these "secrets," with the possible exception of "eat vegetables," requires trust.

Soulwise Conspirators create environments in which trust can flourish. They foster relationships that enable people to make and keep their promises. And when trust is broken, they don't jump ship. They hang in there and help others on the long, difficult road to reestablishing trust.

I served as a trained intentional interim minister at a church that had been rocked by a scandal involving the sexual indiscretion of its minister. That congregation embodied such genuine trust despite the betrayal that the healing process, although painful, did take place and the mission restored.

Honesty

"Honesty is the best policy" according to the old proverb. Soulwise Conspirators tell the truth, the whole truth, and nothing but the truth.

Integrity is their middle name. You can count on them to be honest no matter what because honesty resides at the core of their being. *Not* to tell the truth isn't in their repertoire.

Soulwise Conspirators are committed to the core conviction of compassion that inspires the value of honesty. Their words and actions are transparent so the world can see the honesty in their hearts.

The difference between honesty and dishonesty can be striking. Honesty expresses self-respect and respect for others; dishonesty expresses disdain for oneself and for others. Honesty seeks and thrives on living in the light; dishonesty seeks and thrives on living in the dark. Honesty reveals the truth; dishonesty conceals the truth. Honesty is open; dishonesty is closed.

As pointed out earlier about the value of wisdom, knowledge and wisdom have a distinct partnership. Knowledge and integrity do as well. One without the other prevents building relationships of trust that could change the world. One in partnership with the other presents the possibility of thriving as a civilization. Eighteenth-century English author Dr. Samuel Johnson described this ageless partnership by saying, "Integrity without knowledge is weak and useless, and knowledge without integrity is dangerous and dreadful." (www.samueljohnson.com)

> *Telling the truth has consequences. The idea that truth hurts is borne out in experience. Corporate whistleblowers know the agony that exposing the truth can bring. However, one doesn't have to be brutally honest and communicate the truth with malice. Telling the truth can be done with sincerity and grace. The mission of The Soulwise Conspiracy requires heart-strong people who can tell the truth and call for change even though they may be unpopular.*

Soulwise Conspirators respect themselves and every member of the global family.

They are upright in principle and action, and care more about their convictions than what people may or may not think. They vigorously uphold truth as they perceive it.

Telling the truth opens to forgiveness and can restore relationships—so essential for peaceful and fruitful international relationships as well as personal ones. Sometimes telling the truth can open new opportunities. When I was in fifth grade and playing baseball at recess, I accidentally hit a ball through the principal's office window. I went right in to confess my error. He thanked me for telling him the truth—and then he surprised me. "Why aren't you on the school's baseball team?" he asked. "See you at practice after school."

James Kouzes and Barry Posner, co-authors of *A Leader's Legacy*, contend that the legacy you leave is the life you lead. Soulwise Conspirators will leave a lasting legacy for the global family by practicing these values inspired by their core conviction of compassion: Generosity, Respect, Openness, Wisdom, Trust, and Honesty.

TAKE FIVE FOR REFLECTION

1. What are *your* sources of inspiration for the core conviction of compassion?

   •

   •

   •

2. Name three times you've witnessed the power of compassion?

   •

   •

   •

3. Recall three times when you've shown compassion to others.

   •

   •

   •

4. Name people who model the values of Soulwise Conspirators.

   Generosity:

   Respect:

   Openness:

   Wisdom:

Trust:

Honesty:

5. Name three people you trust.

- •
- •
- •

CHAPTER **6**

RADICAL GLOBAL SERVANT LEADERS

Let's move on to explore the seven key qualities Soulwise Conspirators possess and practice. Their profile forms the acronym RADICAL. The word "radical" derives from the Latin *radix,* which means "root."

Soulwise Conspirators are, first and foremost, rooted in themselves and then grounded as world citizens. Here's a brief overview of their qualities and how they use them to enrich the lives of members of our global family.

Rooted	Embrace their humanity with humility
Authentic	Celebrate their creation with service
Distinctive	Express their uniqueness with boldness
Instinctive	Anticipate their future with clarity
Competent	Engage their gifts with skill
Accountable	Voice their verses with gratitude
Linked	Share their dreams with grace

To illustrate each of these qualities, I have examples from both historical figures and people I know. At the end of the chapter, I suggest you prepare your own list of Soulwise Conspirators.

ROOTED

Soulwise Conspirators embrace their humanity with humility.

Soulwise Conspirators are, in the original sense of the word, firmly rooted. Like trees planted in rich soil, they have roots that spread down and out to provide a solid foundation for their development as well as stability and nourishment for strength and flexibility. They are therefore able to resist the normal threats of wind and weather, and bend rather than break in the storms they may encounter.

They fully embrace their humanity. They know who they are and who they are not. They know what makes them tick and what ticks them off. They know what gives them meaning and what steals meaning. Knowing what's important to them, they feel secure in their own identity.

From this solid foundation with their feet firmly planted on the ground, they can realize their potential to make a difference in the lives of others. "Peanuts" cartoonist Charles Shultz shared this philosophy. He pointed out that people with roots are the ones we remember. For years, he asked people to take this quiz:

1. Name the five wealthiest people in the world.
2. Name the last five Heisman Trophy winners.
3. Name the last five winners of the Miss America contest.
4. Name ten people who have won the Nobel or Pulitzer Prize.
5. Name the last decade's worth of World Series winners.

Shultz noted that few of us remember the headliners of yesterday, even though they were the best in their fields. When the applause dies, awards tarnish, and achievements are forgotten, he recommended taking another quiz.

1. Name a few teachers who aided your journey through school.
2. Name three friends who have helped you through a difficult time.
3. Name five people who have taught you something worthwhile.
4. Name a few people you enjoy spending time with.
5. Name half a dozen heroes whose stories have inspired you. (www.wltc.org/documents/ShultzPhilo.htm)

Shultz teaches that the people who make a difference in our lives aren't necessarily the ones with the most credentials, the most money, or the most rewards. Those who make a permanent difference simply care—the role models that include family members, teachers, coaches, and community leaders.

Soulwise Conspirators embrace their humanity with humility. They possess character, a word that derives from the Greek "to mark or engrave." Their hearts are engraved with the mark of humility, enabling them to live from the inside out. Compassionate Conspirators stand in awe before the mystery of life and pledge to walk humbly into the future with their neighbor.

In his best-selling book, *Good to Great*, Jim Collins described Level 5 leaders—the leaders with the highest level of capabilities in a hierarchy of executive capabilities identified in his research—as having a unique blend of humility and resolve.[30]

Soulwise Conspirators know that it's not good enough to know yourself, as profitable as that may be. At the highest level, you have the capacity to know yourself *and* exploit that self-knowledge to actively care for the human family.

"A hero," said mythologist Joseph Campbell, "is someone who has given his or her life to something bigger than oneself. When we stop thinking primarily about ourselves and our own self-preservation, we undergo a truly heroic transformation of consciousness."

AUTHENTIC

Soulwise Conspirators celebrate their creation with service.

> *Soulwise Conspirators consider themselves chips off the Creator's block, a sign of their authenticity. They're here on purpose and not by accident. "We are finite beings made for the infinite," asserted Bishop Desmond Tutu in a speech delivered in Grand Rapids, Michigan, on March 25, 2003.*

Every person bears a genuine human identity. By examining a person's deoxyribonucleic acid (DNA), we can attest to his or her authenticity. No two persons are exactly alike. Dr. Timothy Johnson, physician, ordained clergyman, and ABC television medical journalist, wrote concisely about the structure and function of DNA in his book, *Finding God in the Questions: A Personal Journey.* "Every cell in our body contains a string of genetic material about one meter long coiled into a tiny ball five thousandths of a meter in diameter. Every time a cell divides, this coiled strand unzips down the middle into two strands; then each forms a partner strand. The result is two new cells, each containing the entire genetic code which—thanks to the human genome project— we know consists of over three billion 'letters,' containing the blueprint for the entire human being."[31]

Our DNA is our primal link to each other.

Part of our interdependence in the human family is having a genetic authenticity—a unique human identity to share for the betterment of all humankind. And we're linked to each other in a kaleidoscopic chain of rich color and diversity. The world hungers for authenticity. Soulwise Conspirators can satisfy that hunger by acting out of their own sense of common authenticity.

After the World War I, Eglantine Jebb went to Macedonia to organize relief for the victims of war, including millions of children. She struggled for children's rights and founded Save the Children International. At the Declaration of Geneva in 1924, she persuaded the League of Nations to adopt her Children's Charter, and in 1925, she joined the League of Nations Council for the Protection of Children. Jebb's conviction was this: "Help should not be a gift from above but rather help aimed at self-help between equals where everyone contributes according to their ability from a feeling of human fellowship across racial, ethnic and national borders." (www.civilsocietyinternational.org/nisorgs/azerbaij/savekids.htm)

Soulwise Conspirators celebrate and honor their creation by compassionately co-creating with others to ensure the worth and dignity of every member of the global family. Appreciating what they have, the Conspirators' first impulse is to share by serving others. I'm proud to be an active member of Rotary International. Its underlying premise is to improve the welfare of others, which can be summed up in this motto: "Service above self."

Simply stated, Soulwise Conspirators focus on improving the quality of people's lives. When I was setting up Kibera Kids Kitchen, a feeding program for children in Kibera slum in Nairobi, Kenya, I visited a smaller slum where I met a 22-year-old vivacious Canadian woman who was coordinating another feeding program for 50 orphans.

I watched this single, recent college graduate interact with the children, many infected with AIDS, as if they were her own African family. The children looked up to her as one of the only persons on whom they could completely depend. She taught, fed, and played with them. She won their trust—her prize for sharing her authenticity and celebrating her creation with service.

DISTINCTIVE

Soulwise Conspirators express their uniqueness with boldness.

Soulwise Conspirators are originals. Mahatma Gandhi described our distinctiveness as "a divine singular signature." Yes, we have unique fingerprints, unique irises, unique voices. Each of us is simply, wonderfully, incredibly, one of a kind!

Yet we all share a common human authenticity in our DNA. Only 1% of our individual DNA distinguishes us from the other 6.6 billion people on earth and the 4.4 people being born every second.

Sometimes our outer uniqueness is obvious. One glance at Stumpy, a duckling born with four legs in New Forest, Hampshire, England, shows what an unusual creature could be. Other times, in the case of identifying the marks of differentiation in beetles, we need to observe closely from over 60,000 varieties. Our inner uniqueness is usually a little more difficult to determine than our outer qualities. As Rev. Henry Ward Beecher commented, "Every artist dips his brush in his own soul and paints his own nature in his pictures."

> *We are an unmatchable combination of body,*
> *mind, and spirit.*

Once the fourth richest Englishwoman, Anita Roddick, founded The Body Shop, a worldwide chain store of natural beauty and self-care products with more than 2,000 outlets in 49 countries. The Body Shop continues to support political causes such as animal-testing bans, environmental protection, Third World debt relief, rain forest preservation, and protecting the whales. The London *Telegraph* once described Roddick as "loquacious, wacky, and opinionated." But one can't deny her uniqueness and her belief that one person has the power to make a significant difference in the world. As she once stated, "If you think you're too small to have an impact, try going to bed with a mosquito."

Soulwise Conspirators take on missions of heroic importance and guide their dreams to fulfillment with their singular distinctiveness. My father used to say that if you want meaning in life, measure yourself against a worthy challenge. Or as Billy Crystal's character said in the 1998 movie *My Giant,* "The size of the villain determines the size of the hero. Without Goliath, David is just a punk throwing rocks."

In 1788, William Wilberforce, a British member of Parliament who remained politically independent, took on a "giant" and embarked on a 19-year struggle to abolish the slave trade. He secured the abolition of slavery in the British West Indies in 1807 but died a month before Parliament passed his Abolition of Slavery bill. Wilberforce described himself this way: "If to be feelingly alive to the sufferings of my fellow-creatures is to be a fanatic, I am one of the most incurable fanatics ever permitted to be at large." (www.britannia.com/bios/wilberforce.html)

Soulwise Conspirators come in all shapes and sizes—no two exactly alike. Some express uniqueness with a fiery mind and a sizzling soul; others demonstrate sensitivity with a quiet demeanor. Together, they serve the mission of The Soulwise Conspiracy by accepting, developing, and employing their own unique qualities and spirit to offer love to humanity.

INSTINCTIVE

Soulwise Conspirators anticipate their future with clarity.

"Follow your instincts," successful entrepreneur and television host Oprah Winfrey counseled her audience in a university commencement address. "That's where true wisdom manifests itself."

Jonas Salk, an American physician, joined Thomas Francis at the University of Michigan School of Public Health in 1942 to develop an immunization against influenza. In 1947, Salk moved to the Pittsburgh School of Medicine where he researched various strains of virus that cause polio. That research led to the first safe vaccine to reduce the incidence of polio. At the time, Salk reflected, "It is always with excitement that I wake up in the morning wondering what my intuition will toss up to me, like gifts from the sea. I work with it and rely on it. It's my partner." (www.salk.edu)

Soulwise Conspirators are instinctive. They anticipate the future with an inborn pattern of behavior characteristic of a species. This instinct evolves from an innate capability or aptitude, resulting in a powerful motivation or impulse, a seemingly unconscious internal alarm that signals danger or opportunity. Most Soulwise Conspirators don't remember a time when they didn't have this capacity to look ahead by instinct. Perhaps they're born with this quality. "I can't tell you about jazz," said jazz legend Louis Armstrong. "You know it when you hear it."

Soulwise Conspirators know a need when they see it and know instinctively what to do. Some call it a "gut instinct," a feeling for making the right move at the right time. Perhaps an animal instinct. Albert Einstein thought so when he said, "It is better for people to be like the beasts... they should be more intuitive; they should not be too conscious of what they are doing while they are doing it."

Dr. Temple Grandin, professor of animal science at Colorado State University and author of *Thinking in Pictures*, said her experience as a person with autism instinctively helps her think primarily in pictures not words. "Visual thinking," she noted, "has enabled me to build entire systems in my imagination. During my career I have designed all kinds of equipment, ranging from corrals for handling cattle on ranches to systems for handling cattle and hogs during veterinary procedures and slaughter.... One third of the cattle and hogs in the United States are handled in equipment I have designed." (www.grandin.com/inc/visual. thinking.html)

Soulwise Conspirators anticipate the future with clarity. They don't have a crystal ball; they just *know.* They put the puzzle pieces of the future together, follow their internal processing system, and move to fulfill the future they've instinctively imagined. Intuition is definitely a quality you want in your attorney, your broker, and your realtor.

Edie Weiner doesn't have a crystal ball, but she does have an amazing capacity to see the future with new eyes. She's president of Weiner, Edrich, Brown, Inc., a futurist consulting group in the United States. One of the most influential practitioners of social, technological, political, and economic intelligence-gathering, her clients range from the U.S. Congress to Fortune 500 companies. With her partner,

Arnold Brown, she has co-written four books, the latest of which is *FutureThink: How to Think Clearly in a Time of Change*.[32]

I've known Edie for two decades through our membership in the World Future Society, and I value her insight and friendship. She also shares her instinct through Esteem Teams, an innovative program she founded in which executive women mentor at-risk girls in the inner city. In addition, she chairs ThinkQuest NYC, which helps bridge the technology gap for inner-city students.

Anticipating the future with clarity is a key leadership quality of Soulwise Conspirators that can benefit society. Malcolm Gladwell, in his book *Blink: The Power of Thinking without Thinking* discusses the genius of intuition and the power of unconscious thought. He contends that truly successful decision-making relies on a balance between deliberate and instinctive thinking.[33]

Wesley Autrey, 50, showed his instinctive ability at the 137th Street and Broadway Harlem subway station in New York City on January 2, 2007. Autrey, father of two, noticed a man suffering a seizure fall on the subway tracks and jumped in to save the stranger, Cameron Hollopeter. When Autrey looked up, he saw the lights of an oncoming train. He grabbed Hollopeter in a bear hug and together they flattened themselves between the tracks in the shallow trough filled with dirty water. Five cars roared over them before the train screeched to a stop. Autrey was humble about putting his life on the line, or rather between the tracks. He said, "I just saw someone in distress and went to his aid."[34]

COMPETENT

Soulwise Conspirators engage their gifts with skill.

Conspirators identify, develop and share their gifts. For example, Albert Schweitzer obtained a doctorate in philosophy in 1899 and a doctor of medicine in 1913. He had a distinguished musical career as an internationally known concert organist and also wrote *The Quest for the Historical Jesus*. He founded a hospital at Lambaréné in French Equatorial Africa. In 1917, he and his wife were sent to a French internment camp as prisoners of war. In 1953, Schweitzer won the 1952 Nobel Peace Prize for his phlosophy of "reverence for life" expressed in many ways, but most famously for founding the Albert Schweitzer Hospital in Lambaréné, France. The world would have been poorer had Albert Schweitzer not made the supreme effort to use his gifts.

Identifying the constellation of gifts we possess takes effort and determination. The strongest gifts in the constellation are variously described as one's dominant competence or genius. Peter Drucker, the father of modern management theory, once said, "The most important thing is to know what you're good at." It's no secret that some possess a richer constellation than others. However, each of us has a purpose in life and all purposes are important. The key? To identify our competent gifts as honestly as we can and put those gifts to work in the best way possible to benefit humanity.

Soulwise Conspirators engage their gifts with skill. Yet it's not enough for them to identify their competence. Unless competence is purposely put to work, it has no value in the great scheme of things. So Soulwise Conspirators engage their competence with their whole being to effect change in the world. They recognize their tremendous power to receive and perform acts of kindness in the world, and they let their love loose in the human family.

Polish-born French physicist, Marie Curie, put competence, discovery, and application in perspective this way: "Humanity needs practical men, who get the most out of their work, and, without forgetting the general good, safeguard their own interests. But humanity also needs dreamers, for whom the disinterested development of an enterprise is so captivating that it becomes impossible for them to devote their care to their own material profit."

> *It's not enough to have the ingredients for a recipe.*
> *We need to employ cooking competence to combine*
> *the elements according to the recipe to achieve*
> *the desired result.*

Everyone has a contribution to make.

ACCOUNTABLE

Soulwise Conspirators voice their verses with gratitude.

On consciously forging the future of humanity, American poet Walt Whitman mused, "That the powerful play goes on and you may contribute a verse." Indeed, Soulwise Conspirators hold themselves accountable for creating their own verses and helping others create theirs. They feel a strong sense of responsibility for and accountability to the human family to ensure that the powerful play goes on.

This internal desire is borne of a commitment to stewardship for life and a strong desire to contribute to the welfare of all people in the world. Convinced they've been given the ability to create their own verses, Conspirators voice those verses and offer them in the spirit of compassion—the primary principle of The Soulwise Conspiracy.

Celebrated Russian poet Yevgeny Yevtushenko stunned the graduating class of 1991 at Juniata College in Huntington, Pennsylvania, with these words: "Forget the vulgar, insulting, patronizing fairy tale that has been hammered into your heads since childhood that the main purpose of life is the pursuit of happiness. It is not! The main purpose of life is the pursuit of holiness—a holiness that comes through entering the suffering of others."

Still, millions around the globe die with their verses still in them. Not that they haven't thought about them—and perhaps even formulated them. Human beings dream of how they could make the world a better place. In traveling around the world, I've never met anyone who didn't have a dream. But for one reason or another, these people haven't actually voiced their verses.

It doesn't have to be a long, complicated, earth-shattering verse. Sometimes minuscule is marvelous. Marion Wright Edelman, president and founder of the Children's Defense Fund, once said, "You just need to be a flea against injustice. Enough committed fleas biting strategically can make even the biggest dog uncomfortable and transform even the biggest nation."

LINKED

Soulwise Conspirators share their dreams with grace.

Born in Scotland, Andrew Carnegie immigrated to the United

States and settled in Pittsburgh. After the Civil War, he invested in the iron and steel industry, which made him a wealthy man. For the rest of his life, he donated large amounts to worthy causes in Britain and America, including public libraries and universities. Carnegie, who believed that individual wealth should be used for public good, stated, "Teamwork is the ability to work together toward a common vision. It is the fuel that allows common people to attain uncommon results."

Even though all people dream, Soulwise Conspirators appreciate dreaming differently than the billions of other dreamers. They realize they're not the sole owners of their dreams and don't selfishly protect them fearing they might be stolen. On the contrary, they consider themselves fortunate to be trustees of their dreams and willingly share them so their dreams for the welfare of the human family can come true. They endorse what Sir Isaac Newton advised when he said, "If I have seen further, it is only by standing on the shoulders of giants."

> *Soulwise Conspirators realize their dreams can never be achieved by their efforts alone. So they reach out and cultivate friendships with like-minded people who will actively support the fulfillment of their common dream. I'm reaching out to friends and their networks to achieve my own dream of establishing The Soulwise Conspiracy to perform CPR to save our global family.*

Advances in technology have made it possible for us to be in touch with anyone, anywhere, any time. We can create a virtual community to address our problems and opportunities. According to futurist David Pearce Snyder, more than one-third of the world's population will be online in less than a decade. So I'm conspiring with information technology experts to perform their magic for The Soulwise Conspiracy website.

Friendships in the global family are becoming critical these days. If we saw each other as friends, we would have a bond that enables us to work together in harmony to face and work out our differences. As Ralph Waldo Emerson asserted, "God evidently does not intend us all to be rich, or powerful, or great, but he does intend us all to be friends."

On a visit to the Edison & Ford Winter Estates in Fort Myers, Florida, I noticed a photo of these five 20th-century giants: Thomas Edison, Henry Ford, Harvey Firestone, Alexis Carrel, and Charles Lindbergh. Below the photograph was this caption: "Uncommon Friends Association." These gentlemen formed bonds of friendship over the years, as recorded in *Uncommon Friends* written by James Newton who knew all five personally. Newton pointed out the personal traits they had in common as being a love of adventure, a sense of purpose, unending personal growth, and commitment to helping friends.[35]

Denis Hayes had a dream he shared with grace. *Time* magazine selected him as "Hero of the Planet" in 1999 for his dream that became reality—Earth Day. At the age of 24, Hayes became national coordinator for the first Earth Day held on April 22, 1970. He organized 2,000 events involving 20 million Americans to promote awareness of the deterioration of the environment. Now president and CEO of the Bullitt Foundation in Seattle Washington, Hayes continues to chair the board of the international Earth Day Network.

All it takes to change the world is for one Soulwise Conspirator to share his or her dream with grace by lighting a single candle. Then another lights a candle, and another and another until light covers the earth. A statement attributed to the Buddha noted that "thousands of candles can be lit from a single candle, and the life of the candle will not be shortened. Happiness never decreases by being shared."

Soulwise Conspirators are linked, and they share their dreams for the benefit of humankind.

Part I of the book described The Soulwise Conspiracy. Part II described Seven Inconvenient Truths and Seven Deadly Attitudes and Part III The Soulwise Conspirators. Part IV, A Guide to Becoming a Soulwise Conspirator, presents the seven necessary steps to make your dream for the global family come true.

TAKE FIVE FOR REFLECTION

1. Describe your understanding of the role of a servant leader.

2. Name three ways you consider yourself to be distinctive.

   •

   •

   •

3. To what three persons or organizations are you accountable?

   •

   •

   •

4. Name people in your life you would nominate for Soulwise Conspirators who exemplify the seven characteristics of Soulwise Conspirators discussed in this chapter.

   Rooted – Embrace their humanity with humility:

   Authentic – Celebrate their creation with service:

   Distinctive – Express their uniqueness with boldness:

   Instinctive – Anticipate their future with clarity:

   Competent – Engage their gifts with skill:

   Accountable – Voice their verses with gratitude:

   Linked – Share their dreams with grace:

5. Take the Charles Shultz quiz.
    a. Name three teachers who aided your journey through school.

    ◆

    ◆

    ◆

    b. Name three friends who have helped you through a difficult time.

    ◆

    ◆

    ◆

    c. Name three people who have taught you something worthwhile.

    ◆

    ◆

    ◆

    d. Name three people you enjoy spending time with.

    ◆

    ◆

    ◆

    e. Name three heroes whose stories have inspired you.

    ◆

    ◆

    ◆

A GUIDE TO BECOMING A SOULWISE
CONSPIRATOR

CHAPTER 7

DISCOVER YOUR PASSION

Soulwise Conspirators naturally love to explore. They can't help it. Their RADICAL nature described in Part III demands they take responsibility for their place in the world. Theirs represents no ordinary connection to the human family. Theologian and writer Frederick Buechner summed up the Soulwise Conspirator's adventure with these words: "Find the place where your greatest love meets the world's greatest need."

Part IV, A Guide to Becoming a Soulwise Conspirator, introduces you to the basic theory and the practical skills needed to breathe hope into humanity. Each of the seven chapters in this part focuses on one of the essential steps:

- Discover Your Passion
- Define the Need
- Dream the Need Fulfilled
- Draft Your Dream Team
- Develop Your Strategy
- Declare Your Dream
- Deliver Your Dream

Part IV begins the exploration by sharply focusing your attention to discover your passion, a process that can be overwhelming. Examining your heart, the muscle of compassion, to find out whether it's soft and supple or hardened and brittle may cause you to tremble. Everywhere you turn, needs appear: needs where you live, needs right around the corner, and needs on the other side of the earth. They shout. They scream. They cry out. Sometimes, they wake us in the middle of the night.

So approach your task with relaxed intensity. As French philosopher Rene Descartes believed, "There is nothing so far removed from us as to be beyond our reach or so hidden that we cannot discover it."

To discover your passion, this chapter guides you to:
- See with your heart's eyes,
- Experience the world in motion,
- Employ all your senses,
- Watch out for limbo dancers, and
- Follow your hunches.

SEE WITH YOUR HEART'S EYES

As Gandhi stepped aboard a train, one of his shoes slipped off and landed on the track. He was unable to retrieve it because the train was moving. To the amazement of his companions, Gandhi calmly took off his other shoe and threw it back along the track to land close to the first. Asked by a fellow passenger why he did so, Gandhi smiled. "The poor man who finds the shoe lying on the track," he replied, "will now have a pair he can use."

Where Do You Start?

Remember, you've been preparing all your life to discover your passion. Everything you've done so far prepares you for this moment: your upbringing, your education, your expertise, and your experience. You bring your own unique perspective to discern what needs to be done in the world.

It's normal to feel both attraction and resistance to the needs you find. Reality by its very nature allures and seduces. It's challenging, often dangerous, yet irresistible. However, there's no room for excuses such as, "I'm only one person." Yes, only one person, but an incredible one. Or "I'm not the governor," unless, of course, you *are* the governor.

You're embarking on an exciting odyssey, an adventure of many turns, a long adventurous quest. Explore your world with honesty, generosity, and objectivity. Identify the needs you encounter in the context of the big picture. Historian Arnold Toynbee thought that civilizations grow and survive by overcoming successive challenges and break down when they fail to meet new challenges. If there ever existed an era of incredible challenge and change, it's now.

When John Quincy Adams was 10 years old and on his way to England with his father, his mother, Abigail, sent him an inspirational letter. She wrote, "These are the times in which a genius would wish to live. It is not in the still calm of life or the repose of a pacific station that great characters are formed. The habits of a vigorous mind are formed in contending with difficulties. Great necessities call out great virtues. When a mind is raised and animated by scenes that engage the heart, then those qualities which would otherwise lay dormant wake into life and form the character of the hero and the statesman."[36]

Look Where Your Heart Leads

"Only the heart," said Russian novelist Fyodor Dostoevsky, "knows how to find what is precious." Trust your heart. Let it lead you to view the world with all its intricacies and nuances. Let it pull you like a strong magnet to pay attention to what it considers important and show you what you absolutely must see and experience.

Be open and receptive. Take it all in. But be prepared for peak and pit experiences. With eyes wide open, you'll discover people and places that warm your spirit. You'll also witness terror and tragedy that will disturb your sensibility.

National Geographic photographer Dewitt Jones provided good advice about taking photographs guided by the heart. He recommended putting yourself in "the place of most potential." That means intentionally position yourself where you can see the details of life with a panoramic view. Jones coaches using your internal light to chase the external light and has said, "Allow your heart to reveal where to stand to get the best possible light." (www.dewittjones.com/html/videos.shtml)

In his book *What Should I Do With My Life? The True Story of People Who Answered the Ultimate Question*, Po Bronson commented, "We all have passions if we choose to see them. Most of us don't get epiphanies. We don't get clarity. Our purpose doesn't arrive neatly packaged as destiny. We only get a whisper. A blank, non-specific urge. That's how it starts."[37] When your heart whispers, listen.

John Wesley heard a whisper. While at a meeting at Aldersgate Street in London, England, he heard a reading of Martin Luther's preface to Paul's letter to the Romans. He reported that his "heart was strangely warmed" and that God called him to live with a passion for social justice. He went out "on fire" and founded the Methodist Church, the symbols for which are the flame and the cross. Active in the anti-slavery movement, he fought for equal rights for women, and established the first Sunday School in England that released children from the slave shops. Today, persons seeking ordination in the United Methodist Church are asked if their hearts are warmed.

Focus on the Faces

Compose your picture. Choose your lens. And then focus on the faces of real people in the real world. Put their faces at the center of your photo-graph-of-the-heart. You're taking a global family portrait, a picture of the people, the derivative meaning of *demographics.*

> *Soulwise Conspirators discover their passion by looking with their eyes-of-the-heart into the eyes-of-the-heart of those they meet—a heart-to-heart connection. Soul meets soul, confirming the wisdom of the ancient proverb that the eyes are the windows of the soul.*

Authentic passion always has a face. And whenever you put a face on your passion, you personalize a concept, an idea, or an issue. You frame your passion in human terms. It becomes real for you, the way cystic fibrosis took on special significance for Frank Deford, senior writer for *Sports Illustrated,* when his daughter died from the disease. Deford's book *Alex: The Life of a Child* put a face on the disease and demonstrated his passion as chair emeritus for the Cystic Fibrosis Association.

Capture the Moment

Moments change our lives for better or worse. Moments change our lives in a heartbeat. Without warning, a car accident claims the life of a loved one. A financial fiasco wipes out your lifetime savings in an instant. The Twin Towers collapse in New York City. A baby enters the world. Your 20-something kids finally leave home. You land the job of your dreams. You bring hope to abused women in a shelter. You help build a house with Habitat for Humanity.

Soulwise Conspirators capture moments on their heart-drive. They remember faces vividly—profiles, laugh-lines, scars, frowns, tears, smiles, and the volumes of stories revealed in the eyes of those they encounter.

Jean Vanier saw the faces of people with developmental disabilities and resonated with their distress at being shut away in psychiatric institutions. After teaching at St. Michael's College, University of Toronto, he returned to France. In 1964, he welcomed two men from an institution to live with him in a little home he called L'Arche, named after Noah's ark, in the French village of Trosly Breuil. He put his passion into action by founding L'Arche, an international movement in which people who have developmental disabilities and the friends who assist them create homes and share their lives. Today, 130 L'Arche communities grace 30 countries on six continents.

Beware of the consequences when you see with your heart's eyes. Vanier observed, "Once in contact with the poor, they [the rich] will become taken up by distress; not the distress of a bad conscience which refuses compassionate contact, but the distress of wounded people whom they will have seen and touched. Having seen and touched people in distress, they will begin to love, begin to dispossess themselves of their riches, begin to share."[38]

> *On June 23, 2007, Ronald Tschetter, director of the United States Peace Corps, told graduates at Daystar University's Commencement in Nairobi, Kenya, that "life is calling. How far will you go?"*

What's your compassion quotient? What's your capacity to love yourself and others? These are critical questions for Soulwise Conspirators whose core conviction is compassion.

EXPERIENCE THE WORLD IN MOTION

The British artist William Turner wanted to experience a storm on the sea at its height, so he lashed himself to the mast of a ship coming into the harbor in a blizzard. This harrowing research resulted in his painting Snow Storm Steam-Boat off a Harbor's Mouth, a watercolor ca. 1841. It's usually housed in the Slate Art Museum in London, England, but is hanging in the Yale Center for British Art, New Haven, Connecticut.

> *To truly experience the world in motion, you have to be there in person, collide with meaning, and get overwhelmed.*

Be There in Person

"Live" trumps "virtual" every time. Virtual reality is a pale substitute for reality because life isn't a spectator sport. You can fully enjoy the richness of surround sound only if you're the one who's surrounded. You can get an idea of what San Francisco is like by watching the San Francisco Chamber of Commerce visitor's video, but actually riding the squealing, open-air cable cars down the city's hilly streets toward the Bay exhilarates you with the feel of the city. And while I'm not sure why, a hot dog eaten at the ball park always tastes better than one eaten in your living room watching the game on TV.

The world accelerates with the speed of technology. CableLabs, the industry's standard-setting unit, recently endorsed technology that will let cable operators boost speeds from 400% to 1600% over their existing lines. That means consumers will soon be able to download an entire high definition movie in about one minute.

> *Yet, significant advances require significant adaptations that summon our intelligence and spirit of optimism. Unfortunately, many will be left in the dust of swift change with needs that are neither identified nor met.*

On the flip side, change provides endless needs calling your name and you can pick and choose what piques your purpose and passion. Engage the world in motion. Be fully present. Immerse yourself in the culture. Absorb like a sponge. Show up early and stay late. Be receptive, open, and alert. "Go to the edge," challenges anthropologist Margaret Mead, "and look into the abyss." Like an embedded reporter, be in the action.

Embrace the world with compassion. Open your arms wide and hug your brothers and sisters in the global community. We're all related. We're one human family. Then kick off your shoes and put on theirs. Experience their journey. This Native American saying rings true: Don't judge a person until you've walked a mile in his moccasins.

Walk and ride with the police on their night-shift rounds as I have in the role of chaplain. Walk with the poor in the streets in India, Jamaica, or America. Walk with a prostitute on a downtown street. Walk with the mentally challenged. Walk in a soldier's boots. Too often in the last few years, I've said good-bye to men and women being deployed for duty in Iraq and elsewhere. I've felt their pride in serving their country as well as their agony in leaving family and friends, often for the third or fourth time.

Collide with Meaning

As you explore, I hope you collide with meaning. I hope you feel like somebody slammed on the brakes and abruptly stopped your world. I hope reality shocks you—not a "reality" TV dramatization, but real drama with real people in real circumstances. Encounter a slice of life that stops you in your tracks so you can't turn away. You may try, but you're drawn back irresistibly. Your gut tells you that you're witnessing something unfair or unjust, and turning away isn't an option.

Malcolm Muggeridge, a British journalist, was assigned to travel to Calcutta to interview and report on the work of Mother Teresa. Extremely skeptical about anything that even hinted of religion, he encountered this saint of the slums as she worked with the poor and was moved by her compassion. He subsequently became an outstanding Christian writer and activist.

I, myself, had a major collision with meaning. I heard that the movie *Hotel Rwanda* was worth seeing. So I went to see it, not thinking about the impact it might have. This movie jolted my spirit in a way I can hardly express. I felt angry. I felt numb. I felt guilty. I felt a sense of shame because the same kind of genocide was happening in Sudan at that very moment.

And here I sat, in a climate-controlled theater, riveted to my comfortable, memory-foam seat, doing nothing about it. I had trouble sleeping for several nights, particularly because I kept thinking about Sierra, a bright female student from Sudan who'd been in my MBA class at Daystar University in Nairobi. Was she okay? How could I help her?

Today, I lobby for justice in places like Darfur by writing letters to politicians expressing my concerns and requesting that we engage in dialogue. I once mailed a letter every Monday for three months, hoping that repetition would break the pattern of polite responses. Unfortunately, I seem to have sparked little action to relieve the escalating suffering and death.

It takes guts to experience the real world in motion. And when we encounter pain firsthand, we should be prepared for the door of compassion to burst wide open.

Get Overwhelmed

Can you recall a time when you were overcome by an experience? One of my students at the University of Phoenix, Sabira Pervanic, a Bosnian refugee, tells about her first trip to the library when she was about eight, accompanied by her 16-year-old sister. Overwhelmed with the number of books, Sabira broke into tears and exclaimed, "There are too *many*—I'll never read them all!"

Here's another example. A few years ago while on a business trip to Oklahoma City, I visited the memorial to the 1995 bombing of the Alfred P. Murrah Federal Building on a quiet, warm summer evening. I sat across from where the building once stood and watched the reflection on the water of the 168 large chairs. They represented the innocent men and women. Beside them were 19 small chairs representing the children killed in the blast. A young woman sat down next to me and we shared in the silence for five minutes. Then she pointed to one of the small chairs and said softly, "That's my son's chair." We wept.

Experience the world in motion. Actively participate in life's ebb and flow. Identify with the people you encounter. Feel their joy and pain, their laughter and tears, and also their successes and frustrations.

EMPLOY ALL YOUR SENSES

The church says: the body is a sin.
Science says: the body is a machine.
Advertising says: the body is a business.
The body says: I am a fiesta.[39]
– Eduardo Galeano

Ole! Your body is truly a fiesta. It's a marvelously integrated sensory machine. It's connected with your whole being. "There is nothing in the mind," theologian Thomas Aquinas contended, "unless it's first in the senses." So honor your body. Be passionately present to the world.

Employ all your sense organs—eyes, ears, hands, tongue, and nose—to discover your passion.

Your senses open doors for you to recognize your passion—what your heart desires for your ultimate fulfillment. Experts in the field refer to the use of all the senses as sensory integration. It's quite amazing and emotionally powerful to have all the senses alive at the same time. Holding the small hand of a young child may spark your heartfelt desire to provide food, shelter, education or protection. Witnessing a glorious sunrise may trigger your concern for environmental causes. I discovered my own passion for preventing malaria in small children when I contracted the disease with all its sensory symptoms.

Activate your senses to give you clues about the depths of your being and your passion for humanity.

Distance runner and running coach George Sheehan in his book *Personal Best* describes the mind/body/spirit phenomenon this way: "The person that I am is a body and a mind expressing a spirit. When I run, my entire personality participates to a greater or lesser degree. My highs, therefore, vary from a purely physical reaction to the deepest spiritual experiences. My feelings span the spectrum from simple sensual pleasure to joy, from commitment to a peace beyond understanding."[40]

I have that kind of sensory-rich experience in the summer when I sit on the beach with family and friends. I watch the sun with its reds and oranges and yellows slowly disappear on the horizon. I hear the crackle of dry wood on the campfire. I feel a gentle breeze off Lake Michigan on my face. I savor the refreshing taste of ice-cold Diet Coke with lemon. I smell the sweet, irresistible aroma of marshmallows roasting to perfection to melt the chocolate on our s'mores.

How utterly magnificent, the body! Fully accept it as a precious gift. Not only does is provide us with many pleasures, it acts as a great teacher and offers valuable life lessons. For example, at the onset of a headache, most people rush to take an extra-strength pain reliever instead of determining what caused the headache and addressing that. But listen to the body's early-warning system when it gives you a heads-up (or, in this case, a pain alert). Your headache tells you that something isn't quite right. The pain can be a clue about how you're dealing with your concerns.

Your body is a tremendous asset in recognizing the troubled spots, not only in your own world but in our world. Look, listen, touch, taste, and smell. You'll need all your senses to discover the depths of your personal passion to breathe hope into humanity.

Look

I thoroughly enjoy watching people. In fact, I've taken up people-watching as a hobby. I like to guess where they're from, what happened to them that day, what they're looking forward to or dreading, who's important in their life, what joys and tragedies they've encountered, what they do for a living, what obstacles they've overcome, what they're dreaming, how they feel about current events, what their passion is, and what need they're fulfilling.

When my daughter, Jill, was nine years old, we'd wait until it was pitch black, set up lounge chairs where we had an unobstructed view on the deserted road by our cottage, and watch the stars dance in the night sky. Occasionally, we'd see the shimmering northern lights, and she'd say, "Look Daddy, the stars are winking at us!"

Yogi Berra noted, "We can observe a lot just by watching." Yogi's doubly right. You need to be an astute observer of the human condition so as a Soulwise Conspirator with your unique visual perspective you can identify the real challenges in the world and find ways to meet them.

With your own eyes wide open, see it all—the good, the bad, and the ugly. "The price one pays for pursuing any profession or calling," wrote James Baldwin, "is an intimate knowledge of its ugly side."

See life unfold around you with a full 360-degree view. Filmmakers refer to this as the panoptical view, from the Greek *panoptos*, meaning visible from all angles. Take on the role of a filmmaker who selects and arranges material for maximum effect. So much life to frame on your personal viewfinder. So many moments to capture on your internal memory card.

Take pictures in your mind. Snap away. Short shots. Long shots. Wide angle. Telephoto. Close up. Shoot your video from a variety of angles. Try different lighting. Look through your unique lens of discovery. Look for the invisible. Borrow the eyes of genius. "You can't see with your eyes," Mark Twain commented, "when your imagination is out of focus." Your eyes provide you with a window not only on the present but on the future that you intend to create. When you can see clearly, you'll be able to help others see or appreciate humanity's needs and work together to fulfill your vision of those needs.

Who knows what you might see? You take a risk to look carefully at our global family. As a member of the human family, observe the world with compassionate purpose and resolve. Your task is to be aware of the full range of conditions under which people are living. Be assured that occasionally, you may witness extreme situations.

In my own life, I have witnessed the destruction caused by war. We've no shortage of conflict today. As I write, 137 wars rage on around the world. Only 27 years in recorded history have been war-free. In our technologically advanced age, you can observe the slaughter "live" and in full color on your TV screen.

I've seen the pain on veterans faces from service in World Wars I and II, the Vietnam War, the Gulf War, and the wars in Iraq and Afghanistan. They all describe the horror they experienced. They told me they had to look away. It was too much to take, too horrible for words, a personal nightmare that many reported continued on.

It's sometimes excruciatingly painful to look. But look we must. And we must do something about the pain and suffering we see. I have resolved to work for peace wherever and whenever possible.

Look and listen.

Listen

The Torah exhorts the faithful to "be still and know that I am God." We are created with the capacity to listen.

Everywhere, we see clear indications that listening is essential to communication and to life. Listen not only to the beat of your own heart, but to the beat of the hearts around you. You may find it helpful to close your eyes. People who are visually challenged do it all the time. That's why their auditory sense becomes so advanced. Listening is always an interpretive exercise—both a skill and an art. You hear what others say and interpret what they mean.

In addition to using your eyes to make your "documentary film," take advantage of your hearing. The sound track will undoubtedly enhance the findings of your other senses. Listen closely to the sounds of our world. Hear the laughter and the cries of both young and old. Listen to the sounds of people across the globe. Your observations will expand your awareness of the totality of the human family and its richness and diversity.

We live in a time when voice communication has become accessible and immediate around the world. Listen to the stories of the world's 22 million refugees fleeing for their lives. Listen to the veterans who tell of these sounds of war: a bullet whizzing overhead, a grenade exploding, an automatic weapon firing, a missile striking and blowing up a build-ing, a Humvee bursting into flames, a shriek of agonizing pain from a wounded comrade. They hear them as distinctly now as the instant they first heard them.

Look, listen, and touch.

Touch

In the 2005 Academy Award-winning movie *Crash*, set in Los Angeles, cars crash, and so do people. In fact, the movie reflects a head-on cultural collision, an explosion of race and class warfare. In the opening scene, when a car driven by a black policeman, played by Don Cheadle, got rear-ended, he reflected, "We're always behind this metal and glass. In any real city, people brush past people, bump into them. I think we miss that so much that we crash into each other just so we can touch somebody." People yearn to touch and be touched.

Our growth largely depends on the essential sense of touch. As an ordained pastor, I've enjoyed the privilege of holding a tiny baby during the ritual of baptism as this dependent infant radiates awesome beauty and innocence. I hold the baby's tiny hand in mine and welcome the child into the wider family.

A sense of touch can bring the feeling of safety and caring. Veterans have told me in minute detail how they were rescued from battle. They described how they were wounded, and then how the medical response teams retrieved them and took them to a hospital for treatment. They invariably reach out and physically touch me when they're telling me their stories, recalling the reassuring touch of their comrades.

Taste

My friend psychologist John Moore loves hot, spicy food. "The hotter, the better," he assured me. So, for his birthday, I gave him a bottle of Dave's Insanity Sauce, one of the hottest sauces on the planet. On the bottle, the label said, "For more product information, call 911." Afterward, I received this note from John: "Opened the bottle and nearly passed out. Put four drops on a sandwich and cried for half an hour and screamed for an hour and a half. Tried again with the same result. Great stuff. Thanks."

Soulwise Conspirators need to actually taste the different foods and beverages people prepare and consume around the world—one of the most enjoyable dimensions of discovering your passion. For example, my dinner at Carnivore restaurant in Nairobi introduced me to Maasai culture and cooking. As I entered the restaurant, I saw a huge barbecue with about 20 varieties of meat sizzling on Maasai spears. Although the menu at the Carnivore changes daily, I tried lean pink giraffe, moist and tender waterbuck, tough zebra, and chewy hartebeest. Pork, chicken, lamb, and beef are also available—all served on a Maasai spear at the table.

The Phoenix Sister Cities organization recognizes the importance of taste. From February 27 to March 1, 2009, it presented the 4th annual WorldFEST that invited people to celebrate the world we live in and its cultures, and enjoy the arts and foods from Phoenix's sister cities. Visitors could see, hear, smell, taste, touch, and actively participate in this hands-on multicultural festival. (www.phoenixsistercities.org)

Tasting the world may cause you to think about people who don't have adequate food for daily living. For example, the world has a desperate need for the sweet taste of safe drinking water. Worldwide, between 1.7 and 2.2 million people die from waterborne diseases each year. Each day, between 5,000 and 8,000 children die from infectious diarrhea acquired from unsafe drinking water. United Nations World Health Organization Director-General Lee Jong-Wook has said that the collective failure to tackle diarrheal disease, which is killing 30,000 people a week, is a "silent humanitarian crisis."

Smell

When my kids were young, one of their favorite books was *The Party*, a scratch-and-sniff book. Scents of hot dogs, popcorn, cola, licorice, and chocolate cake wafted from its pages. Reading it, along with the scratching and sniffing, was like having a party at bedtime. Best of all, it provided lots of fun without the cleanup.

Soulwise Conspirators use their amazing sense of smell to appreciate a culture quickly. Two scientists, Richard Axel of the Howard Hughes Medical Institute at Columbia University in New York and Linda Buck of the Fred Hutchinson Cancer Research Center in Seattle, won the 2004 Nobel Prize in medicine for discovering how the nose knows one odor from another. In a 1991 paper in the journal *Cell*, they revealed that an extensive family of genes produces nasal cells capable of differentiating, with the brain's help, at least 10,000 separate smells. Later studies showed that about 350 smell sensors or olfactory receptors embedded in nasal cells are derived from the gene family identified by Buck and Axel, one that comprises about 3% of the human genetic makeup. Finding that each nasal cell type is attuned to only one smell-producing chemical was unexpected.

The importance of smell is highlighted by The Smell and Taste Center, founded in 1980 at the University of Pennsylvania. The first National Institute of Health (NIH)-funded Clinical Research Center in the United States devoted to the senses of taste and smell, it has achieved worldwide prominence for both its research and clinical activities. It offers numerous databases for Conspirators to diagnose smelling problems and provide treatment. (www.med.upenn.edu/stc/)

Soulwise Conspirators may experience bad smells, too—ones that really stink. The sense of smell is the strongest memory-provoker of all the senses. (http://library.thinkquest.org/co11029/science/factors/senses/php) As an example, veterans tell me about the unforgettable, pungent odor of tear gas they ingested and the stench of rotting bodies. Then there's the acrid odor of cigarette smoke from the 45 million smokers in the U.S. and millions more worldwide.

To discover your passion and how you might help the world, employ all your senses.

WATCH OUT FOR LIMBO DANCERS

Once, just before I gave a speech to a convention in New York City, I went to the hotel washroom. As my cheeks warmed the porcelain throne, I noticed a line of tiny marks on the bottom of the stall door. Curious, I leaned forward slightly and read the beautiful lettering, hand-crafted by a graphic artist. Sorry to say, this "lavatory art" was unsigned. The intriguing message read, "Watch out for limbo dancers." Coincidentally, the same hand had labeled the toilet tissue holders "Leaded" and "Unleaded."

Soulwise Conspirators expect the unexpected and pay close attention to their surroundings.

Expect the Unexpected

> *Expect the unexpected. You never know what will happen. And you certainly don't want to miss a substantial clue to discovering your passion. Cultivate an attitude of openness, readiness, and receptivity. Live each day with anticipation. And keep watching.*

I've noticed that people who approach life this way experience surprise more than others. It's like being on a police stakeout. Sometimes you have to wait a long time before you see something noteworthy, but when something does occur, you're on it. Live in the moment. And be surprised. "Life is not measured by the breaths you take," said comedian George Carlin, "but by the moments that take your breath away."

Nassim Nicholas Taleb, founder of a risk research and trading firm, and author of *Fooled by Randomness: The Hidden Role of Chance in Life and in the Markets*, wrote in the *New York Times* article "Learning to Expect the Unexpected" that the 9/11 commission should focus on the future, not the past. He argued convincingly that the commission, in its mandate "to provide a full and complete accounting of the attacks on September 11, 2001, and recommendations as to how to prevent such attacks in the future," failed to understand the "black swan" concept.

He defined a "black swan" as a surprise, something that occurs outside normal expectations. Most people expect to see white swans because that's what they've known and experienced. However, when they do see a black swan, they create plausible explanations that make black swans appear more predictable and less random than they really are. Taleb calls this distortion "hindsight bias," which severely restricts learning from the past.

Supporting the thesis of his book, Taleb wrote, "The greatest flaw in the commission's mandate, regrettably mirrors one of the greatest flaws in modern society: it does not understand risk. The focus of the investigation should not be on how to avoid any specific black swan, for we don't know where the next one is coming from. The focus should be on what general lessons can be learned from them. And the most important lesson may be that we should reward people, not ridicule them, for thinking the impossible. After a black swan like 9/11, we must look ahead, not in the rear-view mirror."[41]

Let yourself be surprised. Look for the breakthrough that points the way to your passion.

Pay Close Attention

An old farmer in Florida owned a large farm with a recreation area that had a swimming pond, picnic tables, horseshoe courts, and apple and peach trees. One evening, he decided to go down to the pond so he grabbed a five-gallon bucket to bring back some fruit. As he approached the pond, he heard voices shouting and laughing. He came closer and saw a group of young women skinny-dipping in the pond. He made the women aware of his presence, and they all swam to the deep end of the pond. One of the women shouted, "We're not coming out until you leave!" The old man frowned and yelled, "I didn't come here to watch you ladies swim naked or make you get out of the pond." Holding up the bucket, he continued, "I'm here to feed the alligator."

> *Sometimes you may be shocked by what you hear or encounter. You won't know exactly what to do, where to turn, or what to say. It may not be alligators, but the foundations of your world may shake when you witness violence on the street where you live or a burglar breaks in next door.*

I had such an immobilizing experience when I visited Yad Vashem, the Holocaust Memorial in Jerusalem. I turned a corner in the museum and there it faced me—a huge pile of children's shoes. Little shoes. Empty shoes. Sad shoes. My heart sank like concrete. I felt rage. Suddenly, I had a million questions. No, six million questions—about the atrocities committed to six million human beings.

You pay close attention when you watch out for limbo dancers. Although a moment could be one of horror, it could just as easily stun you with beauty and wonder. "The moment one gives close attention to anything, even a blade of grass," wrote playwright Arthur Miller, "it becomes a mysterious, indescribably magnificent world in itself."

Another writer, Evelyn Underhill, echoed Miller. "For lack of attention, a thousand forms of loveliness elude us every day." Pay attention and new thoughts may break through the habitual drone of consciousness. A University of Montreal study on scientific discovery found that 50-70% of useful conclusions of laboratory research were found accidentally.

This means you've got to concentrate in spite of all the distractions that might be whirling around you. The AAA auto club conducted a survey that yielded the following statistics. Of people driving, 71% eat or drink, 46% groom themselves, 30% use their cell-phones, and 40% read or write. In all, these numbers underestimate the problem of distractions on the road. Researchers at the University of North Carolina used miniature cameras to track 70 volunteer drivers for a week. Even though they knew the researchers were scrutinizing their driving, they allowed themselves to be distracted an average of 16% of the time.

The Institute of Medicine has estimated that every year at least 98,000 Americans die and millions more become injured as a result of errors. Mistakes with medication alone, either in or out of hospital, are estimated to account for more than 7,000 deaths a year. Hospital costs to treat patients affected by preventable adverse drug events amount to about $2 billion a year.[42]

According to an article in the *New England Journal of Medicine*, medical interns made 36% more serious mistakes when working more than 80 hours a week—from prescribing overdoses to sticking a tube in the wrong vein—than did their more rested colleagues. A study of 20 first-year interns showed they nodded off more than five times a night during long shifts.[43]

Watch out for limbo dancers and you may, as poet William Blake wrote, "See the world in a grain of sand." Or prevent an accident. Or make a discovery that will benefit the world.

FOLLOW YOUR HUNCHES

"If I had thought about it," claimed Spencer Silver, inventor of the adhesive used on Post-it Notes, "I would not have done the experiment. The literature was full of examples that said you can't do this." (www.edu/itds/courses/bcis5650.htm) To discover your passion and a need in the world, follow your hunches, think and act like a detective, look for patterns, and stay on the case.

Think and Act Like a Detective

People actually spur me on when they tell me I can't do something. I guess I'm hard-wired for that kind of challenge. It's like they're double-daring me to find a way to accomplish what they consider beyond the realm of possibility. It's one of the reasons I'm drawn to the concept.

By all means listen to the concerns and warnings of others, but follow your own hunches. Robert Sternberg and Todd Lubert confirmed this guidance in their book, *Defying the Crowd: Cultivating Creativity in a Culture of Conformity.* To be creative, "...you have to (a) generate the options other people don't think of, and recognize which are the good ones (intelligence); (b) know what other people have done in your field of endeavor so that you will know what they are not doing or have not yet thought to do (knowledge); (c) like to think and act in creative and contrarian ways, and see the forest from the trees in your creative endeavors (thinking styles); (d) be willing to take risks and overcome the obstacles that confront those who buy low and sell high, and to continue to do so throughout the course of your life (personality); (e) not only like to think and act in contrarian ways, but have the drive actually to do so rather than just to think about it (motivation); and (f) work at a job, live in a country, or be in a relationship to others that lets you do all these things (environment)."[44]

Think and act like a detective. You have the wonderful capacity to figure things out, just like the whodunit legends Sherlock Holmes, Columbo, Perry Mason, and the Texas Ranger. My favorite TV detective is Monk, played by Tony Shaluba, described affectionately as the

Defective Detective. Monk demonstrates in a bizarre, quirky way the essence of a great investigator. He trusts himself, looks for patterns, and perseveres until he cracks the case.

Monk trusts his gut implicitly and often drives his colleagues crazy by pursuing his hunches. But, like a good investigative reporter, he trusts everyone and no one. An irresistible idea that might solve the case lures him, and he's compelled to act on it as if haunted by the idea until he follows his hunch. He's mercilessly diligent.

"Diligence," remarked Benjamin Franklin, "is the mother of good luck." Thomas Edison proved that by his tireless effort to invent a storage battery. He tried over 2,300 times unsuccessfully. In 1877, Edison was working on 40 different inventions at the same time. Inventing takes persistent detective work and following up on hunches.

At times, prediction seems so obvious when you follow your hunches and passion without thinking. Someone with a flare for clothes becomes a fashion designer or someone naturally graceful becomes a ballerina. I asked a friend of mine who is a physician why he chose to practice medicine. He simply replied, "I never thought about doing anything else."

At other times, it's just a feeling that keeps on attracting your attention. You're attracted to the inner city but you don't know why. You're attracted to Native Americans but you don't know why. You're drawn to work with orphans in Africa when you haven't even been there. You're not quite sure what it means, but you know it's there. Follow your hunches.

And pay attention to your dreams. I once parked my car at the Gerald Ford International Airport in Grand Rapids during a snowstorm. When I got inside the terminal, I realized I'd lost my wedding ring. I searched in and around the car without success. Three months later, I had a recurring night dream that I went to the airport police and retrieved my ring. So on a whim, I went to the airport police and inquired about my ring. Eerily, the scene was precisely as it was in my dream. When I told the officer at the station who I was, she immediately reached into a box overflowing with jewelry and pulled out my ring. "What's the date inscribed on your ring?" she asked. "June 6, 1998," I answered. She handed me my ring and added, "Have a nice life."

As an explorer and detective, be aware of what's called observer's paradox—that is, the observer's subjective viewpoint always influences scientific findings, even though the observer tries to be neutral and objective.

For Soulwise Conspirators, this paradox highlights the difficulty of sampling natural or spontaneous speech or activity in the presence of an investigator where the goal is to observe people as if they were not being observed. Occasionally, I have witnessed people saying things they think I want to hear rather than what's really on their minds.

Sometimes following a hunch can save someone from dire straits. Because of a hunch, Walter Arvinger became a free man after 36 years behind bars in a Maryland prison for a 1968 murder he didn't commit. Arvinger was 19 when he entered prison. He was freed from prison in November, 2004, after Maryland Governor Robert Ehrlich commuted his sentence. He was granted clemency and released with the help of a law professor and some of his students who followed a hunch.

How did it happen? In December, 2002, Michael Millemann, a teacher in the clinical program at the University of Maryland Law School, received a handwritten note from Arvinger in which the prisoner proclaimed his innocence. On a hunch, Millemann followed up. "I read his trial transcript," said the law professor, "and I was instantly appalled at what I read." Millemann blamed Arvinger's situation on a bad defense, gross error by a young, inexperienced trial judge, and a botched appeal.

Follow your hunches and look for patterns.

Look for Patterns

TV detective Monk always looks for patterns. He wants everything in what he considers its proper place. He shuns chaos and processes information as if playing an elaborate game of Clue. He loves the challenge of solving the mystery, and his hunches tell him right where to look.

Patterns reveal both congruity and incongruity. The incongruous doesn't seem to fit a pattern and generally piques our interest. A song on the children's TV program *Sesame Street* asked, "Which of these things is not like the others? Which of these things is not the same?" In your exploration to find your passion, make a special note of the things that don't fit. Take, for example, these statistics: 14,000 people drive off bridges into water each year in the United States; 5,000 children world-wide die daily from contaminated water; two out of three people with diabetes die of heart disease or stroke. When you notice something odd, something that shouldn't be happening, or something outrageous, what does it spark in you? Do you, like Monk, have the urge to "solve the mystery"?

Probably America's greatest living inventor, Dean Kamen, the inventor of the Segway Human Transporter, gets these urges. An entre-preneur and advocate for science and technology, Kamen holds more than 440 U.S. and foreign patents, many for innovative medical devices that have expanded the frontiers of health care worldwide. His other inventions include the first wearable infusion pump and the first insulin pump for diabetics.

Dean's proudest accomplishments include founding FIRST (For Inspiration and Recognition of Science and Technology), an organiza-tion dedicated to motivating the next generation to understand, use, and enjoy science and technology. In 2000, he was awarded the National Medal of Technology by President Bill Clinton, and in 2002, he won the Lemelson-MIT Prize. Dean was inducted into the National Inventors Hall of Fame in May 2005.

Stay on the Case

Morgan Spurlock knew people face a serious health problem in the United States with 100 million adults—66% of all adults—being seriously overweight or obese; a record number of children are overweight; obesity in adolescents has doubled in the last 25 years; 400,000 die annually because of complications of obesity; the annual treatment costs have reached $110 billion. Researchers predict that, if left untreated, this problem will soon overtake smoking as the major preventable cause of death. (www.acponline.org/patients_families/ diseases_conditions/obesity)

Spurlock suspected that eating fast food contributed in a major way to the problem of obesity, with one in four Americans going to a fast food restaurant every day! So he set out to discover personally the effect of eating for 30 consecutive days at McDonald's. This leading global foodservice retailer in the world has more than 31,000 outlets in 118 countries on six continents, serves 58 million customers each day. (www.about mcdonalds.com/mcd/our_company.html)

In his experiment, Spurlock set these four rules for himself: he could only Super Size when asked, he could only eat food from McDonald's, he had to eat everything on the menu at least once, and he had to eat three meals a day—breakfast, lunch, and dinner.

This intrepid researcher recorded his adventure in his 2004 documentary *SuperSize Me*. In 30 days, he went from 185.5 pounds to 210 pounds (an increase of 24.5 pounds), his triglycerides rose from 165 to 225 (up 65 points), he doubled his risk of coronary disease, and consumed 30 pounds of sugar and 12 pounds of fat. In addition, according to his wife, their sex life was, well, nonexistent. Spurlock's hunch paid off. He proved what Dr. David Satcher, former United States surgeon general, has stated, that fast food is a major contributor to the national epidemic of obesity.

Follow your hunches to discover your passion and a worthy need. Think like Monk. Trust yourself, look for patterns, and stay the course until you crack the case.

This chapter encouraged you to discover your passion, push the emotive envelope, and feel the needs of the world. But Soulwise Conspirators need both passion and reason. The next chapter shows you how to think critically to define the need that reflects your passion.

TAKE FIVE FOR REFLECTION

1. When you see with your heart's eyes, describe what you see happening.

2. When you see with your heart's eyes, name three faces you see.

    -

    -

    -

3. Theologian Frederick Buechner invited people to "find the place where your greatest love meets the world's greatest need." Describe that "place" for you.

4. What interesting or surprising information did your "detective work" uncover in discovering your passion?

5. What organizations or people in the world currently address the need you've uncovered and how effective have they been in dealing with it?

CHAPTER **8**

DEFINE THE NEED

"**R**idiculing idealism is shortsighted, but idealism without the rigors of pessimism is misleading," was a comment in the *2006 State of the Future* report, an annual overview of the global situation including prospects and strategies published by the Millennium Project. "We need very hardheaded idealists who can look into the worst and best of humanity and can create and implement strategies of success." (www.acunu.org/millennium/sof2006.html)

Chapter 7 showed you how to discover your passion. This one will help you define the need you've discovered by taking the following steps:

- Put on your thinking cap,
- Use multiple intelligences,
- Ask really good dumb questions,
- Assess the urgency, and
- Connect the dots.

PUT ON YOUR THINKING CAP

The phrase "put on your thinking cap" (previously known as a "considering cap"), originally meant to take time to consider a question. So put on your thinking cap, blend passion with reason, let logic loose, and think in synch.

Blend Passion with Reason

Soulwise Conspirators blend passion with reason to fulfill their calling. They combine feeling and love with logical thinking. They believe in the necessity of using both emotive and cognitive capacities to unleash their love for the global family.

Although Soulwise Conspirators affirm the integral relationship of passion and reason in decision-making, they often vigorously debate the relative influence of reason and passion.

Some vote for passion's influence. Alexander Pope in *Moral Essays* maintained, "Be it what it will, the ruling passion conquers reason still." And Aristotle confirmed the importance of passion in the process of weighing alternatives when he wrote, "One who attempts to move people to thought or action must concern themselves with their emotions. If he touches only their minds, he is unlikely to move them to action or to change of mind—the motivations of which lie deep in the realm of the passions."

Others align with essayist and poet Ralph Waldo Emerson, who cautioned, "Ideas must work through the brains and the arms of good and brave men, or they are no better than dreams."

When Pierre Elliott Trudeau became Prime Minister of Canada in 1968, he offered the people a new vision of their country. An intellectual and charismatic, Trudeau promised that a strong and more visible government would rule from the head not the heart, and the slogan he repeated to reinforce his perspective was simply "Reason over Passion."[45] Evan Simpson, in his book, *Reason Over Passion: The Social Basis of Evaluation and Appraisal*, presents scholarly arguments to support the philosophy of reason over passion.[46] College students from Israel and Palestine take a practical approach by seeking to bring their two homelands together in peace.[47]

So put on your thinking cap and let logic loose.

Let Logic Loose

Think critically about your passion and the needs you're uncovering in the world. French chemist and biologist Louis Pasteur, who proved the germ theory of disease and invented the process of pasteurization, wisely said, "Chance favors the prepared mind."

> *It's not enough to have a passion, even if it's sizzling hot. As a Chinese proverb counsels, "It is not economical to go to bed early to save candles if the results are twins."*

It's critical to apply the rigorous discipline of critical thinking to define the need. That requires cultivating an acute awareness of and a generous capacity to challenge assumptions that you and others hold. Observe the context in which you and others live, and imagine and explore alternative ways of looking at and living in the world.

Critical thinkers engage in reflective skepticism, a frame of reference that questions everything, particularly quick-fix solutions and silver bullets. Critical thinkers don't accept the ideas of those in power just because they hold positions of authority. Psychiatrist Dr. Carl Hammerschlag has said that "the key to new learning is to accelerate the unlearning of old certainties."[48]

Regrettably, people didn't scrutinize the underlying assumptions about apartheid in South Africa with compassionate criticism until recently. Through the Truth and Reconciliation Commission, the country has made great strides for freedom, though much remains to accomplish.

Critical thinking enables you to assess local situations at home, at work, or in the global community, so you can create solutions for the common good. According to Stephen Brookfield in his book *Developing Critical Thinkers: Challenging Adults to Explore Alternative Ways of Thinking and Acting*, critical thinking usually involves five phases: a trigger event, a period of appraisal and analysis, a time of exploration, the development of alternative perspectives, and integration.[49]

I have adapted Brookfield's model to further describe The Soulwise Conspiracy.

Consider these five phases of critical thinking in the development of ONE: The Campaign to Make Poverty History, launched in April 2005. (Information stated here comes from www.ONE.org.)

1. **The awareness phase**

   You experience a negative (and occasionally a positive) trigger event that causes discomfort or perplexity. For example, U2 lead singer and social activist, Paul David "Bono" Hewson, recalled his trip to Ethiopia in 1984. On his last day there, a man handed him his baby and begged, "Take him with you." He knew in Ireland his son would live, but in Ethiopia his son would die. Bono said his journey to help eradicate poverty began at that moment.

2. **The examination phase**
You appraise and analyze why and how the situation arose. The founding members of ONE, including Bono and celebrities Brad Pitt, Al Pacino, Tom Hanks, and Cameron Diaz, visited impoverished locations to personally witness poverty. They also conducted research on the state of the "Third" World where they learned about these overwhelming needs: extreme poverty, AIDS, a child dying every 15 seconds from diseases caused by contaminated water, and 77 million children going without school because neither their families nor their governments have the resources to provide them with a basic education.

3. **The consideration phase**
You explore new ways to live and do things that reduce the discomfort. The ONE Campaign faced this choice: it could do nothing to alleviate the suffering in the world or actively engage the American public in caring for sisters and brothers in the global family. As Bono explained, "It's not about charity, it's about justice. Together as ONE, we can do even more. This is our civil rights movement."

The campaign's promotional materials explain the research that produced the name of the campaign, stating, "The ONE Campaign derives its name from the belief that allocating an additional one percent of the U.S. budget toward providing basic needs like health, education, clean water and food would transform the futures and hopes of an entire generation in the world's poorest countries."

4. **The transition phase**

   You develop alternatives with new assumptions and activities. The following statement reveals the campaign's approach: "The ONE Campaign is an effort by Americans to rally Americans—one by one—to fight the emergency of global AIDS and extreme poverty. ONE is students and ministers, punk rockers and NASCAR moms, Americans of all beliefs and every walk of life, united to help make poverty history."

   The campaign invited people to sign this ONE Declaration: "WE BELIEVE that in the best American tradition of helping others help themselves, now is the time to join with other countries in an historic pact for compassion and justice to help the poorest people in the world overcome AIDS and extreme poverty.

   "WE RECOGNIZE that a pact including such measures as fair trade, debt relief, fighting corruption and directing additional resources for basic needs—education, health, clean water, food, and care for orphans—would transform the futures and hopes of an entire generation in the poorest countries, at a cost equal to just one percent more of the US budget."

5. **The resolution phase**

   You integrate the decisions you've made and put them into action. More than two million people have signed the ONE Declaration and stand as ONE. In the 2008 U.S. presidential race, presidential hopefuls from both parties talked about tackling global poverty. For example, former United States Senator John Edwards gave a major policy speech on extreme poverty in Manchester, New Hampshire, on March 15, 2007. His plan included leading a worldwide effort to fund the goal of universal primary education by 2015, with the U.S spending $3 billion a year to educate 23 million children in poor countries. The plan would have doubled the U.S. investment in clean water programs and added a new cabinet position to oversee efforts to increase political and economic opportunities for the poor. On the Republican side, Senator John

McCain continually alerted his audiences to the consequences of not addressing global poverty realities.

The ONE movement gained steam in April 2009 when United States President Obama exceeded ONE's request for at least $850 million for the 2010 budget for agricultural development by committing $1 billion. The funding will be targeted on 25 countries in 8 regions.[50]

> *The ONE Campaign expressed its conviction and resolve in this abbreviated version of its Declaration:*
>
> *WE COMMIT ourselves—one person, one voice, one vote at a time—to make a better, safer world for all.*
>
> *WE BELIEVE*
> *We can beat: AIDS, starvation and extreme poverty.*
>
> *WE RECOGNIZE*
> *One billion people live on less than ONE dollar a day.*
>
> *WE COMMIT*
> *Ourselves, one person, one voice, one vote at a time to make a better safer world for all.*

Let logic loose. Engage your mind in critical thinking to define your need, and then reap the rewards of clarity.

Think in Synch

Careful, exact evaluation and judgment characterize the "critical" in critical thinking. Such thinking involves detecting and analyzing assumptions that underlie the actions affecting our lives. When we suspend judgment and take time for thoughtful reflection, we increase the odds of identifying and challenging assumptions without the pressure of having to make a snap decision.

Sometimes it's difficult to make sense of the world. So many factors keep changing without notice. That's why it's important to think contextually, to look at all sides of an issue and understand why people have different points of view before making a definitive conclusion. Let your good ideas incubate for better results.

It's amazing to me how many business leaders fail to take even a quick look at the economic landscape before pressing on with significant expenditures. For example, in 1903, the Mercedes Corporation conducted a survey to test the market potential of automobiles and find out how many cars they could expect to sell. The study's conclusion was that the manufacturer could sell only one million cars because there would never be more than a million men trained as chauffeurs. The leaders at Mercedes failed to think in synch. In contrast, Toyota carefully analyzed the economic landscape and decided to manufacture more energy efficient vehicles to meet the public's demand.

Likewise, the Second Harvest Gleaners Food Bank in Grand Rapids, Michigan, saw that the 2008 recession would continue to deepen and with increased unemployment estimated to reach between 17 and 20 percent by the end of 2009, prepared for a substantial increase in families needing food support. (www.mackinac.org/article.aspx?ID=10532)

World leaders especially need to think in synch in 2009 as the world grapples with its worst economic downturn since the Great Depression. Leaders who believe they've got to do something—anything—without even a cursory appreciation of our global circumstances, put all of us in danger. For example, borrowing our way out of this current recession may put our future and the future of our grandchildren at risk.

USE MULTIPLE INTELLIGENCES

"Yathink?" I hear this common expression and I want to respond "NO!" Many people *don't* think well.

Studies confirm that we don't use our brainpower effectively or efficiently. Research in the area of intelligence has exploded in the last few decades. Turns out there's not just one kind of intelligence but many. In this section, you'll discover the kinds of intelligences at your disposal to help you fulfill your dreams. You can use your own head, gather intelligence, expand into Gardner's eight intelligences, and explore emotional and spiritual intelligence.

Use Your Own Head

We're learning more and more about the brain, why it works the way it does, and how. (For a taste of this news, I suggest checking out *The Owner's Manual for the Brain: Everyday Applications from Mind-Brain Research* by Pierce J. Howard.)

At the turn of the 20th century, Alfred Binet, a French psychologist, developed a way to measure intelligence. He formulated a test capable of measuring a child's capacity to learn and called it the Intelligence Quotient or IQ test. Binet's original purpose was to discover a student's intellectual shortcomings. The average score is 100; a student with a score of 131 is considered gifted; a score of 81 places a student in special education.

In the United States, regrettably, the IQ test quickly became an accepted way to rank students. But it can never reflect the full range of intelligence, which you'll see as you read on.

You have an intricate gift on your shoulders. The human brain is comprised of more than a trillion cells, including 100 billion neurons devoted to the thinking process. These neurons are connected by trillions of chemical transmitting junctures called synapses to provide us with incredible brainpower. To define a need, you've got to use your head—that is, you must use your own greatest natural resource, your intelligence.

Gather Intelligence

We hear every day something about "intelligence," especially after the events of 9/11—intelligence operations, intelligence reports, and intelligence failure. In this sense, intelligence is information that we use our own intelligence to gather.

The United States Intelligence Community (IC) includes federal government agencies, services, bureaus, or other organizations within the executive branch that play a role in the business of national intelligence. IC members include the Central Intelligence Agency, the Department of Homeland Security, the Department of State, and the Federal Bureau of Investigation among others. (www.intelligence.gov/index.shtml)

The Intelligence Community has broken down its field into four major disciplines called "INTs." They include:

- HUMINT – Human Intelligence (the collection of intelligence from human sources, including defectors, voluntary sources, spies);

- IMINT – Imaginary Intelligence (information gleaned from aerial or satellite photographs of a foreign target);
- SIGINT – Signals Intelligence (interception of communications sometimes requiring decryption); and
- MASINT – Measures and Signatures Intelligence (space-based or airborne sensing devices used to detect particles in the air, soil composition, and water impurities).

If IMINT represents the eyes and SIGINT the ears, then MASINT represents the nose of intelligence.

Take on an intelligence mission of your own. These "INTs" provide an invaluable resource, and when combined, they make your task of defining a need much easier and more productive.

For example, when gathering intelligence on the state of the environment, Human Intelligence or direct human observation of conditions such as melting of ice in the Arctic and Antarctic or rain forest depletion can help. Imaginary Intelligence can provide detailed aerial photographs of forests and bodies of water. Signals Intelligence can record the sounds of the planet, including birds and mammals. Measures and Signatures Intelligence can precisely quantify the impurities in water supplies. Use any and all data and something may strike you as an area of need you are passionate to fill.

Expand into Gardner's Eight Intelligences
In 1983, psychologist Howard Gardner published *Frames of Mind: The Theory of Multiple Intelligences*, in which he challenged conventional wisdom. Gardner proposed that people were endowed with seven intelligences, and he's subsequently added an eighth, naturalistic intelligence. These intelligences, he demonstrated, are unevenly distributed, coexist, and can change over time. His idea was revolutionary because traditional psychologists measured general intelligence with IQ tests focused on only these two intelligences Gardner identified: logical mathematical and linguistic skills.

The theory of multiple intelligences has claimed three major tenets:

- First, that human beings have evolved to have several distinct intelligences and not one general intelligence;
- Second, that each intelligence is relatively independent or semi-autonomous, although they work together, and any significant achievement involves a blend of intelligences; and
- Third, that the intelligences are valued by cultures around the world, although not always to the same degree.[51]

Gardner's eight multiple intelligences are noted here with examples of how Soulwise Conspirators can use them.

1. Verbal-linguistic – knowing and understanding the world through words and language. This intelligence can be helpful in testing the rates of progress in literacy programs in specific locations around the world.
2. Logical-mathematical – inductive and deductive thinking, numbers, and abstract patterns. A Soulwise Conspirator can track the trends and countertrends statistically in any area of research, including poverty and mortality rates, and income and aid distribution.
3. Intrapersonal – relates to self-reflection and awareness of internal states of being. Interviews in particular circumstances can reveal the inner thoughts and feelings of people whose human rights are being violated.
4. Interpersonal – involves person-to-person relationships and communication. For the Soulwise Conspirator concerned about violence in the world, this intelligence can yield information about the root causes of conflict and how to address and resolve them effectively.
5. Visual-spatial – the sense of sight and the ability to create mental images. Research in the area of poverty indicates that the poor generally have an image of themselves as poor until they die. Use this intelligence to provide clues for how to help them re-image their situation.
6. Bodily kinesthetic – relates to physical movement and the wisdom of the body. This intelligence offers creative possibilities in helping people take care of their physical well–being through simple means like diet and exercise.

7. Musical-rhythmic – recognition of tonal patterns, sounds, rhythms, and beats. If you are defining a need in a specific culture, you'll want to access the wealth of insight that can be gained by identifying its particular kind of music.

8. Naturalistic – sensitivity to the world of nature. This intelligence is perfect for Soulwise Conspirators concerned about the environment. Traveling to various parts of the planet, even outer space, can be stimulating and productive.[52]

I have found in presenting keynote speeches that explaining the application of Gardner's insights produces remarkable results. For example, I had the privilege of presenting to the Million Dollar Round Table (MDRT), "The Premier Association of Financial Professionals," at its 2006 annual meeting in San Diego, California. Out of the starting gate, I had a distinct advantage because I hold an insurance license and know several MDRT members who are highly motivated, successful, and generous achievers. I interviewed five members to discover how I could help them "Be the Change," the meeting's theme. They told me they wanted to know how to champion change. So I titled my seminar "Champions of Change: Clearing the Hurdles of the 21st Century."

Primarily, I used a combination of the intrapersonal intelligence (critical to empathizing with their clients) and the interpersonal intelligence (essential for building relationships through clear communication) to create an outline that demonstrated their critical role as change-agents. I addressed how the concept of change is changing, identified three main hurdles of the 21st century they face, and recommended five strategies for clearing those hurdles.

I also appealed to the audience's musical-rhythmic intelligence by playing a piece of music about change as they entered the ballroom. To their visual-spatial intelligence, I created a live, memorable image of clearing hurdles by literally leaping over chairs in the center aisle.

Use all eight intelligences consciously. Mix and match them. Experiment with a couple of them you don't ordinarily use as much as the others.

> *Whatever action you take, think as you
> experience the world in motion. Develop an
> elasticity of mind. As Voltaire, the French
> philosopher and writer, said, "No problem can
> withstand the assault of sustained thinking."*

But wait—there's more.

Explore Emotional and Spiritual Intelligence

This section could be titled "Beyond Gardner," as inevitably thinkers came along who recognized yet further realms of intelligence. The emotional intelligence movement arose and affirmed what British novelist Arnold Bennett proclaimed to be true when he said, "There can be no knowledge without emotion. We may be aware of a truth, yet until we have felt its force, it is not ours. To the cognition of the brain, must be added the experience of the soul."[53]

The idea of "emotional intelligence" has evolved over time and was further refined by psychologists Dr. John Mayer from the University of New Hampshire and Dr. Peter Salovey from Yale University in 1990. It represents the ability to perceive emotions, access and generate emotions to assist thought, understand emotions and emotional knowledge, and reflectively regulate emotions to promote emotional and intellectual growth.[54] Then in 1995, Daniel Goleman, a psychologist and writer for *The New York Times*, popularized the concept with his best seller, *Emotional Intelligence: Why It Can Matter More than IQ*. Goleman's work has been a boon to educators who wished to more deeply understand the developing young minds and hearts they work to assist.

Even beyond emotional intelligence, we are blessed with having spiritual intelligence. Leading the quest to define and understand this ability, Danah Zohar, a physicist and philosopher, has written works that extend the language and principles of quantum physics into a new understanding of human consciousness, psychology, and social organization. Her books *SQ* and *Spiritual Capital* move us beyond IQ and EQ to SQ, spiritual intelligence. Through them, we can transform ourselves and our culture, acting from higher motivations such as exploration, cooperation, mastery, and service. A most appropriate intelligence for the Soulwise Conspirator's repertoire.

Use every one of your magnificent intelligences, know that your synapses are leaping for joy, and allow yourself to be guided to your perfect place in the world.

ASK REALLY GOOD DUMB QUESTIONS

The philosopher Socrates taught his students 2,500 years ago what has come to be called the Socratic Method, which encourages people to ask questions as if they were ignorant of the answers. In other words, he recommended asking really dumb questions. Fall in love with questions, ask lots of questions, and never stop asking.

Fall in Love with Questions

To discover a pressing need, you need to fall in love with questions.

Sister Joan Chittister loves questions. In fact, this Roman Catholic nun is addicted to them. She wholeheartedly believes this Biblical promise: "Ask and it will be given to you" (Luke 11:9). In her book *Called to Question: A Spiritual Memoir*, she revealed her calling to ask questions. In an interview, she claimed that "defiance is a form of obedience and that silence in the face of injustice is a sin."[55]

She has described society's resistance to questions this way: "We see people die spiritually every day. Sometimes they look very religious in the doing of it, in fact. They keep believing, reading, praying, thinking what they have always thought. In the face of new questions, they dare no questions. At the brink of new insights, they want no insights. They want comfort and a guarantee of the kind of heaven they imagined as children. They think that to think anything else is unfaithful."[56]

An indispensable part of your toolkit, questions help define a need. The skill of asking questions enhances all professions, including law, psychology, science, the arts, information technology, and engineering. In medicine, questions constitute the very heart of a definitive diagnosis.

Four years ago, I became quite ill. Seven specialists examined me. Finally, in desperation, I traveled to the Mayo Clinic in Rochester, Minnesota. Let me tell you that the physicians at this world-renowned medical center really love questions. And they're thorough. I now have an in-depth understanding of probing!

Dr. Connie Jennings, my primary physician at Mayo and a phenomenal diagnostician, asked the right questions in the right way—brief, clear, and focused. To her, diagnosis is an interrogative game, but a serious one. She inquired about who I am, what I thought was wrong, where and when I felt pain, and how severe it was. Questions. Questions. Questions. Then came the answers and corrective treatment. Thanks, Dr. Connie!

Ask Lots of Questions

Socrates, the ancient Greek master interrogator, engaged his students in what has been named the "100 Questions" exercise. He invited his students, in one sitting, to quickly make a list of a hundred questions that were important to them. He discovered that the first 20 questions were quite random, while the next 30 or 40 registered recurring themes. In the second half of the list, however, the surprisingly enlightening material revealed the students' deepest hopes and fears.[57]

Sometimes asking questions can yield extraordinary results. That's what occurred in the 1993 lawsuit that Erin Brockovich, an American legal clerk and environmental activist, constructed against the Pacific Gas and Electric Company. Despite her lack of a formal law school education, Brockovich asked hundreds of questions to gather proof for her case against the company for pollution and drinking water contamination. She drilled down with relevant questions like these: "What's happening here? How did it get this way? Who's responsible? How do people cope? What will happen if nothing is done?" Brockovich won her case for a settlement of $333 million, and the entire drama was made into a 2000 movie *Erin Brockovich* nominated for five Academy Awards. It pays to ask questions.

> *We can learn a lot by observing and adopting the curious and open approach that children take to the world. They persist in asking "Why? Who? What?" questions with disarming innocence, all the while building their databank of information about their surroundings. While walking in our neighborhood, I encountered such a curious three-year-old standing at the end of her driveway. She looked at me and inquired sincerely, "Are you a stranger?"*

Never Stop Asking

Scientists can affirm the necessity of asking questions to make new discoveries. March 2005 marked the 100th anniversary of the publication of Albert Einstein's "Special Theory of Relativity," which found that the timing, length, and mass of an object or event is relative to how close to the speed of light each participant and observer is traveling. As this science superstar advised, "Learn from yesterday, live for today, hope for tomorrow. The important thing is to not stop questioning."

Leadership specialist Peter Block, in his book *The Answer to How is Yes: Acting on What Matters*, reframed leadership as adopting the role of social architect, where engaging and defining the question replace vision, charisma, and driving change. "Transformation," Block asserted, "comes more from pursuing profound questions than seeking practical answers."[58]

Profound questions are elusively simple. Fortunately, questions have a longer lifetime than answers.

Go ahead. Ask really good dumb questions. But be prepared. "One who asks questions," warns the Cameroonian proverb, "cannot avoid the answers."

ASSESS THE URGENCY

Suppose you're responsible for identifying and addressing the pressing needs in the world. But which needs take precedence? It's one of the toughest questions you'll have to address in your efforts to define a need.

In medicine, the process of determining which patient has the most urgent need is called triage. After triage, doctors and nurses must assess each patient the same way. What needs to be done first? Medical emergency physicians deal skillfully with this process every day. They're smart, swift and savvy. They check all the patients' vital signs and determine with insight and accuracy what needs to be done first. The pressure's on because their response often means the difference between life and death.

When you assess the urgency of the need you've uncovered, set your priorities, don't obsess with the urgent, and keep your perspective.

Set Your Priorities

What should one do first? In October 2004, the Copenhagen Consesus posed and answered this question. The project brought together 38 of the world's top economists to create a list of global priorities. Using cost-benefit analysis, this expert panel concluded that HIV/AIDS, hunger, free trade, and malaria were the world's top priorities. They rated urgent projects in response to climate change extremely low, calling these ventures "bad projects" because they would cost more than the benefit they could produce.

A coalition of environmental and development organizations published a report responding to these findings, stating that the Kyoto Protocol and even stricter policies should be our first priority. The Kyoto Protocol, an international agreement, links to the United Nations Framework Convention on Climate Change.

The major mandate of the Kyoto Protocol sets binding targets for 37 industrialized countries and the European community for reducing greenhouse gas emissions. These targets amount to an average of 5% reduction against 1990 levels over the five-year period 2008 to 2012. The coalition criticized the Copenhagen Consensus as "intellectually corrupt" reaching "bizarre conclusions" through "intellectual illiteracy."

Often, it's difficult to determine priorities. What's *your* number one priority—terrorism, racism, economic justice, health care? At this stage of the discovery and definition process, don't allow yourself to be overwhelmed. The task of being in charge of the world—even if it's only in your imagination—can be daunting!

> *Throwing up your hands and walking away won't help. Focus on reality to assess the urgency of the world's long list of needs and decide what, in your opinion, should get attention first.*

Nobody said that the Soulwise Conspirator's job would be easy. What you choose to address may not be the most urgent problem in the world but will be based more on what you're drawn to or attracts your attention or perhaps on your personal experience. "Urgent" can be relative; focusing on "important" might be your best route.

Don't Obsess with the Urgent

Some people operate totally on the urgency principle, often with disastrous results. Business owners can slide into a tyranny-of-the-urgent mode during economic downturns and stay in that mode even when the economy has recovered.

In an article in *Fast Company*, Seth Godin, author of *Free Prize Inside*, stated, "If it's urgent, ignore it. Smart organizations ignore the urgent. Smart organizations understand that important issues are the ones to deal with. If you focus on the important stuff, the urgent will take care of itself."[59] With simple planning, one can avoid manufactured emergencies like having to rush to the airport to catch a flight. We all face circumstances that cause legitimate delays. But I encounter many travelers who don't plan ahead to arrive at the airport early; as a result, they constantly have to make a mad dash to the gate.

Each person has a particular sense of priorities based on who they are, their experiences, and their circumstances. For example, if a drunk driver kills one of your family members, you'll probably get mad and join MADD (Mothers Against Drunk Driving). If you're diagnosed with cancer, you'll be eager to find a cure. If you're a reporter facing a black bear in the woods, you won't be thinking about freedom of the press.

One morning in 1888, the inventor of dynamite, who had spent his whole life amassing a fortune from the manufacture and sale of weapons of destruction, awoke to read his own obituary in the newspaper. The obituary resulted from a simple journalistic error. Alfred's brother had died in the night, and an inexperienced reporter carelessly reported the death of the wrong brother.

Anyone would have been disturbed under the circumstances, but Alfred Nobel was horrified. So this was how the world saw him—as the dynamite king! It seemed the general public thought that blowing things up constituted the entire purpose of his life. None of his true intentions to break down the barriers that separated people were recognized, or even given serious consideration. He was quite simply a merchant of death. For that alone he would be remembered. In response to this injustice, he established the Nobel Peace Prize.

Sometimes, it's just time. It's time to act. Musician and performer Bruce Springsteen wrote the article "Chords for Change" published in the *The New York Times* to explain how he decided it was time to express his views about the 2004 presidential election. He joined with some of his fellow artists, including the Dave Matthews Band, Pearl Jam, R.E.M., the Dixie Chicks, Jurassic 5, James Taylor, and Jackson Browne, in the Vote for Change Tour around the United States.

Springsteen concluded his article with this call to action: "It is through the truthful exercising of the best of human qualities of respect for others, honesty about ourselves, faith in our ideals that we come to life in God's eyes. It is how our soul, as a nation and as individuals, is revealed. Our American government has strayed too far from American values. It is time to move forward. The country we carry in our hearts is waiting."[60]

Keep Your Perspective

When you're assessing the urgency, it's essential to keep your perspective. Consider that the estimated number of 150,000+ fatalities from the giant tsunami in the Indian Ocean on December 26, 2004, remains well within the margin of error for estimates of the number of deaths every year from malaria. Two million people die annually of malaria, most of them children and most in Africa. Every month, more people will die of malaria (165,000 or more) and HIV/AIDS (240,000) than died in the tsunami, and almost as many will die because of diarrhea (140,000).

> *Remember, you don't have to address a giant need. But it does have to be a need that you consider to be worthy of your attention. So whether it's tackling one of the world's big three diseases—malaria, TB, or AIDS—or helping your child with ADHD, be inescapably drawn to do what others may consider impossible.*

CONNECT THE DOTS

The focus of the previous chapter, Discover Your Passion, began with Frederick Buechner's invitation to "find the place where your greatest love meets the world's greatest need." The five practical guidelines recommended were:

- See with your heart's eyes,
- Experience the world in motion,
- Employ all your senses,
- Watch out for limbo dancers,
- Follow your hunches.

In this chapter, Define the Need, suggestions have been to:

- Put on your thinking cap,
- Use multiple intelligences,
- Ask really good dumb questions,
- Assess the urgency.

Now it's time to connect all these dots to get a picture of your passion and the need you've defined. This essential part of the process will *connect your greatest love with what you consider the world's greatest need*. You'll also focus on one need and take the litmus test.

Solve the Nine-Dots Puzzle
Try to connect all nine dots below using no more than four lines without lifting your pencil from the paper or retracing any lines.

How did you do? (You'll find a solution to the Nine-Dots Puzzle at the end of this chapter.)

When most people are faced with this puzzle, they connect the outside dots to form a square or a box. The key to solving the puzzle, however, is thinking *outside* the box. When you restrict your thinking to the normal boundaries, you may not consider other solutions. But by being open to connecting the dots in uncommon ways, you expand the creative possibilities.

I asked my client, the president of a Fortune 100 company, if he considered himself an outside-the-box thinker. He responded that he needed time to think about the question. That was a good clue. When we met two weeks later, he indicated that he didn't think he was. I appreciated his surprisingly honest answer. "All I want," he reflected, "is a bigger box."

Albert Einstein masterfully used linking in his creative process of thinking. He had an amazing capacity to link things that seemed to be unrelated, and likewise, to bring together the obvious and find not-so-obvious connections to produce fresh innovative ideas.

Soulwise Conspirators catalyze connections in the world, linking their greatest love with the world's greatest need and being open to new, creative, and sometimes unexpected links. Futurist Eric Hoffer claimed, "In a time of drastic change, it is the learners who inherit the future. The learned usually find themselves equipped to live in a world that no longer exists."[61] Another futurist, Alvin Toffler, author of the best seller *Future Shock*, agreed with Hoffer when he wrote, "The illiterate in the future will not be those who cannot read or write, but those who will not be able to learn, unlearn and relearn."[62]

Focus on One Need

By now, you have an idea of what, in your view, are the world's greatest needs. Make a list of the needs you've uncovered, and then reduce the list until you've isolated the one need you passionately want to address. Articulate the need you've identified simply and clearly in the context of the big picture.

People ask how they'll know it's the right need to fulfill. You'll probably have more than one need you wish to address, but just pick one for now. Make your best choice based on the available information and your own inclinations. I've found that everyone who engages in this adventure experiences a struggle. The needs of the world can be overwhelming.

Unless you focus on one need, you run the risk of diluting your efforts. Thomas Merton, an American Roman Catholic priest, once issued this warning: "To allow oneself to be carried away by a multitude of conflicting concerns, to surrender to too many demands, to commit to too many projects, to want to help everyone in everything is itself to succumb to the violence of our times."

Give yourself enough time to make creative connections. Occasionally, people tell me they knew instantly what need arrested them, but in my experience, that's rare. Usually, the process involves weighing a myriad of factors over time, carefully discerning direction.

Multitudes of legitimate options exist, including sharing our resources, finding a cure, educating for life, feeding the hungry, building community, bringing justice, fostering peace, protecting the planet, and so on. Like Henry David Thoreau, American writer, philosopher, and naturalist, you may want to retreat to the woods and discern your direction from the perspective of peace and quiet.

Take the Litmus Test

The litmus test consists of microscopically observing the need you've discovered. Magnify its every detail.

Joe Califano Jr. engaged in this kind of magnification and reports on it in his book *High Society: How Substance Abuse Ravages America and What to Do About It*. During his extensive history of investigating this topic, Califano declared smoking tobacco "public enemy number one" when he served as Secretary of Health, Education, and Welfare in the Carter administration. He has called for a revolution in American attitudes toward all substance abuse and addiction, and the way we deal with these problems. In *High Society*, Califano pointed out it's virtually certain a child who reaches 21 without smoking, using illegal drugs, or abusing alcohol will never do so. He chronicles the fearful cost in personal pain and public dollars of our nation's failure to act on this truth.

Califano showed how substance abuse perpetrates violent and property crime, soaring Medicare and Medicaid costs, family break-ups, domestic violence, the spread of AIDS, teen pregnancy, poverty, and low productivity. He has taken on alcohol and tobacco interests that buy political protection with campaign contributions and seed a culture of substance abuse among our nation's children and teens. He explained the importance of parent power and proposes revolutionary changes in prevention, treatment, and criminal justice.[63]

Califano's book *High Society* is a clarion call to every individual and institution to confront this plague—one that has maimed and killed more Americans than all our wars, natural catastrophes, and traffic accidents combined.

> *Don't rush into deciding what need you're personally called to fill. Take time to magnify the details, but don't take forever, either. Constant analysis may lead to paralysis.*

Malcolm Gladwell, in *Blink: The Power of Thinking Without Thinking*, presented the case for the power and accuracy of snap judgments. Using research on a wide variety of topics including selling cars, marriage, emergency room procedures, speed-dating, and golf, he argued that too much data can actually lead to making bad decisions.[64]

Jack Cornfield, in *After the Ecstasy, the Laundry*, offered this advice: "Sometimes it is necessary to march, sometimes it is necessary to sit, to pray. Each in turn can bring the heart and the world back to balance. For us to act wisely, our compassion must be balanced with equanimity, the ability to let things be as they are. Just as our passionate heart can be touched by the sorrows of the world, so too we must remember that it is not our responsibility to fix all the brokenness of the world—only to fix what we can. Otherwise we become grandiose, as if we were put here to be the savior of the humanity around us."[65]

Once you've discovered your passion and defined a need, it's up to you to dream your need fulfilled, the focus of the next chapter.

TAKE FIVE FOR REFLECTION

1. In considering your own personal blend of passion and reason, does one usually trump the other, and why?

2. What insights did you gain by applying Gardner's eight multiple intelligences to yourself?

3. What three really good dumb questions did you ask about the need in the world you want to address?

   -
   -
   -

4. What are your priorities in addressing the need in the world you've identified?

5. What does the litmus test reveal about the need you've identified in the world?

A Solution to the Nine-Dots Puzzle

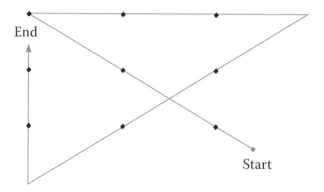

CHAPTER 9

DREAM THE NEED FULFILLED

In *Seven Pillars of Wisdom: A Triumph*, T.E. Lawrence, the famous Lawrence of Arabia, wrote, "All men dream dreams, but not all men dream equally, for there are those who dream at night in the empty recesses of their minds, and they awake in the morning to find that, behold, it was just a dream. But there are other men and women who are dangerous dreamers. For these are men and women who dream in the daytime with their eyes open, that they might fulfill their dreams."[66]

Soulwise Conspirators dream dangerously. They believe their dreams can come true and that their dreams *can* and *will* change the world. They dare to be optimistic. They believe that where the people dream, the people flourish.

The big bonus is this: Dreamers generally live longer because they have a purpose for living. They conspire to transform themselves and the world with compassion.

So far in Part IV, A Guide to Becoming a Soulwise Conspirator, you've seen how to discover your passion and define your dream. This chapter will inspire you to dream the need fulfilled—to claim it, frame it, name it, and flame it. Let's start with claiming your dream.

CLAIM IT

Perceive the Dream

Soulwise Conspirators believe their dreams reveal a glimpse of the future. Most people contend that seeing is believing. Soulwise Conspirators, however, approach their dreams with a different perception than most. They know they'll see it when they believe it. They claim their visions of the future as those visions take shape in their hearts and minds. This key process moves their dreams forward.

You claim your dreams a long time before they become reality. Everything you've experienced to this point in your life contributes to your dreaming. Perceiving or understanding your dreams is an inside job, so welcome your dreams into an environment of anticipation and possibility. Study your dreams to comprehend their texture, color, and nuance.

Clara Barton's dream evolved over two decades. When the American Civil War broke out in 1861, she took up nursing and also worked to get badly needed medical supplies to the battlefields. After the war, while in Europe recovering from an illness, she joined the International Red Cross and nursed the wounded during the Franco-Prussian War of 1870-71. She finally returned to America to claim her dream by establishing an American branch of the Red Cross in 1881. She served as the organization's first president until 1904. Largely as a result of her campaigning, the United States signed the Geneva Conventions for international humanitarian law in 1882.

> *Claim your dream and live with it day and night.*
> *Live with the seeds of your dream that you may later*
> *choose to plant and nurture to fruition.*
> *Live and breathe your dream as if it's already*
> *been accomplished. Long before Olympic champions*
> *give their medal-winning performances, they've*
> *imagined themselves performing at their best.*
> *To these super athletes, their dream is a*
> *magnificent obsession.*

Michael Phelps dreamed of winning eight Olympic gold medals at the 2008 Summer Olympic Games long before he dove into the swimming pool in Beijing. Every year, Phelps would lay out his goals on a sheet of paper, which he'd give to his coach, Bob Bowman. Neither would say a word to anyone about what's on that paper. At least neither did until Phelps accomplished what he'd set his mind to do and won eight medals in a single Olympic Games. Apparently, eight is a lucky number not only for Chinese culture but for Phelps, who swam his way to eight gold medals at the Games that started on 8-8-08 at 8 p.m.

Listen to the voice of your dream. See it in your mind's eye. Think about it. Ruminate on it. Be silent in its presence and meditate on it.

Soulwise Conspirators consider their dreams to be a calling, their vocations. By far the happiest people I know are those actively and passionately fulfilling their calling. They resonate with it and pursue it with courage, even in the face of danger, often entering uncharted territory with conviction.

A Soulwise Conspirator's calling embodies compassion, a primary sign of a person's inner growth. Actor Christopher Reeve put it this way: "Go see the human beings who are suffering, and then ask yourself, is the work I did today relevant to human suffering? Did I do something that is going to help change somebody's life, maybe not today but sometime soon?"[67]

My compassion was put to the test during a trip to Nairobi, Kenya, in June 2004. I visited Kibera, Africa's largest urban slum and home to over a million people, one third of the population of Nairobi. The most densely populated informal settlement in sub-Saharan Africa, Kibera covers an area of approximately 250 hectares (four square miles) with a population density of more than 2,000 people per hectare. Kibera consists of 12 interlocking villages with approximately 8,000 dwellings in each village. Its name, Kibera, comes from the Nubian word *kibra*, meaning forest or jungle.

I met wonderful families with whom I remain dear friends to this day. However, I experienced the biggest dichotomy in my life—the pure joy and rhythm of their lives alongside the stark realities of unbelievably harsh conditions of poverty, hunger, pollution, disease, and death. I saw firsthand why people often refer to Kibera as "the forgotten city."

My heart broke that day. I cried until I had no more tears.

And then, through my brokenness, I began to dream of how I could apply my gifts to help these fellow members of my global family. By comparison, I was extremely wealthy. I considered how I could use my influence to stand alongside these slum survivors. I realized that my calling consisted of these four interconnected missions: feed the kids, prevent malaria, transform the slum, and educate leaders.

Only I could decide whether I would take the next step to receive this gargantuan dream.

Receive the Dream

In 1969, after my ordination, I had been appointed senior pastor of the St. Anthony Pastoral Charge of the United Church of Canada, which served one large and 10 small churches on the northern coast of Newfoundland and Labrador. One Sunday afternoon, I traveled 40 miles on my snowmobile to conduct a service in a small white clapboard church that could probably hold 25 adult worshippers in an out-port village. I waited for about 15 minutes and only one person showed up for worship—a fisherman in his early fifties who'd traveled about 20 miles to get there. He stood about 5'5", wore a dark blue parka that he kept zipped up, and wore black snowmobile boots and gloves. He had a weathered face and a full salt and pepper beard.

Momentarily, I considered just saying a prayer and calling it a day. But on reflection, I realized that together we'd already logged 60 miles of travel, with 60 more miles to return. So I decided to conduct the whole service as if the church were filled with a few hundred worshippers. I did it all—the hymns, readings, prayers, sermon, Eucharist, and benediction. I even took the role of the choir by singing the hymns solo. During my sermon, my congregation of one never looked up. I wondered why I'd bothered.

I greeted him at the door as he left and thanked him for coming. And then he surprised me. He said, "Reverend, I've been thinking about becoming a Christian for about thirty-odd years. And today's the day!"

> *Soulwise Conspirators give a resounding Yes! to their calling with an open-eyed, carefully considered acceptance. They sign an internal contract with their hearts and minds. They cast their vote for their dream and make their commitment to themselves official. Anyone with a willing heart and mind can receive the gift of a dream. As an African proverb advises, "You don't have to be tall to see the moon."*

Usually a trigger prompts receiving or accepting the gift of a dream. By 1998, John Wood had spent seven years working unbelievable hours at the software giant Microsoft as director of business development for China. He decided to take a three-week trek in Nepal to recharge his batteries. Wood chronicled the chance encounter that changed his life and the reception of his calling in his book *Leaving Microsoft to Change the World: An Entrepreneur's Odyssey to Educate the World's Children.*

While in Nepal, Wood met a provincial school administrator in charge of securing resources for 17 schools in a country where the illiteracy rate is 70% and resources minimal at best. He visited a school and saw firsthand the injustice of how one's place of birth determined access to books and education. This experience triggered a dream he ended up fully embracing. A year later, after leaving Microsoft, he arrived at the same remote village school leading eight donkeys carrying thousands of books for the children. As the children rushed to grab their new treasures, John Wood's joy rivaled theirs.

Soulwise Conspirators graciously acknowledge and accept the responsibility of their dreams as dream trustees. They realize that, according to the old adage, "If it's to be, it's up to me." Dream trustees are entrusted with the responsibility of making their dreams come true.

Sometimes the trigger to receive a dream comes in the form of a life-altering event or disease. In 1991, award-winning television and movie actor Michael J. Fox was diagnosed with young-onset Parkinson's disease. Here's how he described his wake-up call in *Lucky Man: A Memoir:* "I woke up to find the message in my left hand. It had me trembling. It wasn't a fax, telegram, memo, or the usual sort of missive bringing disturbing news. In fact, my hand held nothing at all. The trembling was the message."[68]

Seven years later, he made his condition known to the public and established The Michael J. Fox Foundation for Parkinson's Research. The organization has what may seem to be an impossible dream—to find a cure for Parkinson's within the decade. In 2009, Fox released another book, *Always Looking Up: The Adventures of an Incurable Optimist.* It tells about his continuing courageous struggle with the disease. Such a situation has provided him with intense motivation to follow through—both for himself and for others who suffer from this debilitating condition.

In addition to the challenges of receiving a dream, trustees gain immeasurable benefits. As a young and starving comedic actor, Danny

Thomas vowed that if he found success, he would open a hospital dedicated to St. Jude, the patron saint of hopeless causes. In 1962, he founded St. Jude Children's Research Hospital in Memphis, Tennessee, which annually treats 4,600 children suffering with leukemia, cancer, AIDS, sickle cell anemia, and other diseases. Thomas not only achieved success in his acting career, he reaped satisfaction from knowing his philanthropy was helping save children's lives.

I've witnessed the joy people experience by serving others in inner city soup kitchens, mentoring children and adults in reading, repairing homes for the elderly, visiting the sick, or working tirelessly for a cause that has touched their lives.

Each of the four inter-related dimensions of my African dream had a distinct trigger. I decided to feed the kids when I witnessed 150 children vomit after eating their one meal a week because their stomachs weren't used to food. I committed myself to prevent malaria in children after I contracted and recovered from the disease myself. After considerable resistance, I accepted my call to transform the slum when I stood in the pouring rain in Kibera. I realized that God had chosen me at this time and in this place for this purpose. And I accepted my responsibility to educate leaders in Africa while watching the television coverage of riots in the slums of Nairobi after the 2007 presidential elections.

Soulwise Conspirators proudly and humbly receive their torches representing their dreams. They bear their torches and maintain the flames until the dream is fulfilled. Then they share the responsibility, guidance, and joy with all those who involve themselves in the dream. Unconditionally, they accept the challenge that India's spiritual and political leader Mahatma Gandhi put out—to "be the change you want to see in the world."

Conceive the Dream

To this point, you've perceived your dream and taken that important leap to receive it. Now it's time to conceive the gift of your dream, to nurture it with imagination for its eventual delivery.

Before you dash out and declare your dream, take the necessary time to appreciate and understand the nature of your dream and enable it to grow to its full potential. Use commitment and enthusiasm to engage your whole being in this integral stage of development.

Conceive means to become pregnant with or to develop an idea in the mind. As you conceive your dream, give it the dedicated care and attention that mothers give their babies during and after pregnancy. Cradle and cultivate your dream during its gestation. You'll provide it with significant mental and emotional energy in this period of development.

Napoleon Hill, perhaps America's foremost motivational author and the founder of what's often referred to as the "science of success," stated, "Whatever your mind can conceive and believe, it can achieve." He also said, "Cherish your visions and your dreams as they are the children of your soul, the blueprints of your ultimate accomplishments."

Engaging in the process of conceiving your dream is essentially an act of servant leadership. Dr. Peter Senge, who popularized the concept of the "learning organization" in his best seller, *The Fifth Discipline: The Art and Practice of the Learning Organization*, clarified the leadership role of the Soulwise Conspirator this way: "Especially in the West, leaders are *heroes*—great men (and occasionally women) who 'rise to the fore' in times of crisis... So long as such myths prevail, they reinforce a focus on short-term events and charismatic heroes rather than on systemic forces and collective learning. Leadership in learning organizations centers on subtler and ultimately more important work... In a learning organization, leaders' roles differ dramatically from that of the charismatic decision maker. Leaders are designers, teachers, and stewards."[69]

Soulwise Conspirators appreciate and accept their leadership roles in the world as designers, teachers, and stewards. They are committed to conceiving their dreams by framing, naming, and flaming them.

Framing denotes how you will shape and formulate your dream. Soulwise Conspirators could be called dream "imagineers" or "social sculptors," who possess prophetic powers of discernment, wisely engage these powers to predict and prepare for what's ahead, and then shape our individual and collective future.

Once you've framed it, you'll want to name your dream so it reflects your uniqueness and confers an identity to this new entity you've created.

Naming your dream is a critical piece of your dream puzzle because it communicates to the world what you've imagined and arouses curiosity about your idea. Think of a name like "Tears for Fears," the African hunger initiative.

I recommend the name you give your dream serve these purposes:

- Sell and tell,
- Vow and wow,
- Shout and tout,
- Click and stick.

The last step in the claim-your-dream process is to flame it. By this I mean following the tradition of testing your vision by "fire" to see if it can withstand the heat of rigorous evaluation. This process reflects the theme of "Refiner's Fire" sung by Brian Doerksen. It goes like this: "Purify my heart, let me be as gold and precious silver. Purify my heart, let me be as gold, pure gold." (www.briandoerksen.com) Doerksen's song refers to a silversmith who holds a piece of silver in the middle of the fire where the flames are hottest and burns away all the impurities. The testing of a dream indicates where it needs to be refined.

FRAME IT

Trust Your Inner Artist

American poet Carl Sandburg wrote, "Nothing happens unless first a dream."

A few years ago, I had the honor of being a corporate coach to Bill Odom, former president of the Ford Motor Credit Company, one of the largest credit companies in the world. At one of our monthly three-hour meetings, I asked him to sit opposite me at the end of a long table in the boardroom. Without prior notice, I invited him to imagine himself as the conductor of the "Ford Credit Orchestra." After presenting him with a brand new baton, I sat down. Without missing a beat, President Bill began directing, and for 17 spectacular minutes, creatively expressed his dream for the company. He already held the dream inside; I just gave him a gentle nudge to let it out.

We're born with the capacity to dream and a vast reservoir of resources ready to be released to shape the future. The premise of education holds that we have everything we need to realize our potential. Great teachers accept the responsibility and challenge to draw out what's already inside the student.

Soulwise Conspirators see in their mind's eye a clear, compelling picture of the fulfillment of their defined need. They know that dreaming begins internally; they visualize both need and solution. As author Eudora Welty expressed it, "All serious daring starts from within."

Like professional golfer Tiger Woods, who's known to visualize the ball rolling into the cup before he even hits it, Soulwise Conspirators imagine the resolution of a need before they take action.

One must take a leap of imagination to create the future. As stated eloquently by Friedrich Nietzsche, a German philosopher of the late 19th century, "You must carry the chaos within in order to give birth to the dancing star."

Soulwise Conspirators are challenged to carry their "star child" with all the accompanying concerns, uncertainties, and fragility so it fully develops to term and emerges from the chaotic environment of incubation with discernible purpose and momentum.

No painless way to forge the future exists; no quick solution to the world's problems will emerge. Soulwise Conspirators have no magic wand to wave over the earth to right humanity's wrongs. However, they do believe transformation of the global family is possible, and that they can be the catalysts of that transformation. Believing must be the first step of creation.

Soulwise Conspirators radiate a positive idealistic spirit that permeates their dreams from conception to reality. They fit this profile offered by Felix Adler, founder of the Ethical Culture movement: "An optimist is a person who sees only the light in the picture, whereas a pessimist sees only the shadows. An idealist, however, is one who sees the light and the shadows, but in addition sees something else: the possibility of changing the picture, of making the light prevail over the shadows."

The Jerome and Dorothy Lemelson Center for the Study of Invention and Innovation, a part of the Smithsonian Institute's National Museum of American History, promotes nurturing our inventive sides. Through its traveling exhibition, Invention at Play, the center encourages young people and their families to be creative. It makes the case that inventiveness and innovative thinking are not granted to a few inspired visionaries among us, but rather are qualities granted to all human beings. But they do need fostering, which is why the center reaches out to both adults and children, encouraging them to think of themselves as inventors.

> *Soulwise Conspirators need a solid knowledge base, plus a keen, well-developed sense of imagination to dream needs fulfilled, find a solution, seize an opportunity, discover a cure, solve a riddle, crack a code, or resolve a dispute. Didn't the great scientist Albert Einstein consider imagination more important than knowledge or intelligence?*

Athletes recognize the critical nature of imagining a destination. Whether it's football, baseball, or hockey, players formulate a mental picture of completing the play. For example, football quarterbacks imagine the receiver catching the ball in the end zone for a touchdown. Hockey and basketball players balance speed and distance when passing the puck or the ball on the way to the net or basket. "Imagination gives you a destination," observed Duke University's famed men's basketball coach, Mike Krzyzewski. "The greatest gift a coach can give a player, a teacher can give a student, and a parent can give to their child is the opportunity to imagine great things. These dreams in childhood pave the way for future success."[70]

For Soulwise Conspirators, the destination is of ultimate importance. They begin by living the vision as if it has already happened. As legend has it, during an election, Abraham Lincoln visited the church of his opponent, a Methodist minister, to hear him preach. The minister asked for those who'd like to go to heaven to stand. Lincoln didn't. When asked where he was going, Lincoln replied, "Congress."

My own mind envisions a mile-long line of young hungry children in Kibera slum in Nairobi just before eight in the morning. They're waiting to receive their one meal of the day—porridge in a forest green mug with a special logo on it. Parents accompany some of the children, but most are orphans who've survived another day. I see them smiling because they know that today they won't go hungry.

Whereas I'm still framing my dream in my mind, photographer David DeJonge of Zeeland, Michigan, has done so literally. He had the vision to photograph and preserve the stories of the few remaining World War I veterans. DeJonge refers to WWI vets as a forgotten group in the U.S., often ignored by public officials and foundations. Because most people who served during that war were born around the turn of the last century, the remaining survivors were well over age 100. DeJonge's nine portraits of WWI veterans are on permanent display in the Pentagon.

The first step in framing your dream is to trust your inner artist. The second step is to imagine the impossible.

Imagine the Impossible

As Soulwise Conspirators, we imagine the impossible. What's the difference between the possible and the impossible? The impossible may take a little longer to achieve.

Dreaming the impossible involves a big risk. Some may think we've lost our minds. But as Soulwise Conspirators, we believe we have no choice. We're not bound by the possible but liberated by imagining the impossible and spurred on by an inescapable drive.

Ann Roulac, author of *Power, Passion and Purpose: 7 Steps to Energizing Your Life*, wrote that "extraordinary people visualize not what is possible or probable, but rather what is impossible. By visualizing the impossible, they begin to see it as possible."[71]

In August, 1996, Christopher Reeve showed his agreement when he addressed the Democratic National Convention. This actor who had played Superman in the movies but was confined to a wheelchair due to his paralysis from an accident, said, "So many of our dreams at first seem impossible, then they seem improbable, and then, when we summon the will, they soon become inevitable. If we can conquer outer space, we should be able to conquer inner space too—the frontier of the brain, the central nervous system, and all the afflictions of the body that destroy so many lives and rob our country of so much potential."

Never let it be said that "Superman" gave up.

Reeve's own misfortune gave him the impetus to establish a foundation and co-found the Reeve-Irvine Research Center to find new treatments for spinal chord injuries. Not everyone would react that way to a tragedy—but Christopher Reeve was a Soulwise Conspirator.

Sometimes you need to enlarge yourself to achieve your dream. At the 1992 Corporate Design Foundation Conference, design guru Sara Little Turnbull delivered an address that included this poem with spatial significance projected on a screen:

If you don't
Stretch
You don't know
Where the   edge
Is

Yes, Soulwise Conspirators push the limits. They're willing to stretch out of their comfort zones to fulfill their dream. They follow this advice from Ralph Waldo Emerson: "Do not go where the path may lead, go instead where there is no path and leave a trail." Miles Hilton Barber, a British adventurer, created a new trail in the skies by flying a microlight from London to Sydney. Not so impossible, you say? Consider that Barber has been blind for 25 years!

Make the impossible a habit. Author Madeline L'Engle, best known for the children's classic *A Wrinkle in Time*, claimed, "I live by the impossible. Like the White Queen, I find it a good discipline to practice believing as many as seven impossible things every morning before breakfast."

> *Soulwise Conspirators refuse to lower their*
> *expectations to appease opposition or disbelief.*
> *In my experience, naysayers can actually be valuable*
> *in the process of dreaming. When people tell me that*
> *my dream for a future of abundance for Africa*
> *is impossible, I thank them. They've confirmed*
> *that my dream is worthwhile.*

Daniel H. Burnham, Director of Works for the World's Columbian Exposition in 1893, said, "Make not little plans; they have no magic to stir men's imagination." Dreaming big is essential for gathering the support of others for a dream.

How about a 20-foot inflatable Super Colon for big? The coordinators of the National Colorectal Cancer Awareness Month wanted to stir the imaginations of both men and women, helping them possibly save their own lives. The American Cancer Society estimates in 2008 that 148,810 men and women will be diagnosed with colon cancer, and that 49,960 Americans will die of the disease. Overall, 91% of the new cases and 94% of deaths occur in individuals 50 and older. Half of these deaths could have been saved with recommended screening. So the Society created the 20-foot inflatable colon to show what healthy colon tissue looks like as well as stages of cancerous colon tissue. Visitors can actually walk through it and learn about prevention, risk factors, symptoms, and treatment.[72]

Jeffrey Sachs also imagines big. Really big. A visionary economist, former director of the UN Millennium Project, and president and co-founder of Millennium Promise Alliance, Sachs imagines the global eradication of extreme poverty—a $200-$250 billion-a-year dream! That amount is double what the developed world spends on foreign aid. Sachs punches the air for emphasis when he speaks to audiences around the globe. "The basic truth is that for less than one percent of the income of the rich world, nobody has to die of poverty on the planet."

Sachs is the director of The Earth Institute, Quetelet professor of Sustainable Development, and professor of Health Policy and Management at Columbia University. He's also special advisor to United Nations Secretary-General Ban Ki-moon. From 2002 to 2006, he was Director of the UN Millennium Project and Special Advisor to United Nations Secretary-General Kofi Annan on the Millennium Development Goals, the internationally agreed-upon goals to reduce extreme poverty, disease, and hunger by 2015.

Like Sachs, I imagine the impossible—my dream of transforming Kibera slum in Nairobi. When I tell people in Kenya, especially "slummers," about it, most laugh out loud and say I'm out of my mind. They know that others have valiantly attempted to improve the conditions of poverty, unemployment, disease, and crime with little or no success.

A bright spot on the horizon is "Cities Without Slums," an action plan developed by the Cities Alliance in July 1999 and launched by Nelson Mandela at the inaugural meeting of the Cities Alliance in Berlin in December 1999. Subsequently endorsed by the 150 heads of state and government attending the UN Millennium Summit in September 2000, the plan is reflected in the United Nations Millennium Development Goals. It states, "By 2020, to have achieved a significant improvement in the lives of at least 100 million slum dwellers."

I see in my mind's eye a picture-perfect Kibera. My impossible dream projects a vision of Kibera transformed forever, a city of opportunity and prosperity within the city of Nairobi. Its citizens work together to foster an environment of collective responsibility in a spirit of cooperation for the good of all. Whereas the majority of people living in Kibera in 2009 have no deed to the land they live on, in my dream, they all share in the title to the land.

The transformation of Kibera will serve as a model for slums in other parts of Africa and the world. According to the 2006 United Nations World Water Development Report, half of the world's population lives in urban areas compared with less than 15% in 1900. That means the world's urban population increased more than tenfold in the 20th century. Unfortunately, in 2006, 930 million people—nearly one-third of all urban dwellers—live in slums. The United Nations estimates that the number of people living in slums passed 1 billion in 2007 and could reach 1.39 billion in 2020. In Asia and the Pacific, 2 out of 5 urban dwellers live in slums, compared with 3 out of 5 in Africa. (http://filipspagnoli.wordpress.com/2009/04/23/humanrights-facts-114-urbanslums)

To frame your dream and see it fulfilled, be sure to trust your inner artist and imagine the impossible. Then you must express your vision.

Express Your Vision

The third part of framing your dream consists of expressing your inner artist's impossible dream. Your picture-perfect future could take a creative combination of forms including prose, poetry, speeches, models, painting, photography, sculpture, dance, drama, pottery, film, cuisine, aroma, or theater. Suppose you choose to use painting as your medium of expression. You'll need to include two aspects: broad strokes and significant detail.

Using a wide brush, paint the broad strokes that give an overall sense of the dream you imagine as if it's already been fulfilled. You want to convey the big picture, the IMAX perspective that articulates the scope and breadth of your dream. If the viewer doesn't appreciate the big picture, then the details will be irrelevant. If you've identified the need for children to be protected against malaria, for example, then your broad strokes would reveal what life would look like if children were living malaria-free. You might want to show insecticide-treated bednets preventing pesky mosquitoes from getting in and infecting a vulnerable child.

Next, use a fine brush to provide details that complement and enhance the broad strokes of your dream. Make them crystal-clear. What colors, textures, and images can you add to the picture? What interactions and relationships, moods and movements can you depict? In your mind, bring your painting to life with feelings, conversations or written words, silence or sounds. What metaphors, similes, or analogies come to mind? What do you see, hear, taste, smell, and feel when you look at your painting?

In the 1984 movie *The Karate Kid*, Mr. Kesuke Miyagi, a handyman/martial arts master meets Daniel LaRusso, a bullied boy. When Daniel expresses interest in bonsai, Mr. Miyagi encourages him to trim a juniper in minute detail. The following dialogue reveals the master's advice for Daniel:

> Miyagi: "Close eye. Trust. Concentrate. Think only tree. Make a perfect picture down to last pine needle. Wipe mind clean everything but tree. Nothing in this whole world—only tree. You got it? Open eye. Remember picture? Make like picture. Just trust picture."
> Daniel: "But how will I know if my picture's the right one?"
> Miyagi: "If come from inside you, always right one."

When the broad strokes and the intricate detail come from within your heart and mind, your authenticity will shine through in your picture of the need fulfilled.

I've already indicated my love and affection for Africa and its people. But what about its future? What's my picture of what could happen in the future? My undergraduate and graduate business students at Daystar University in Nairobi, Kenya, repeatedly asked me if I thought Africa ever had a chance to be a key player in the global economy. One student asked poignantly, "Do we have a snowball's chance in hell?" My simple qualified answer was and remains, "Yes. But only with exceptional leadership." The continent's future will ultimately depend on the social, technological, economic, political, and spiritual guidance of its member nations.

In an article in the *Minneapolis StarTribune* on January 5, 2008, Ward Brehm, chair of the United States African Development Foundation, commented on the turmoil following the Kenyan presidential elections on December 27, 2007, by saying, "The 'cure' for Kenya, and indeed for all of Africa, is to democratically elect leaders with good hearts."

I am committed to help Daystar University fulfill its mission by establishing The Daystar University Global Leadership Center. Programs in this Center will inspire servant-leaders with good hearts and minds to transform Africa for a future of promise.

> *For Soulwise Conspirators, the future stretches before them as a canvas ready for them to paint. They subscribe to the wisdom of this African proverb: "Tomorrow belongs to the people who prepare for it today."*

They trust their inner artist, imagine the impossible, and express their vision both in broad strokes and significant detail. Like parents of a new child, they bear the honor and responsibility of choosing a name that best identifies their baby.

NAME IT

Congratulations! You've successfully framed your dream fulfilled. Your next task is to name your dream, to give it a specific identity. If you've ever named a child, you know how difficult a task choosing an appropriate "given" name can be. You have to weigh a multitude of factors in search of the perfect name. Witness this process:

Two doctors opened an office in a small town and put up a sign that read "Dr. Smith and Dr. Jones, Psychiatry and Proctology." The town council was not happy with the sign, so the doctors changed it to "Hysterias and Posteriors." This was not acceptable either, so in an effort to satisfy the council they changed the sign to "Schizoids and Hemorrhoids." No go. Next, they tried "Catatonics and High Colonics." Thumbs down again. Then came "Manic Depressives and Anal Retentives." Still no good. Another attempt resulted in "Minds and Behinds." Unacceptable again. So they tried "Lost Souls and Butt Holes." No way. "Analysis and Anal Cysts?" Nope. "Nuts and Butts?" No. "Freaks and Cheeks?" Still no go. "Loons and Moons?" Forget it. Almost at their wit's end, the doctors finally came up with "Dr. Smith and Dr. Jones, Odds and Ends." Everyone loved it.

What's in a name? A lot! The name you assign to your dream pinpoints and articulates the fulfillment of the need you've identified. It serves eight purposes: sell and tell, vow and wow, shout and tout, and click and stick.

Let's begin by considering how to choose a name to sell and tell.

Sell and Tell

We live in a sell and tell world. A study conducted by Marity Dialogue Marketing group found that every day we're bombarded with approximately 3,000 messages that vie for our attention. They attract and repel, entice and provoke, stir and irritate, draw and disturb. According to new research, our brains record all of these messages and store them. But only a few of these messages stand out enough to capture our attention and perhaps our action or business. (http://rubiconconsulting. com/mt4/mt-tb.cgi/570)

Ads everywhere clamor for our attention as advertisers go beyond the ends of the earth to make their pitches. The European Incoherent Scatter Scientific Association, a science consortium that runs a space center on an Arctic Ocean archipelago, even transmits signals into outer space. It has teamed up with a sponsor, Frito-Lay, which has invited the British public to submit 30-second commercials about life on our planet. The winning entry will be transmitted via ultra-high-frequency radar to a solar system 42 light years away in the constellation Ursa Major, which scientists say could be teaming with life forms.

Skilled advertisers devise campaigns targeted at specific audiences in particular environments. They recognize these three key factors combining to induce a behavioral change: the motivation, the ability, and the trigger. For example, a man falls in love with the woman of his dreams and is motivated to marry her. Then he decides to buy her a diamond ring and checks his bank account to see if he can pay for it. Finally, he realizes that Valentine's Day is only two weeks away, which triggers his purchase of a diamond.

Authors name their books to attract readers to buy. They realize that book titles sell and book subtitles tell. The title must grab potential readers emotionally and the subtitle cognitively. Together, they act as the trigger to persuade people to buy the book and reveal its content. I titled this book *Soulwise: How to Create a Conspiracy of Hope, Health and Harmony* with these criteria in mind.

The following three examples of nonfiction book titles also illustrate this principle:

- *The World Is Flat: A Brief History of the Twenty-first Century* by Thomas Friedman
- *Tuesdays with Morrie: An Old Man, a Young Man, and Life's Greatest Lesson* by Mitch Albom
- *Good to Great: Why Some Companies Make the Leap... and Others Don't* by Jim Collins

Sometimes, a single book title will serve to both sell and tell:
- *The Seven Habits of Highly Successful People* by Stephen Covey
- *1001 Ways to Be Romantic* by Gregory Godek
- *Juggling for the Complete Klutz* by John Cassidy & B.C. Rimbeaux

As you can appreciate from these examples, naming your dream to "sell and tell" requires condensing your idea into a word or phrase. You may want to seek the advice of an idea guru or a wordsmith who majors in the art and science of naming. By articulating and sharing your dream with another pair of eyes and ears, you may uncover insights that will help you name your dream and also help develop a strategy for its fulfillment.

> *Look outside the box. You may even want to throw the box away. Play with names. "You're Hired" is the name of a new cocktail inspired by Donald Trump for toasting. The Steak and Shake Restaurant offers a banana/strawberry milkshake called "Banawberry."*

I'm fortunate that my night dreams often name things for me. My subconscious analyzes the information I take in and processes it while

I'm sleeping.

For example, I've expressed my concerns for the health and welfare of Africa, especially for the children and families in Kibera. My heart aches for these people who live under the most oppressive conditions. On the first night of my visit to Kenya in the summer of 2007, I had an amazing technicolor dream about the slum. I had the same dream of transformation the second night and the third—in fact, every night for six weeks. I thought I was going crazy, so I checked in with an African friend who's a psychologist. I poured out my story in detail. He listened intently. And then, after a long pause, he took my hands in his, looked me in the eye, and said, "KaraKibera. God chose you to transform Kibera. Let's celebrate."

Hearing my friend say "KaraKibera," although it had no particular meaning for him in Swahili, held special meaning for me because my wife's Swedish name is Kara, which means "dear ones." The transformation of the slum would be for the "dear ones of Kibera." God obviously believes that the slummers are capable of creating a future of promise and prosperity. And like Nehemiah, the Biblical figure given a dream, I'm the keeper and catalyst for the dream called KaraKibera— transforming the slum for good forever.

Here are some commercial and organizational examples of names that sell and tell.

Sell and Tell commercial examples:
- Disney Dream Vacations
- Brann's Sizzling Steaks
- Desperate Housewives
- Krispy Kreme Doughnuts
- My Big Fat Greek Wedding

Sell and Tell organizational examples:
- United Nations
- Greenpeace
- Help Stop Hunger
- Amnesty International
- Doctors without Borders

Vow and Wow

The name you choose for your dream vows to passionately fulfill what you've imagined. A sign in the window at the Old Hamlin Café in Ludington, Michigan, confidently states this promise: "Eat our brunch ... get gas." Well, maybe. Old Hamlin's owners created its tongue-in-cheek promotion when the price of fuel was shooting through the roof. For the record, the café's food tastes great, especially its breakfast.

A name represents a vow or covenant between you and others. It tells succinctly what you promise to do and embodies your intention of fulfilling your promise. When you, yourself, have developed and are fully confident in your plan, put your promise out there. Ignore the skeptics and keep the faith. You'll attract those who resonate with your dream.

My vow to readers of *Soulwise: How to Create a Conspiracy of Hope, Health and Harmony* is to do everything in my power to save the global family from choking to death by sparking a movement of Conspirators to work with compassion for the future of civilization. Similarly, my promise to the citizens of the slum in Nairobi reads "KaraKibera—transforming the slum for good forever."

Translate your vow into a consistent wow experience for your intended audience. Blow them away with their first impression of your named dream. Create an unforgettable encounter that makes them smile or nod or scream "Yes!" Good newspaper headlines always do this. You want to capture attention so people clamor to know more about your dream and consider being a part of it.

> *"Wow" consists of a well-crafted combination of originality, pizzazz, and coolness. Think of the birth of a child, which perhaps is the epitome of Wow. But don't spend a lot of money to create the buzz that Wow delivers. Simply connect with your target audience in an expressive way.*

When I was considering how to brand my business—Dr. Phil Johnson, The FireStarter—I wanted to include a car that embodied the image I wanted to convey. So I decided to test drive a variety of cars to see which one best fit. I wanted to use a car that supported my vision of people radically alive and my mission to set people's hearts on fire, igniting their passion for life, love, and work. My brand personality is spirited, purposeful, passionate, provocative, and playful. My brand packaging I saw as bold, dynamic, clean, upbeat, and evocative. I wanted my audiences and coaching clients to have an embracing, engaging, energizing, and empowering experience.

I had fun test-driving these superb lines of sporty cars to see how they felt and handled:

Mustang, Corvette, Acura, Lexus, Saab, and Porsche. But no. My last stop was the BMW dealer. The moment I got in the fire-engine-red Z4 with its tan interior, I knew I'd found my perfect match. This car engendered a Wow experience almost like falling in love. The Z4 fulfilled my expectations, but more important, when I showed a few of my clients a photo of me in the driver's seat of this car, they pointed to the car and exclaimed, "It's you!"

People are yearning for Wow experiences that stimulate meaning in their lives. They long to experience the human family in all its glorious dimensions. Soulwise Conspirators have the opportunity and the responsibility to communicate their dreams to the global community through simple and profound experiences that touch and move the heart and mind.

Soulwise Conspirators are by definition provocative. In his book, *The Provocateur: How a New Generation of Leaders Are Building Communities, Not Just Companies*, Larry Weber described the roles provocateurs play in leading what I call the Wow Revolution.

Weber wrote:

Successful provocateurs are a combination of educator, entertainer, Sherpa guide, and head concierge. The educator establishes the organization's mission clearly and visibly and uses every opportunity to teach through example, word, and deed. The entertainer creates an environment in which people feel connected; they entertain in such a way that people do not feel they are being passively amused. The Sherpa guide is able to conduct others—customers, employees, suppliers, even entire companies—along an uncertain path, developing skills and strengthening commitment at every step. The head concierge knows both what customers want and where to find it.[73]

Live Aid certainly vowed and wowed. The rock music concert

organized by Bob Geldof and Midge Ure held on July 13, 1985, vowed to raise funds for famine relief in Ethiopia. Simultaeously, it wowed 82,000 people in Wembley Stadium, London, England, and another 99,000 people in JFK Stadium in Philadelphia, Pennsylvania.

This "global jukebox," as some named it, inspired concerts in other countries, including Australia and Canada. It constituted one of the largest-scale satellite linkups and television broadcasts of all time with an estimated 400 million viewers from 60 countries who watched the live broadcast. Live Aid raised $300 million. Unfortunately, very little of the money acutally relieved the famine in Ethiopia.

Creating a name that vows and wows is both challenging and rewarding. Here are a few examples of commercial and organizational names that vow and wow.

Vow and Wow commercial examples:

•	Medtronic	*Alleviating Pain. Restoring Health. Extending Life.*
•	AT&T	*Your World. Delivered.*
•	Travelocity	*You'll Never Roam Alone.*
•	WalMart	*Save Money. Live Better.*
•	Septic Company	*One Call: We'll Take It All.*

Vow and Wow organizational examples:

•	American Heart Assn.	*Learn and Live.*
•	Bread for the World	*Seeking Justice. Ending Hunger.*
•	World Bank	*Building a Better World for Children*
•	Oxfam	*United for a More Equitable World*
•	Habitat for Humanity	*Building Dreams*

Shout and Tout

You want the name you choose to get the attention of a world where noise levels continue to increase dramatically. Be heard above the noise. That means your name must shout and tout so that your message lands in the ears and minds and hearts of your target audience.

When I refer to shouting, I don't mean to scream your message at the top of your lungs. Shouting refers to having a clear, compelling message delivered uniquely at an opportune time.

Comedian Jerry Seinfeld went to great heights to get his *Bee Movie* off the ground at the Cannes Film Festival in May, 2007. The movie tells the story of a bee that sues humanity over the misappropriation of honey. To create buzz, Seinfeld donned a bee costume and leaped off the Carlton Hotel attached to a gondola cable. He flew several times across the Promenade de la Croisette (French for Avenue of the Little Cross) 60 feet above this prominent road in Cannes. It was, you might say, a stinger of a promotion.

Some names shout naturally, such as the Minneapolis-based rock band that calls itself "Bleeding Hickies." And x-ray patients at the Mayo Clinic have their choice of "barium treats" in various gastro-gourmet flavors like Simply Strawberry, Mango Tango, Very Cherry and Coca Mocha.

Some place names naturally stand out. Consider Tickle-Me-Ass Cove in Newfoundland and Climax, Pennsylvania. The sign for the latter has become one of the most photographed—and, I might add, stolen—in the world.

To ensure your name will be heard above the noise, differentiate it from others in the marketplace. Be aware that the competition to be heard is fierce and often unforgiving. Differentiate or die. We remember Alexander the Great, but we've never heard of Alexander the Lesser.

Condense your dream as if you're going to put it on a license plate—a splendid exercise to help you forge a shout and tout message. These examples will prime your pump: ILUMIN8, WAS HIS, ANTISUV, AH 2 SKI, IHAMMER and WING NUT (a Detroit Red Wings fan).

"StoryCorps: Recording America" (a great name in itself) is a National Public Radio oral history project describing the lives and history of Americans. One story relates that Lucky Osborne's parents divorced when he was seven. He grew up with his grandparents, "Mama Willie and Daddy Charlie," in the Mississippi Delta. His grandparents bought a little cafe. One day, a sign painter wandered in and told Daddy

Charlie, "If you'll feed me, I'll paint a sign—any sign you want—on the front of your cafe. Just write it out and give it to me." Daddy Charlie printed out "Ferrell's Café" on a piece of paper and handed it to him. A little while later, the painter returned. "Your sign's ready. I'm ready to eat."

Daddy Charlie and the painter went outside to look at the sign. It was painted upside-down because the man couldn't read. The sign stayed that way for years. People would ask, "Charlie, why don't you have that sign fixed?" He'd say, "No, people come by here and they'll stop and come in and ask me why that sign's upside-down. They're always gonna drink a cup of coffee, eat a piece of pie, hamburger, something. [It's] the best advertising I ever had."

My name and tagline, "KaraKibera—transforming the slum for good forever," shouts and touts. It shouts loudly and clearly that I aim to achieve the impossible by transforming the slum, and touts that the slum citizens can accomplish this feat. Tout your dream and its intended results without exaggeration, pretense, or arrogance. As professional baseball pitcher and the National League's 1934 MVP, Dizzy Dean, asserted, "It ain't braggin' if you can back it up."

Sometimes, a cause cleverly shouts and touts its message primarily because of what's missing. On Monday, March 6, 2006, a full-page advertisement appeared in *USA Today*. Most of the page is white space. In the top third of the page, the following letters are printed in substantial point size: H NGER. Under these letters a line in a much smaller point size reads, "The problem can't be solved without you." Bottom-of-the-page copy states, "This month Wal-Mart is matching the first $5 million in-store donations dollar for dollar to America's Second Harvest, The Nations' Food Bank Network. So the next time you are at the checkout, donate your dollars and make twice the difference in eliminating hunger."

Let's look at more examples of commercial and organizational names that shout and tout.

Shout and Tout commercial examples:
- Haagen-Dazs
- Google
- Heinz
- Porsche
- Godiva

208

Shout and Tout organizational examples:

- One Laptop Per Child
- Human Rights Watch
- Save the Children
- American Cancer Society
- Second Harvest Gleaners

So far we've covered these six purposes the name you give your dream will serve: sell and tell, vow and wow, shout and tout. Now let's consider how to choose a name that will...

Click and Stick

When asked in a study what sounds animals make, preschoolers gave these usual answers: sheep baa, cows moo, cats meow, and dogs bark. However, when the children were asked what sound ducks make, they replied "AFLAC" based on an insurance company's commercials.

You want the name you give your dream to click with your audience so it sticks in their minds. There's an art and science to clicking and sticking. Research definitively shows that when people have an image related to an idea, business, or dream imprinted in their mind, the odds increase that they'll be able to recall both the image and the corresponding idea.

In the case of AFLAC, the advertising team took an unheard of name and coupled it with the image of an endearing and unforgettable duck. As a result, millions of people recall the image of the duck and the name of the insurance company it represents. Even children have become imprinted— but they probably can't tell you AFLAC is an insurance company.

> *"Clicking" refers to the positive connection you make with your audience. Your message resonates with them for a host of reasons, some of which are obvious while others remain a mystery. Something attracts, captures, and keeps our attention. The stars align. Everything converges as one.*

In relationships, we're occasionally drawn to someone we feel a strong connection with, as if we've known that person for a lifetime even though we've just met. Clicking with others comprises the root of the connection among members of the human family. Soulwise Conspirators agree with Eleanor Roosevelt that "the future belongs to those who believe in the beauty of their dreams." So clicking with one another to communicate dreams is essential for the future of the global family.

From time to time, a phrase in a movie clicks and sticks with us. In the Academy Award-winning 1939 film *Gone with the Wind,* who could forget this immortal line that Rhett tossed off to Scarlett: "Frankly, my dear, I don't give a damn." Likewise, who could forget the line "Hasta la vista, baby!" made famous by Arnold Schwartzenegger in the 1991 film *Terminator 2: Judgment Day.* In his thick Austrian accent, he bids farewell ("See you later, baby!") in Spanish to whomever he's going to blow up.

Memory and music go hand in hand. Perhaps you have in your musical memory bank lyrics sung by Julie Andrews in the 1965 movie *The Sound of Music.* I bet this first word triggers the rest of the verse: "Supercalifragalisticexpialidotious."

For my undergraduate degree, I majored in Greek and learned all my declensions under the "musical direction" of my professor, Dr. Arthur Little. He would tap out the beat like a conductor and almost sing the declensions. As a result, years later I can still remember my declensions without hesitation.

Some song melodies and lyrics seem to stick for life. Just for fun, test your memory and see how quickly you can complete the following five lyrics.

1. Twinkle, ...
2. Take me out to the ....
3. O say can you ....
4. Old McDonald had a ....
5. I want to hold your ....

In my home of Grand Rapids, Michigan, where the weather changes on a minute-to-minute basis, the local ABC affiliate television station cleverly uses rhyme to help viewers interpret the meaning of different colors on the station's "Weatherball" (an actual ball lit up so neighbors can see it as well as being on the air).

13 Weatherball red, warmer weather ahead.

13 Weatherball blue, cooler weather in view.

13 Weatherball green, no change foreseen.

Colors blinking bright, rain or snow in sight.

Using acronyms also makes names stick. Acronyms comprise abbreviations of several words in such a way that the abbreviation itself forms a word that's easy to pronounce and remember. Some acronyms have become so accepted into the language that we automatically know what they mean but don't think about the actual words they stand for.

Did you know that "RAdio Detecting And Ranging" is "RADAR"? We often don't even capitalize it anymore. Who thinks "North Atlantic Treaty Organization" when they see "NATO"? What about "Self-Contained Underwater Breathing Apparatus" for SCUBA? Organizations often use acronyms that will trigger meaning for their cause, such as MADD, Mothers Against Drunk Driving.

Uno clicked with the public when he became the first beagle named Best in Show at the 2008 Westminster Kennel Club Dog Show—the first beagle winner *ever* in the entire 132-year history of this premier canine competition. Uno not only won the hearts of the audience at the event, but captured the hearts of the public who fell even more in love with one of America's most popular dog breeds of the century.

Uno clicked with the audience and his name will stick for a long time to come. We'll also remember his name because "uno" means one in Spanish and Italian. The slang expression "Numero Uno" refers to first in rank, order, or importance. Uno definitely proved to be "Numero Uno"—best in show, best in name.

For an excellent summary of how to make ideas click and stick, get your hands on the book *Made to Stick: Why Some Ideas Survive and Others Die.* The authors, Chip and Dan Heath, organized their observations and recommendations in what they call a SUCCESs system. Their memorable system incorporates the principles of:

- Simple (Helps people find and share the core),
- Unexpected (Helps people pay attention),
- Concrete (Helps people understand and remember),
- Credible (Helps people believe and agree),
- Emotional (Helps people care), and
- Stories (Helps people act).[74]

Here are other examples of names that click and stick.

Commercial examples:
- Coke
- Kodak
- Kraft
- Starbucks
- Smuckers

Organizational examples:
- Red Cross
- Scouts
- Peace Corps
- UNICEF
- United Way

Consider several names for your dream fulfilled, narrow the list, and then test two or three. Do they have the capacity to sell and tell, vow and wow, shout and tout, and click and stick? Before you broadcast your exciting news to the world, take the time to do what they do at NASA (a good acronym for National Aeronautics and Space Administration): test before launch.

FLAME IT

I buy Eddie Bauer jeans because they wear well, look great, and give me superb quality. I know that two people inspected my jeans. In a front pocket of my last pair, I found two pieces of paper with these notifications: "Inspected by #14" and "Inspected by #45." That's who tested these jeans.

Be sure to "flame" your dream before you launch it. Test it rigorously. The process of flaming derives from an ancient strategy of refining by fire. A silversmith, for example, takes a piece of silver and holds it in the middle of the fire where the flames are hottest. The refiner's fire purifies. It melts the silver and separates out the impurities that ruin the silver's value, burning them up and leaving the silver intact. Your dream deserves to be flamed.

My "Flame It" test forms the acronym DISAPPEAR, which stands for **D**efinitive, **I**nspiring, **S**imple, **A**ttractive, **P**ositive, **P**roactive, **E**mpowering, **A**ttainable, and **R**elevant.

This acronym embodies the intention that, when you fulfill your dream, it will disappear as a dream, making way to formulate your next dream. Each of the nine qualities engenders five questions to help you discern whether your dream passes the "flame test," then five commercial and five organizational examples illustrate the quality.

Let's put your vision to the test.

Definitive

Is your dream:
- specific?
- measurable?
- on a timetable?
- comprehensive?
- precise?

Commercial examples:
- BMW — *The Ultimate Driving Machine*
- FedEx — *The World on Time*
- Visa — *Life Takes Visa*
- Walgreens — *The Pharmacy America Trusts*
- Minutelube — *Some People Want to Change the World. We Just Want to Change Your Oil.*

Organizational examples:
- Better World Campaign — *Peace. It's Cheaper than War.*
- The Salvation Army — *Doing the Most Good*
- World Bank — *Working for a World Free of Poverty*
- U.S. Air Force — *Above All*
- Kauffman Foundation — *The Foundation of Entrepreneurship*

Inspiring

Is your dream:
- substantial?
- significant?
- energizing?

- exciting?
- awesome?

Commercial examples:
- Dupont — *The Miracles of Science*
- GE — *Imagination at Work*
- Lexus — *The Pursuit of Perfection*
- Lowe's — *Let's Build Something Together*
- Carnival Cruise Lines — *The Fun Ships*

Organizational examples:
- Peace Corps — *Life is Calling. How Far Will You Go?*
- The ONE Campaign — *Making Poverty History*
- Ford Foundation — *Working with Visionaries on the Frontlines of Social Change Worldwide*
- United Methodist Committee on Relief — *Be There. Be Hope.*
- Foundation for a Better Life — *Be Inspired. Pass It On.*

Simple

Is your dream:
- understandable?
- clear?
- lucid?
- straightforward?
- uncomplicated?

Commercial examples:
- MasterCard — *Priceless*
- Lazy-Boy — *Comfort. It's What We Do.*
- Bissell — *We Mean Clean*
- Duracell — *Trusted Everywhere*
- Philips — *Sense and Simplicity*

Organizational Examples
- Habitat for Humanity — *Building Dreams*
- Ford Foundation — *A Resource for Innovative People*
- UNICEF — *Do What It Takes.*
- Reebok Human Rights Fn. — *A Life Free of Fear and Want*

214

* W.K. Kellogg Fn. — *To Help People Help Themselves*

Attractive

Is your dream:
* inviting?
* appealing?
* engaging?
* intriguing?
* magnetic?

Commercial examples:
* MacDonald's — *I'm Lovin' It*
* General Motors — *Hummer – Like Nothing Else*
* Geico — *Want to Save 15% on Car Insurance?*
* Microsoft — *Your Potential. Our Passion.*
* Logitech — *Designed to Move You*

Organizational examples:
* Skoll Foundation — *Uncommon Heroes. Common Good.*
* Rotary International — *Service above Self*
* The SmileTrain — *Changing the World One Smile at a Time*
* CARE — *Defending Dignity. Fighting Poverty.*
* MacArthur Foundation — *Building a More Just, Verdant, and Peaceful World*

Positive

Is your dream:
* helpful?
* optimistic?
* confident?
* upbeat?
* promising?

Commercial examples:
* BD — *Helping All People Live Healthy Lives*
* Citibank — *Citi never sleeps*
* Staples — *That Was Easy*
* Ford — *Bold Moves*

- LensCrafters — *Open Your Eyes*

Organizational examples:
- Oxfam — *Lasting Solutions to Poverty, Hunger, and Social Injustice*
- Festival of Children — *Together We Can Make a Difference*
- WorldWatch — *Vision for a Sustainable World*
- Heifer International — *Ending Hunger, Caring for the Earth*
- ChangingThePresent — *Changing the World. One Gift at a Time.*

Proactive

Is your dream:
- purposeful?
- life-changing?
- future-oriented?
- stretching?
- responsible?

Commercial examples:
- America's Milk Processors — *Think About Your Drink*
- Allstate — *Are You In Good Hands?*
- Exxon Mobil — *Taking On the World's Toughest Energy Challenges*
- Pfizer — *Working Together for a Healthier World*
- Cialis — *When the Moment is Right, You Can Be Ready.*

Organizational examples:
- American Cancer Society — *Walk for the Cure*
- Bread for the World — *Seeking Justice. Ending Hunger.*
- American Diabetes Assn — *Cure. Care. Commitment.*
- Parents — *The Anti-Drug*
- Mercy Corps — *Be the Change*

Empowering

Is your dream:
- supportive?
- enabling?
- trusting?
- affirming?
- encouraging?

Commercial examples:
- MassMutual — *You Can't Predict. But You Can Prepare.*
- Nike — *Just Do It!*
- Cargill — *collaborate create succeed*
- Pfizer — *Working together for a healthier world*
- Enterprise Rent-A-Car — *We'll Pick You Up.*

Organizational examples:
- Arthritis Foundation — *Take Control. We Can Help.*
- American Heart Assn. — *Learn and Live.*
- Civic Ventures — *Helping society achieve the greatest return on experience*
- Grameen Foundation — *Empowering people. Changing lives. Innovating for the World's Poor.*
- FINCA* — *Small Loans-Big Changes*

*Foundation for International Community Assistance

Attainable

Is your dream:
- realistic?
- possible?
- conditional?
- feasible?
- achievable?

Commercial examples:
- Home Depot — *You Can Do It. We Can Help.*
- WeightWatchers — *Stop Dieting. Start Living.*
- Target — *Expect More. Pay Less.*
- Bristol-Myers Squibb — *Together We Can Prevail.*
- SWIFT Wind Turbine — *harness the power of the wind*

Organizational examples:
- World Vision — *Building a Better World for Children*
- Melville Charitable Trust — *Finding and Fighting the Causes of Homelessness*
- Calvert Foundation — *Create Jobs, Build Homes, and Change Lives*

- Geraldine R. Dodge Fn. — *Making Our Society More Humane and Our World More Livable.*
- Desmond Tutu Peace Fn. — *A World Committed to Peace*

Relevant

Is your dream:
- applicable?
- timely?
- pertinent?
- suitable?
- meaningful?

Commercial examples:
- Medtronic — *Alleviating Pain. Restoring Health. Extending Life.*
- Waste Management — *Think Green*
- ConocoPhillips — *Energy for Tomorrow*
- University of Phoenix — *Thinking Ahead*
- American Airlines — *OneWorld Revolves Around You*

Organizational examples:
- United Nations — *It's Your World*
- United Way of America — *What Matters*
- United Church of Christ — *God Is Still Speaking*
- Global Hunger Foundation — *Help Stop Hunger*
- Russell Life Skills & Reading Fn — *Opening Books To Open Doors*

So far in Part IV, A Guide to Becoming a Soulwise Conspirator, you've seen how to discover your passion, define a need, and dream that need fulfilled: to claim it, frame it, name it, and flame it. You're well on your way to changing the world.

It's a wonderful feeling to realize you're pursuing a dream that will contribute to the welfare of the human family. Together, we can do the impossible. The next chapter will help you draft your dream team to make your dream come true.

TAKE FIVE FOR REFLECTION

1. Verbalize your vision of the need you want to fulfill.

2. What three possible names have you given to your vision?

   •

   •

   •

3. In what three specific ways have you claimed your vision?

   •

   •

   •

4. Name three persons with whom you've shared your vision.

   •

   •

   •

5. If you put your vision to the "flame it" test, what results do you think you'd find?

CHAPTER 10

DRAFT YOUR DREAM TEAM

Draft a dream team to achieve your vision. This seems like a no-brainer, but it takes considerable foresight, imagination, and tenacity to attract the right people in the right place at the right time for the right reason to fulfill a common compassionate calling.

Let me illustrate how to draft a dream team by sharing how I, as the founding executive director of the Daystar University Global Leadership Center (DUGLC) in Nairobi, Kenya, chose my Heart for Africa Dream Team.

The key was choosing people who, together, could fulfill the Center's clear and compelling vision—"Africa transforming for a future of promise"—and its corresponding mission—"to inspire servant leaders to transform Africa for a future of promise."

I know my well-articulated vision will attract people to offer their unique gifts and skills and provide me with a touchstone for choosing the best possible combination of Soulwise Conspirators. I'm building the dream team principally around the dream.

I've arranged the qualities I want team members to possess in the form of this acronym DREAM TEAM: Dedication, Resilience, Enthusiasm, Artistry, Magnetism, Talent, Endurance, Agility, and Muscle. However, I found it difficult to choose my dream team because so many people were already working diligently for Africa's present and future. All possess the qualities noted, but I want to emphasize a dominant quality each demonstrates. So I'm choosing these two teams with a heart for

Africa: a team of celebrities and a team of people I know personally.

At the end of the chapter, you're invited to choose your own dream team in an exercise that will clarify your thinking about your vision as well as about those you'd like to be part of your team.

DEDICATION

First, look for a dedication to your compassionate vision and mission as the foundational quality in your team members. Ashley Judd, actor and United Nations Youth/AIDS ambassador, explained the kind of dedication displayed by a Soulwise Conspirator (also called a humanitarian) this way: "A humanitarian is a person who understands that we are all interconnected and interdependent, who understands that the same divine spark resides in every single soul, and who understands that life's greatest reward comes from service."[75]

Your team members need to demonstrate their passionate dedication to serving others—like Rick and Kay Warren do, as well as Dr. Bill Sprague.

Rick and Kay Warren

Why did Saddleback Church, a congregation of 22,000 in Lake Forest, California, commit to address the pandemic of AIDS in Africa and its attendant ills of poverty?

Because Kay Warren had an epiphany about the essence of her Christian faith. It inspired her to take dedicated action, with her husband and their congregation following suit. Kay is married to Rick Warren, the founding pastor of Saddleback Church and author of *The Purpose Driven Life*, which has sold 30 million copies and been translated into 56 languages.

The Warrens use the wealth and fame from the success of the book to invest, especially in the people of Rwanda. Together, they are dedicated to an ambitious initiative to address poverty, illness, and illiteracy globally.

As executive director of the Saddleback HIV/AIDS Initiative, Kay has publicly urged her congregation and others to repent for their past indifference to the AIDS crisis and for stigmatizing people with AIDS. She has built bridges between religious and secular relief groups, refusing to insist on abstinence or condoms as an either/or moral choice.

The initiative has brought together leaders to discuss a partnership of government, business, and the church to stop HIV/AIDS.

Dr. Bill Sprague

Dr. Bill Sprague, a retired physician of obstetrics, dedicates himself to the dream of eradicating polio—one he shares with 1.2 million members in 32,000 Rotary International clubs. In 1985, Rotary established the PolioPlus Program, which works globally, and especially in Africa, to eradicate this debilitating disease. Rotarians, whose motto is "Service above Self," have contributed more than $600 million to support the program.

Dr. Bill served as a medical corpsman with the 1st Marine Division in the South West Island campaign during World War II. He witnessed the devastation of war, social injustice and poverty—experiences that sparked his compassion and a lifetime of international service. His most challenging work took place in Somalia where he saw his colleagues in Doctors Without Borders executed. He's led teams with the World Health Organization, United Nations Children's Fund, and the Center for Disease Control. Every year since 1962, he has volunteered somewhere in the world.

Dr. Bill's interest in polio began when he witnessed iron lungs being used during the polio epidemic in the United States in the early 1950s. For several years, he was the Rotary International Coordinator of the PolioPlus program in the South Pacific Region. Dr. Bill has vaccinated over a billion children for polio. He describes his efforts to eradicate the disease as his calling, and his dedication inspires others, including me, to work toward a world without polio.

> *Teamwork makes the dream work. You can't do it alone. You need others who are dedicated to work together to fulfill your dream.*

RESILIENCE

Two words I saw on a baby's bib reveal this reality: "Spit Happens." Sure, everyone experiences "spit." It's universal. As human beings, we differ not so much in the "spit" we encounter, but how we respond to it. Our level of resilience ultimately determines how we react to setbacks.

Albert Einstein assigned three rules to one's work: out of clutter find simplicity; from discord find harmony; and in the middle of difficulty lies opportunity. Soulwise Conspirators face misfortunes with spirit and courage, and look for the opportunities they present. They follow the counsel of Oprah Winfrey, who in her commencement address to Wellesley College in 1997, told the graduates, "Turn your wounds into wisdom."

The following stories relate how two Soulwise Conspirators did exactly that when they emerged from extreme circumstances to change the world. Nelson Mandela and Wangari Muta Maathai are undeniably poster people for the quality of resilience.

Nelson Mandela

For 27 years, Mandela was simply a number: 46664.

Imprisoned on Robben Island off Cape Town in South Africa, Nelson Mandela wore the prison number 46664. He was jailed for leading the liberation movement against apartheid and for his impassioned stance for the right of everyone to live in freedom. He was prisoner number 466, imprisoned in 1964. Because Robben Island prisoners were never referred to by their names, but rather by their numbers and year of imprisonment, Mandela's number was 46664. After being released from prison in 1990, Nelson Mandela became South Africa's first black president, serving from 1994 to 1999. As the resilient Mandela observed, "The greatest glory in living lies not in never falling, but in rising every time we fall."

Mandela has since campaigned to prevent the spread of AIDS through the 46664 (four double six six four) campaign that he began in 2003 to reach youth by engaging support of the people who most appeal to them. To use the power of music, sport, and celebrities to raise awareness about the impact of AIDS, especially in Africa, and to promote HIV-prevention measures around the world, he enlisted Dave Stewart of the Eurythmics, Brian May and Roger Taylor of Queen, and Bono of U2. Together, they persuaded more than 30 of the world's top artists to perform together at a global awareness concert for HIV/AIDS. It was held at Green Point Stadium in Cape Town in November 2003 and broadcast worldwide via TV, radio, and the Internet. The Nelson Mandella Foundation received the proceeds from this concert for its mission of making a just society and convening dialogue around critical social issues.

Wangari Muta Maathai

A Nairobi hotel gift shop clerk held up a book, pointed to a clump of well-manicured trees planted in the hotel's garden, and said, "The author planted those trees. If you want to know about the spirit of African women, read this book." So I bought the book, *Unbowed: One Woman's Story*, by Wangari Muta Maathai and couldn't put it down.

Maathai embodies the quality of amazing feisty resilience. In the 1980s, her husband Mwangi Mathai, a politician whom she'd married in 1969, divorced her, saying she was too strong-minded for a woman and that he couldn't control her. The judge in the divorce case agreed with her husband, and Wangari was put in jail for speaking out against the judge, who then decreed that she must drop her husband's surname. In defiance, Wangari chose to add an extra "a" instead.

During the Kenyan presidency of Daniel arap Moi, Wangari was imprisoned several times and violently attacked for demanding multiparty elections and an end to political corruption and tribal politics. In 1997, in Kenya's second multi-party elections marred by ethnic violence, she ran for the country's presidency, but her party withdrew her as a candidate.

Internationally recognized for her persistent struggle for democracy, human rights, and environmental conservation, Wangari Maathai has addressed the United Nations on several occasions. For the five-year review of the 1992 Earth Summit, she spoke on behalf of women at special sessions of the General Assembly. She has also served on the UN Commission for Global Governance and the Commission on the Future.

In 1977, Maathai founded The Green Belt Movement, a grassroots environmental non-governmental organization, which has planted over 40 million trees across Kenya to prevent soil erosion. She and the Green Belt Movement have received numerous awards, most notably the 2004 Nobel Peace Prize.

ENTHUSIASM

In a 2004 interview, *Fast Company* asked Erick Weihenmayer, the first blind climber to scale Mt. Everest, "What do you look for in teammates?" Weihenmayer replied, "I look for people who have an unrealistic optimism about life. I hear people say, 'Seeing is believing.' I want people who believe the opposite, that 'believing is seeing.'

You've got to believe first in what you're doing and be sure you have a reason to believe it. You can tell who those people are. You say, 'Hey, want to climb Everest with a blind guy?' Pretty quickly, you'll figure out who's a believer."

Enthusiasm doesn't consist merely of wishing and hoping. It's a contagious spirit that begins with Soulwise Conspirators like Desmond Tutu and Mark and Ann Fackler, who strive to satisfy humanity's hunger for hope.

Desmond Tutu

Archbishop Desmond Tutu oozes with unrealistic optimism and bubbles with enthusiasm, a word derived from the Greek that means "inspired by God."

I once saw him at a forum where he sat on the edge of his seat sharing his compassionate presence—exuberant, playful, witty, philosophical, and spiritual. A trained teacher who was later ordained as a Christian minister, he exuded enthusiasm like a special breed of Energizer Bunny.

Tutu has devoted his life to working for human rights. During apartheid, he kept hope alive in the hearts and minds of millions of South Africans. He shared his powerful vision that justice would come and that freedom was unstoppable for all South Africans. In 1984, he was awarded the Nobel Peace Prize, and has received over a hundred honorary doctorates from universities all over the world.

Scheduled to open in 2010, the Desmond Tutu Peace Centre in Cape Town, South Africa, will serve as a landmark of enthusiasm promoting sustainable peace and values-based leadership. Aimed at using the experience of the South African people and the example of Desmond Tutu, the Peace Centre will inspire a new generation of visionary peace builders. Oprah Winfrey and the Dalai Lama are honorary co-chairpersons of the Centre.

Mark and Ann Fackler

"Face the deep-seated problems of the world," commented Dr. David Meyer in his book *The Pursuit of Happiness: Who is Happy and Why*, "but also retain plenty of hope, energy and enthusiasm."[76]

That describes Mark and Ann Fackler, who have an incredible fervor for Africa. They have a realistic sense of the challenges Africa faces, but they look to the future of that continent with hope, energy, and above all, enthusiasm.

One Sunday after church, my wife Melody and I were enjoying a cup of coffee with Mark and Ann at a local Panera bakery. Mark, a communications teacher at Calvin College in Grand Rapids, Michigan, and Ann, a culinary coordinator, were telling stories about their "family and friends" in Africa, as they love to do.

Out of the blue, Mark asked us, "Why don't you come with us to Kenya next summer?" Melody and I quickly looked at each other, confirming agreement, and I replied, "Sure. What are the dates?" That was the beginning of our African adventure, which continues to unfold every day. We responded so positively to their invitation, mainly because of their contagious enthusiasm for Africa. It reminded me of a scene in the 1997 movie *My Best Friend's Wedding* where someone starts singing Dionne Warwick's "I Say a Little Prayer" and the singing spreads like a virus. In the end, everyone is belting out the song.

Melody and I caught their enthusiasm, discovering first-hand in our three-week visit to Kenya that their enthusiasm is rooted in their love for the people of Africa. Mark and Ann showed a genuine respect for African heritage, culture, and traditions, and demonstrated a willingness to stand alongside the people in their struggle, to share in their pain and suffering.

ARTISTRY

Identify people for your team who possess the gift of artistry—and the kind of artistry that will serve your purpose effectively. Individual and collective artistry enables people to interact and creatively address world needs around the international table. Soulwise Conspirators believe that meeting each other is an invaluable art in the process of bringing health, hope and harmony to the global family.

My dream team needs humanitarian activists who will use their artistry to help Africa create a future of promise. In the years ahead, it will take a lot of artistry to capture energy on the African continent with its 54 countries and population of 890 million.

Two excellent examples of Soulwise Conspirators who express their artistry for the less fortunate on the planet are Bono and Ryan Spencer Reed.

Bono

"My name is Bono, and I'm in fightin' form," declared the lead singer of U2, who took the Economic Club of Grand Rapids by storm on May 4, 2006.

"We are watching people being loaded onto the trains, and we know where they are going. But the end of the story need not be the same. The people of Africa need not be condemned. We, you, I will not be complicit.... We will not turn away as the trains roll past. We will go down the tracks, and we will lie across them.

"Africa is more than a cause. It's an emergency. Six thousand five hundred Africans die every day of AIDS because they lack the drugs that anyone can buy at any drugstore. If you look at what happened in South Asia in the tsunami, you had 15,000 lives lost in an instant to that great misnomer of all misnomers, Mother Nature. Well, in Africa, 150,000 lives are lost every month—a tsunami every month. And it's not a natural disaster. It is a completely avoidable catastrophe."[77]

Bono, the impassioned lead singer of U2, transferred his artistry, power, and celebrity to focus on poverty and social injustice in Africa. He was in "fightin' form" when I saw him in Grand Rapids, and he punched his words to jolt his attentive audience into global action. Bono believes that taking action is not about charity, but about justice.

Fluent in Italian and Spanish, Bono uses his artistry in concerts and campaigns and connections with political leaders to advocate for causes he believes in. He's more interested in solutions than problems as he said, "I think it's very important to describe Africa in terms other than tragedy."

People are paying attention. Bono was named *Time* magazine's 2005 person of the year along with Bill and Melinda Gates.

Ryan Spencer Reed

When I was leaving my Maasai friends in Kenya in the summer of 2004, Chief Joseph Oleteleu said to me, "An American photographer named Ryan Reed lived with us on the mountain for about six months. He took a lot of pictures while he was here. If you meet him when you get back to the United States, ask him why he hasn't written." I replied that I would, but thought the odds of meeting this phantom photographer were quite slim.

One month after I returned from Kenya, I dropped into Reed Photography in Ludington, Michigan, near our Lake Michigan cottage. A slight young man in the shop asked how he could help me and I noticed that the name on his badge was Ryan. "Are you Ryan Reed?" I asked. "Yup," he replied. Then I said, "Chief Joseph Oleteleu wants to know why you haven't written." "Pardon?" Ryan asked. "Yes, Chief Joseph wants to know why you haven't written." That's how I met Ryan Spencer Reed, an incredibly gifted photojournalist.

After studying medicine in college, he began documenting social issues in 2002. He moved to Nairobi and went to the Kakuma refugee camp in northwestern Kenya, home to more than 90,000 refugees from conflicts across east Africa, most of whom are Sudanese. From that experience, he's focused his work exclusively on Sudan. Reed has entered Sudan a half-dozen times in both the south and in Darfur, in addition to covering the mass exodus of refugees to eastern Chad. Since 2004, he has expressed his passion for Sudan by lending his artistry to universities in the form of lectures and traveling exhibitions.

Most recently, Reed has collaborated with other photojournalists to publish *DARFURDARFUR: Life/War*. In every shot, Reed looks through his lens of compassion and captures a moment that tells a story about the suffering and pain of people in Sudan. These exquisite photographs are often overwhelming and spark intense rage, sorrow, and shame.

MAGNETISM

To fulfill your mission, you'll need people on your team who are skilled at attracting attention like a magnet. In 1999, I had the privilege of spending three days with the Dalai Lama at a conference on religion and world peace held in Tiberias, Israel. In one of the sessions, I was seated directly behind His Holiness and felt the incredible power of his field of attraction. People there were literally drawn to experience his presence.

My Heart for Africa Dream Team requires members who can naturally attract others to join them as Soulwise Conspirators to perform CPR to save our global family. Oprah Winfrey and Samuel Losuron Poghisio possess this rare quality of magnetism.

Oprah Winfrey

Oprah Winfrey, the super-magnetic talk show host and philanthropist, and I share at least this in common: going to Africa changed us forever. We also both believe that education plays a major role in Africa's future. Winfrey has said, "Education is the path to the future. I believe that education is indeed freedom. With God's help, these girls will be the future leaders on the path to peace in South Africa and the world."

In 1998, Winfrey founded Angel Network that helped fund 28 schools in five African countries. In 2007, she established the Oprah Winfrey Leadership Academy for Girls in South Africa, a 28-building, 50-acre campus in Henley-on-Klip. Winfrey considers the academy an investment in the individuals and in the future of Africa. At the dedication of the Academy she said, "I wanted to give opportunity to girls who were like me. Girls who were poor, who had come from disadvantaged circumstances, but girls who had a light so bright that not even poverty, disease, and life circumstances could dim that light."

The Academy selected 484 girls to be interviewed and Winfrey interviewed the finalists, creating the list of 152 eager students. These girls will pay nothing; and when they graduate, they will be funded by Winfrey to go to the college of their choice anywhere in the world. She sees these girls as the visionaries and leaders of tomorrow.

I dream that one day I can personally welcome the academy's graduates, spirited African leaders, to meet their colleagues at the Daystar University Global Leadership Center in Nairobi.

Samuel Losuron Poghisio

"Sam's here! Sam's here!" The buzz arose at the welcoming table at a golf tournament sponsored by Daystar University at the Royal Nairobi Golf Club in July 2007. "Who's Sam?" I asked. The "welcomers" seated behind the table looked at me as if I was from another planet. "You don't know Sam Poghisio? There he is in the parking lot." I turned and saw Sam, a tall handsome figure, surrounded by his entourage.

One of the tournament organizers indicated I would be playing in a foursome with Sam and invited me to meet him. Up close, I began to appreciate the magnetism of this politician, a member of the Orange Democratic Movement who has represented the Kacheliba Constituency in the National Assembly of Kenya since 2007.

Poghisio draws people to him because he's authentic, trustworthy, and optimistic.

Poghisio is *authentic*. He looks you straight in the eyes as if you're the only person in the world at that moment. Our conversations throughout the day were polite and friendly and, above all, genuine. It felt like we were life-long friends reuniting after a long separation.

Poghisio is also *trustworthy*. In Kenya's December 2007 election, 85.6% of his constituents cast votes for him, an expression of the public trust he's earned. A man of principle, Poghisio holds strong convictions rooted in his Christian faith and supported by his theological training at Wheaton College, Illinois. His convictions are also supported by his friendships with other faithful politicians in the world at the National Prayer Breakfast, a yearly event held in Washington hosted by members of the United States Congress.

In addition, people are drawn to Poghisio because he is realistically *optimistic* about the future of Africa and his country. He acknowledges the huge challenges of governing including poverty, corruption, disease, and violence, yet he remains confident that Africans can rise to these challenges. Poghisio brings his positive presence to the Kenyan government as Minister of Information and Communication.

TALENT

As Soulwise Conspirators, surround yourselves with talented people who are willing to apply their talent to fulfill your collective dream. A successful team effort partly depends on attracting a diversity of talent. In his book, *The Medici Effect*, Frans Johannson claimed that diversity of talent forms the core of creativity where each team member brings his or her combination of talents and skills.

I remind all my corporate coaching clients that if everyone thinks alike, then some of us aren't necessary.

The Soulwise Conspirators Maya Angelou and Godfrey Nguru have each spent a lifetime inspiring the world with their dedication and talent.

Maya Angelou

Surround yourself with talented people like author, poet, historian, director, performer, and civil rights activist Maya Angelou. Born Marguerite Annie Johnson in St. Louis, Missouri, she changed her name in her early 20s to Maya Angelou after her debut performance as a dancer at the Purple Onion cabaret in San Francisco. Her managers at the nightclub recommended that she adopt a more theatrical name that captured the feel of her calypso dance performances. Fluent in French, Spanish, Italian, and West African Fanti, she's a mentor to Oprah Winfrey.

Angelou possesses an extraordinary talent to express in poetry

231

and prose how her heart sees the human condition so people all over the world can live with hope. She's an agent of change who once said, "Love is that condition in the human spirit so profound that it allows me to survive and better than that, to thrive with passion, compassion, and style."

In 1996, Maya was named a national ambassador to UNICEF. Appointed to a lifetime position as the first Reynolds Professor of American Studies at Wake Forest University, she also became the second poet in United States history to have the honor of reciting her work at a presidential inauguration. She's been nominated for two Grammy Awards and has received more than 50 honorary degrees from colleges and universities worldwide.

One of her 12 best-selling books, *I Know Why the Caged Bird Sings*, revealed how she transformed her tragic childhood into a rich life. Today, Maya is regarded as one of the great voices of contemporary literature and a remarkable renaissance woman.

Godfrey Nguru

Like the unique contributions of Maya Angelou, Rev. Prof. Godfrey Mbiti Nguru brings his own combination of talents to Daystar University as its vice-chancellor since 2004. The support of Daystar University, the largest Christian university in Africa, and its vice-chancellor, is critical to the success of the Daystar University Global Leadership Center. On my Heart for Africa team, Nguru acts as internal champion of the Center in the university community.

I witnessed his leadership capacity as he brought the idea of establishing a global leadership center at Daystar University to fruition. I presented my dream of the Center in a proposal to him at a two-day meeting in Evanston, Illinois. He recognized immediately how it aligned perfectly with Daystar University's mission to educate servant leaders to transform Africa and the world. He saw that the Center could be key in the university's long-term development.

Nguru returned to Nairobi and presented my proposal in a special meeting of the University Senate, the governing body of the University. His proactive stance demonstrated that he was serious about championing the idea. The Senate unanimously approved my proposal and appointed me to be the founding executive director.

ENDURANCE

In 2007, actor and human rights activist George Clooney traveled to Chad to film the documentary *A Journey to Darfur*. That's when Clooney reflected, "The more time you spend with the people in the camps who are holding on by a whisper and still believe that their lives will be better, the more you believe that anything is possible."

Although they may be tempted, Soulwise Conspirators do not subscribe to this advice from humorist W.C. Fields: "If at first you don't succeed, try, try, again. Then quit. There's no use being a damn fool about it." Conspirators are committed—like Clooney, George W. and Laura Bush and Peter Okaalet—to a marathon of service.

George W. and Laura Bush

One of the marks of a leader is to see the big picture in the long term. Such foresight is especially crucial for African leaders as they develop their nations in a fast-paced global context.

Fortunately, Africa has a friend in the United States, which has demonstrated its commitment to support and sustain Africa's long-term growth and stability. President George W. Bush and his administration not only recognized the important role of Africa in the world, but also strengthened and expanded the U.S./Africa partnership to empower Africans to alleviate hunger, expand education, and fight disease.

Together, leaders from Africa and the United States are working to pioneer a new era in development on the African continent. Specifically, the plan is for the U.S. to increase total assistance to Africa to $8.7 billion by 2010, double the level of assistance in 2004. In addition, President Bush's Malaria Initiative (PMI), launched in 2005, added to his Emergency Plan for AIDS Relief to combat disease in Africa. PMI, Saving Lives in Africa, is estimated to have already reached 25 million people in sub-Saharan Africa in the fight against malaria. The program continued into 2009 with PMI reaching an estimated 49 million people with lifesaving prevention or treatment services. In Zambia and Rwanda, the overall number of deaths among children has dropped by one-third. (www.fightingmalaria.gov/)

While her husband was in office, First Lady Laura Bush made three independent trips to Africa, visiting South Africa, Tanzania, Rwanda, Ghana, Liberia, Nigeria, Senegal, Mozambique, Zambia, and Mali. She

233

highlighted the partnership between the United States and Africa to expand education, empower women, and fight against diseases such as HIV/AIDS and malaria.

Peter Okaalet

Grandfather Johnson believed the best way to get to know a person was to break bread with them in their home. And from my experience, my grandfather was right. He said sitting around someone's kitchen table gives you the opportunity to learn what's really important to them, how they view themselves and their place in the world, and how they cook vegetables. (Grandfather despised overcooked vegetables and held suspect people who did that.)

I thought about my grandfather's perceptions when I received an invitation to have dinner with Dr. Peter Okaalet and his wife, Sarah, at their home in Nairobi. I met Okaalet, whom *Time Magazine* named a "Global Health Hero" after a speech he made on his work in Africa at the January Series at Calvin College in 2007. Who exactly is this hero and what will he be like in his home? I wondered.

Little did I know when I accepted the Okaalet's invitation that Sarah manages her own catering business. Grandfather would be pleased to know that the vegetables were cooked to perfection. In fact, the whole meal was delicious, especially the baked mango supreme desert.

Okaalet possesses the quality of endurance, which is clearly evident in the compassionate presence of this tall striking Ugandan. His grace before our meal gave thanks for our abundance and sought God's blessing on those less fortunate, especially those families dealing with the burdens of the AIDS epidemic, the focus of his calling in Africa. Beneficially for the Heart for Africa Dream Team, he sits on the Senate of Daystar University.

AGILITY

James Kouzes and Barry Posner, co-authors of *The Leadership Challenge*, point out that the key to excellent leadership is how one responds in the moment. Soulwise Conspirators are imbued with this quality of agility.

Scientist Albert Einstein displayed an unusual degree of flexibility or agility. Strictly true or not, one story indicative of Einstein's persona relates that Einstein's driver, who had a striking resemblance to Einstein, used to sit at the back of the hall during each of his lectures. He once remarked to Einstein that he could probably give the lecture himself. So, at the next lecture, Einstein and his driver switched places. Einstein sat at the back in his driver's uniform and the driver gave the lecture flawlessly. At the end of the lecture, a member of the audience asked a detailed question. The lecturer/driver replied, "The answer to that question is quite simple and perhaps my driver could answer it."

President Bill Clinton and James Ogolla bring the quality of agility to my dream team.

Bill Clinton

I had heard Bill Clinton, the 42nd president of the United States, give speeches on several occasions on television, but was unaware of his versatility in reading and relating to others in person—until June 18, 2007. That's when I observed him address the Economic Club of Grand Rapids with amazing dexterity. I watched President Clinton combine "concepts discerned by interpersonal intelligence with the skills of the consummate actor," as Howard Gardner described in his book *Changing Minds: The Art and Science of Changing Our Own and Other People's Minds.*

Clinton biographer, Joe Klein, described this quality of the former president: "His sonar was remarkable in political situations. He seemed to sense what audiences needed and delivered it to them—trimming his pitch here, emphasizing different priorities there...."[78]

From the moment he started speaking, his internal wheels kept turning and he adjusted his emphases to match the predominantly Republican and conservative audience of 2,100 on that evening. Clinton's opening line, a reference that Bono had been the club's guest speaker the previous year, set the tone: "Thank you for the introduction, the welcome, and for giving me the only time in my life when I drew a bigger crowd than Bono."

Clinton offers his gift of agility in responding to the world's needs through his book *Giving: How Each of Us Can Change the World*, and the humanitarian work of the William J. Clinton Foundation. The foundation's website boldly declares this global perspective: "Our world, our responsibility: Every person, rich or poor, has the right to a healthy life, a promising future, and a genuine sense of belonging. Our work, our promise: Together we can build a world where every person counts, every child enjoys equal opportunity,

and our common humanity means more than our differences."
(www.clintonfoundation.org) The foundation's major thrust includes
three initiatives: the Clinton Global Initiative, the Clinton HIV/AIDS
Initiative, and the Clinton Hunter Development Initiative.

James Ogolla

The Daystar University Global Leadership Center team needs agile
people because contemporary leadership, especially in Africa, demands
the capacity to move quickly from one thing to another. Olympic
athletes train for agility in addition to training for strength and endurance. Leaders, of course, need all three, but without agility, or flexibility,
they're unable to fully realize the potential of their missions.

As a university professor, I occasionally have the privilege of teaching
a student who stands out in the class. That happened when I taught my
first course in communication at Daystar University. I met a young gifted
Kenyan who was exceptionally promising. I recall leaving the evening
session and saying to my colleague with whom I taught the course, "That
young man is going to be the president of Kenya someday."

I would like to draft James Ogolla for my dream team *especially* for
his agility, which is guided by his vibrant Christian faith. A fantastic
juggler, I observed Ogolla's flexibility in the classroom setting organizing thoughts and ideas during discussions about communication theory
and practice. Constantly curious and eager to learn, he asked insightful
questions that demonstrated his willingness to embrace change. An avid
soccer player when he was young, he has adapted his athletic instincts
to handle ideas as means to achieve goals.

Ogolla appreciates present realities in light of the big picture and
can establish priorities and act quickly and effectively. Most importantly for the Heart for Africa team, he understands that one of the
most critical needs in Africa is to educate and encourage leaders who
will transform Africa for a future of promise.

MUSCLE

Soulwise Conspirators surround themselves with global citizens who
demonstrate DREAM TEAM qualities.

Muscle represents the strength of character to use your "currency" to
show compassion for the global family. Everyone has currency, even those

with no cash. Currency comes in as many varieties as there are people, and it includes prayer, parenting, friendship, smiles, or a helping hand.

Select people for your dream team who will use their currency to perform compassionate works for the human family. My mother taught me about the stewardship of resources and using the muscle of one's currency. Every Friday when I was growing up, my mother sat at the kitchen table with my father's weekly pay in cash and divided it among several envelopes spread on the table. The first one to be filled was always our family's contribution to the work of the church.

The following two couples, Bill and Melinda Gates, and Scott and Miracle Balsitis, continue to exercise their muscle in their own unique ways to save the global family.

Bill and Melinda Gates

Imagine the size of the table that the Bill and Melinda Gates would have to have—and the large quantity of envelopes! The couple contends they've been blessed with the currency of financial resources. *Forbes* magazine ranks Bill Gates as the richest man in the world with $58 billion. But money isn't Bill and Melinda's only currency. Perhaps a far more critical currency they offer to the world is their gift of genuinely humble compassionate hearts.

The Gateses became passionate about philanthropy after reading an article about the millions of children in poor countries who die from diseases that have been eliminated in rich countries. They couldn't believe that some lives are worth saving and others not, so they resolved to use their muscle to reduce inequity as the central point of their giving. In an address in Geneva on May 16, 2005 to the 2005 World Health Assembly, the supreme decision-making body of the World Health Organization, Bill said, "I'm optimistic that people's thinking will evolve on the question of health inequity—that people will finally accept that the death of a child in the developing world is just as tragic and worthy of our attention as the death of a child in the rich world." Melinda added, "I believe the connection happens when you see people as neighbors and not as strangers. The people of Africa are our neighbors."

Bill and Melinda established their foundation in 2000 with these two simple values at the core of its work: *All lives, no matter where they are being led, have equal value; and to whom much is given, much is expected.*

In July 2008, Bill left his day-to-day duties at Microsoft to devote himself fulltime to the work of the Bill and Melinda Gates Foundation. He brings a refreshing entrepreneurial approach to philanthropy to confront global health and education issues, with assets on June 30, 2008, of $35.8 billion. The Gates Foundation has spent $8 billion on global health, including the fight against AIDS, malaria, and tuberculosis in Africa and elsewhere. (www.gatesfoundation.org)

Scott and Miracle Balsitis

Few have billions of dollars to share. However, most of us have important resources and currency nonetheless, whether we're millionaires, thousandaires, hundredaires, or centaires.

I received this "currency" letter from my stepdaughter, Miracle, a 29-year-old childbirth educator, and her husband Scott Balsitis, a 30-year-old virologist, who live in Boston.

Dear Father Phil,

As part of our tithe, we've decided to commit $25 a month to your Africa fund. We really believe God is doing great things in you and through you and we want to support you in any way we can. So even though it's not much compared to how much is needed, this is our way of saying we love you and want to do our part to support the ministry God has for you. We know that you're not certain how it will be used in Africa or when exactly you'll be going, but we know you'll find a way to use this for someone who needs it. May God bless you richly for your commitment to his lost and broken children.

Your son and daughter,
Scott and Miracle

Enclosed with the letter was a check for $25. I knew they didn't have much money, at the time living just above the student poverty line and with the responsibility of caring for our granddaughter, Elsa Melody. Reluctant to cash their check, I put it in my desk drawer. I received a check for $25 for each of the following five months and dutifully filed them. On the seventh month, I received a $25 check and this brief message: "Please cash the checks. The kids in the Kibera feeding program are hungry now."

Every month since then, like clockwork, I receive and cash their check so they can flex their muscle to feed the hungry kids in Nairobi.

We all have the privilege and responsibility to share our currency with members of the human family in need. Jamie Scott got to use his currency in the school play. His mother knew he had his heart set on being in it, although she feared he wouldn't be chosen. On the day parts were awarded, Jamie's mother made a point of being at the school door when school got out to lighten what she felt would be a terrible blow to his young ego when he didn't get a part. The school doors burst open letting loose a torrent of children, and among them, Jamie. He rushed up to his mother breathlessly, eyes shining with pride and excitement, as he burst out, "I made it! I made it! I've been chosen to clap and cheer!"

Now it's your turn to draft a DREAM TEAM that meets your vision's requirements.

TAKE FIVE FOR REFLECTION

Given these nine characteristics, whom would you choose to be on your dream team?

- Dedication

- Resilience

- Enthusiasm

- Artistry

- Magnetism

- Talent

- Endurance

- Agility

- Muscle

CHAPTER **11**

DEVELOP YOUR STRATEGY

Soulwise Conspirators work diligently to blend passion and reason to fulfill their calling. They join the capacity to love and feel with the ability to think and reason—emotion plus logic. They believe that both the emotive and the cognitive are necessary to unleash love for the global family.

So they develop their strategy to accomplish their mission by intentionally putting on their strategic thinking caps. In a nutshell, strategic thinking is the art and science of devising a careful plan to use specific resources to manifest a vision.

This chapter will guide you to develop your strategy—to think strategically, track the trends, get your net working and prepare for the worst. Let's first explore how to think strategically.

THINK STRATEGICALLY

Communications expert James E. Lukaszewski described a strategist as "one who is able to analyze effectively, forecast pragmatically, focus realistically on issues and problems, interpret events and ideas and their impact candidly, and generate ethically and morally appropriate options for decision making and progress."[79] Former boxing champion George Foreman added this perspective: "There's more to boxing than hitting. There's not getting hit, for instance."

> *Strategic thinking involves a collaborative effort*
> *of both your right- and left-brain functions.*
> *The good news is that once you commit yourself to*
> *your dream, both of your hemispheres will automati-*
> *cally assist you as strategic thinking allies.*

The research of Daniel Pink, author of *A Whole New Mind*, can provide Soulwise Conspirators with an extremely bright future. Pink has proposed that success in today's world depends on empathy, intuition, spirituality, and right-hemisphere abilities—the very qualities Conspirators add to their left-brain functions. A seismic, though as yet undetected, shift is now underway in much of the advanced world. As Pink wrote. "We are moving from an economy and a society built on the logical, linear, computer-like capabilities of the Information Age to an economy and a society built on the inventive, empathetic, big picture capabilities of what's rising in its place, the Conceptual Age."[80]

Jeffrey Sachs, economics professor and global activist for eradicating poverty, agreed with Pink. In his book, *Common Wealth: Economics for a Crowded Planet*, he referred to this time in history as the "age of convergence" where left- and right-brain come together to shape our collective future.

Because history has proven that the Greeks were excellent thinkers, I've chosen three words of Greek derivation to describe the strategic thinking process: *synopsize*—to condense; *synthesize*—to combine resources; and *synchronize*—to coordinate in time.

Let's consider the first element of the process, synopsize.

Synopsize

The word *synopsize* combines the Greek words *opsize* (to see) and *syn* (together) and means to condense, summarize, or briefly outline.

> *Applied to strategic thinking, synopsize refers to*
> *making a précis or a brief accurate summary of your*
> *established vision.*

As a leadership consultant, I've had the privilege of working with leaders from several Fortune 100 companies including IBM, whose leaders have a remarkable capacity to synopsize. Thomas Watson Jr., IBM's American president who oversaw the company's growth from the 1920s to the 1950s, wove that capacity into the fabric of the company's culture. Watson summarized IBM's philosophy with a motto consisting of one word—THINK. The IBM tradition of strategic thinking continues to this day as the company reinvents itself for a new century. It's not surprising that IBM's highly successful line of notebook computers is called "ThinkPads."

Synopsize your vision into a clear, concise, and compelling picture of the future. Your potential followers need a condensed picture of what you hope to accomplish for two reasons. It will help them put your vision into sharp focus, and it will give them a resonating "picture" they can use to communicate your vision effectively. By synopsizing your vision, you're enabling others to become evangelists for your cause.

I have reviewed hundreds of vision statements and can honestly say that most are platitudinous and meaningless. They bear all the marks of a work cobbled together by a committee who metaphorically intended to design a horse but ended up with a camel. Ten years ago, I worked with a Fortune 500 company that had forgotten its vision. At a meeting of the company's executive team, I put its main competitor's vision statement on the screen without telling them whose vision it was. The entire executive team was convinced that their competitor's vision was their own!

On May 25, 1961, President John F. Kennedy challenged NASA to put an American on the moon by the end of the decade. Clearly, in his mind Kennedy saw a man on the moon. In 1991, the Toronto Blue Jays baseball team resolved to win the World Series and did so in '92 and '93. Rotary International, through its PolioPlus Program, has a vision of a polio-free world. The Juvenile Diabetes Research Foundation has a compelling vision of children living without diabetes.

It's imperative that Soulwise Conspirators hone their vision synopsis skills to attract and keep attention, especially in the fiercely competitive global philanthropic marketplace. Give your dream the chance it deserves to be heard and achieved.

Synthesize

Synthesize, the combination of the Greek words *thesize* (to put) and *syn* (together), means to combine and integrate resources to produce the intended result. Applied to strategic thinking, synthesize refers to developing a system to enable the flow of action toward the goal—a flowchart that indicates who will do what, where, and how. (We'll consider the "when" dimension in the next section, which shows how to synchronize your purposeful activity.)

> *Whereas synopsize reveals what your dream is, synthesize addresses how you will manage the action to realize your dream, or how to get from where you are to where you want to be.*

Thinking strategically does not equal strategic planning. I've endured hundreds of strategic planning meetings and weekend retreats that accomplished group bonding but failed to involve participants in a conscientious and integrated process to create the future.

Henry Mintzberg, Cleghorn Professor of Management at McGill University, Montreal, Canada, pointed out that enlightened congruence—his term for the intelligent alignment of resources in context—combines synthesis, intuition, and creativity. By contrast, formal planning consists of analytical thinking and depends on preserving and merely rearranging established categories. Authentic strategic change invariably requires the invention of new categories from which new perspectives and new combinations emerge.

"The problem," explained Mintzberg, "is that planning represents a calculating style of management, not a committing style. Managers with a committing style engage people in a journey." He concluded that his research, coupled with that of many others, "demonstrates that strategy making is an immensely complex process, which involves the most sophisticated, subtle, and, at times, subconscious elements of human thinking."[81]

The following anecdote shows the importance of thinking through and aligning your resources *before* committing to your plan.

Saddam Hussein was sitting in his office wondering whom to invade next when his telephone rang. "Hallo, Mr. Hussein!" said a heavily accented voice. "This is Paddy down at the Harp Pub in County Sligo, Ireland. I am ringing to inform you that we are officially declaring war on you."

"Well, Paddy," Saddam replied, "This is important news! How big is your army?"

"Right now," said Paddy, "there is myself, my cousin Sean, and the entire dart team from the pub." Saddam paused. "I must tell you, Paddy, that I have two million men in my army waiting to move on my command."

"Jesus, Mary, and Joseph!" said Paddy. "I'll have to ring you back." The next day Paddy called again. "Top o' the mornin', Mr. Hussein! I'm sorry to tell you that we have had to call off the war."

"Why the sudden change of heart?" asked Saddam.

"Well," said Paddy, "We've had a long chat and decided there's no way we can feed two million prisoners."

What's the moral of the story? You may be hot to trot, but if you haven't figured out how to "feed the prisoners," you'd better "call off the war" until you figure it out. Do not pass *synthesize!*

First you synopsize, or condense your vision. Second, you synthesize, or combine your resources effectively. Now you can consider the third aspect of strategic thinking—how to synchronize, or coordinate your strategic thinking with respect to time.

Synchronize

Synchronize, the combination of the Greek words, *chronos* (time) and *syn* (together), means to coordinate in time or to operate in unison. Applied to strategic thinking, synchronize refers to organizing and directing who will do what, where, and how—and when they will do it. The strategic focus moves to when.

> *Synchronization is a necessary life skill.*
> *It constitutes a wide range of activities, including*
> *day-to-day concerns such as getting up on time and*
> *scheduling a dental appointment, to the bigger issues*
> *of investing for retirement or solving*
> *the global climate crisis.*

Timing can be everything. It might mean life or death. The premise of this book, *Soulwise*, is that we must act now to save the lives of millions of people in the global family at risk of dying.

Synchronization can be complicated. For example, baseball batters have to coordinate hundreds of muscles at precisely the right moment to connect with a baseball going over 90 miles an hour. Likewise, trapeze artists know that the synchronization of their whole team depends on their superb ability to judge position, distance, and speed for seamless transitions.

Soulwise Conspirators must synchronize at four specific times: (1) introducing and securing commitment to their vision; (2) launching their vision; (3) coordinating the action to accomplish their vision; (4) anticipating the future.

1. Choosing the best time to introduce your vision to potential Conspirators could make or break your efforts. Probably no perfect time exists to present your dream, but you should weigh the possibilities of timing to increase the chances that people will listen to you and commit their support to your dream.

2. After introducing your vision, the next need for synchronization is launching your vision. Just like the opening of a new store, the introduction of a new product, or the first notes of a symphony, Soulwise Conspirators must be attentive to the details of the official beginning of the journey to your vision. Plan your launch so it openly presents the reality of the problem you've identified, plus the hope you're generating to breathe new life into that reality. The key will be consistency of your message and strategy.

246

3. I've been making plans for the launch of this book, and timing is crucial in coordinating the action of Soulwise Conspirators and their resources to fulfill the book's vision. Excellent timing for going public with a book can send sales through the roof, whereas bad timing can send your book to the remainder table without notice. Fortunately (for my timing only), the issues I address in the book will probably continue for some time to come. So that my voice can be heard above the noise of the crowd, I'll release the book on a day when I can tie in my fresh message with an accepted day of global significance like United Nations Day or World Malaria Day.

4. The fourth time for Soulwise Conspirators to synchronize is in preparing wisely for the future. Native American elders teach that we must plan "unto the seventh generation."

Anthropologist and systems theorist Gregory Bateson tells the story about New College at Oxford University, founded in the early 1600s. When the Great Hall was built for the school, huge oak beams four feet in width supported its roof. In recent years, the caretakers discovered that the beams were severely weakened by dry rot. With this came a dilemma: how to find similar beams today. It occurred to one caretaker to speak to the college forester. The forester smiled at the question and said, "We've been wondering when you would call us. The builder of the hall knew there would eventually be dry rot. So he instructed our predecessors to plant a grove of oak trees to replace them. Those trees are now three hundred fifty years old—just the right size for the beams."[82]

As Soulwise Conspirators, you need to develop your strategy to include thinking strategically: synopsize—condense; synthesize—combine resources; and synchronize—coordinate in time.

TRACK THE TRENDS

Clearly, the future will not be like the past. In fact, it may bear little or no resemblance to what we've known or experienced. As I see it, we have two choices: we can fear the future and cocoon ourselves, or we can embrace the future boldly and move forward with hope and tenacity.

A trend can be defined as the general direction in which something tends to move, a general tendency or inclination, or a pattern evident from past events. A trend identifies the influences that drive or cause change, the changes already taking place, and the changes that appear likely to take place.

Trends range widely, from the growing demand for healthy foods to the predictions of increased violence. Acting on the healthy food trend, Harold Schmitz, a food scientist at the global food company Mars Inc., is working on a "healthy chocolate" initiative. His expensive, five-year investigation studies the molecular composition and nutritional effects of cocoa, one of chocolate's primary ingredients. Schmitz's mission? To "reinvent" cocoa and chocolate to optimize the taste and health benefits and help Mars reap the rewards.

> *Soulwise Conspirators must gear up for trends proactively instead of following fads reactively. Positioning their dreams ahead of the curve will substantially increase their chances of realizing them.*

Recognizing trends is valuable, but being overly focused on them presents a problem that psychologists call "inattentional blindness." Let me explain with the following illustration.

Subjects in an experiment reported in *Scientific American* in March 2004 were told to focus on how many passes a basketball team made in a one-minute video. About halfway through the video, a gorilla emerged and walked across the basketball court. Half of the participants in the experiment didn't see the gorilla. Apparently, the more you focus on something, the less able you are to see unexpected or unanticipated happenings. Overfocusing may cause blindness to other trends, and countertrends as well.

Soulwise Conspirators would be wise to pay attention to five trend categories as designated by the acronym STEPS: **S**ocial, **T**echnological, **E**conomic, **P**olitical, and **S**piritual.

These major trends to track include my subjective suggestions. I encourage you to explore the specific trends that will influence your dream and strategy. For each of the five trends, I've suggested three noteworthy examples.

Social Trends

- The rebirth of social activism
- The redefinition of individual and societal roles
- The rising concern for personal and environmental health

Technological Trends

- Speed: Computer chips can now perform 1.144 thousand trillion floating point operations per second.
- Size: Information will double every 18 months and nanotechnology will flourish.
- Saturation: Internet connectedness and interconnectedness will increase dramatically.

Economic Trends

- Globalization of the marketplace
- Transition to an information-based economy
- Restructuring of world economies

Political Trends

- Clash of systems
- Change of political climate
- Threat of terrorism

Spiritual Trends

- Conflict of ideologies
- Rise of fundamentalism
- Search for significance

Tracking these trends will inform your strategic thinking and influence the development of your strategy. Now let's see how to get your net working.

GET YOUR NET WORKING

Establish Partnerships

"First you must find your trajectory," said Joseph Campbell, American mythology professor and writer, "and then comes the social coordination."

Soulwise Conspirators establish partnerships with people who will invest in their dream emotionally, intellectually, and financially, and conspire or "breathe together" to fulfill their dreams for the world.

When we consciously move from me to we, the ownership of the dream expands and we become partners in prosperity. When you borrow $25,000 from the bank, you're a customer. But when you borrow $25 million, you're a partner. We're stronger together when we combine our collective muscle to do the heavy lifting our contemporary circumstances require.

A full-page newspaper ad (www.wecansolveit.org) declared the power of partnership in large bold-face type:

You can't solve the climate crisis.

It's too big for one person to solve. It's going to take all of us, working together. The good news is, the solutions already exist. But the only way were going to get them is by sending a powerful message to our corporations and our government. More than a million people, from all walks of life and across the political spectrum, have already come together to make their voices heard. Now we need you. Take one minute to join us at wecansolveit.org. Because you can't solve the climate crisis on your own. But together we can.

Tremendous power is generated in a one-plus-one philosophy, whether it's solving the climate crisis or any of the other six inconvenient truths. In my consulting experience with sports teams, I've observed a positive shift in team dynamics when players accept and celebrate the power of "we." They practice better. They play better. And often their partnership results in championship performance.

"Our chief want in life," said Ralph Waldo Emerson, "is having someone who will make us do what we can." Soulwise Conspirators take on the role of cultural mentors/tormentors to do whatever it takes to persuade people that we do have the power to change the world, and then energize them to release their collective power for the welfare of the global family.

Many CEOs embrace a philosophy of cooperation in their speeches but not in their actions. I recall touring a large manufacturing plant with its CEO. He gave every indication that the company was committed to partnership, but I discovered the opposite. On the way, he stopped to ask one of the plant workers on the assembly line how she liked her job. She responded, "Who the hell are you?"

It's essential to establish international partnerships to meet the countless contemporary global challenges. Authentic intentional collaboration, with a combination of hard and soft power, would produce an international synergy that would enable organizations and governments to transform society. Kofi Annan, former secretary-general of the United Nations, showed support for this position by saying, "The United Nations once dealt only with governments. But now we know that peace and prosperity cannot be achieved without partnerships."

Without partnerships, my several compassionate efforts would never have gotten off the ground. With partnerships, however, I've been able to do the things I envisioned. For example, three years before the beginning of the new millennium, I had a night dream that eventually became "2000 wishes: a children's musical for the millennium." The purpose of the musical was to enable members of the global family, especially the young, to celebrate the beginning of a new millennium with hope for the future. I formed partnerships with Allan Stein who wrote a fabulous score and Greg Atkins who wrote a script with a delightful story line. I welcomed several hundred financial supporters who made it possible to launch the production with the dedication of the show's staff and cast and their families and the wider community.

When Soulwise Conspirators work together, they can do anything— even eliminate polio, a goal of Rotary International and The Bill and Melinda Gates Foundation, among other organizations.

Another good example of partnership is Roll Back Malaria (RBM) launched in 1998 by the World Health Organization, the United Nations Children's Fund (UNICEF), the United Nations Development Program, and the World Bank. The RBM Partnership's goal is to cut the burden of malaria in half by 2010 through a coordinated approach to fighting the disease.

The simple, powerful idea called (Red) plays out as a business model where consumers buy a product or a service by a designated (Red) company. It, in turn, gives some of its profits to buy and distribute antiretroviral medicine to people dying of AIDS in Africa. The plan is for (Red) to spread.

The (Red) website expresses its partnership to expand HIV/AIDS treatment in this tightly worded manifesto: "(Red) is not a charity. It is simply a business model. You buy (Red) stuff. We get the money, buy the pills, and distribute them. They take the pills, stay alive, and continue to take care of their families and contribute socially and economically in their communities. If they don't get their pills, they die. We don't want them to die. We want to give them the pills. And we can. And you can. And it's easy." (www.joinred.com)

Soulwise Conspirators get their net working by establishing partnerships and weaving a worldwide web through modern technology. Let's consider how to get connected.

Weave a Worldwide Web

According to the *2008 State of the Future*, about 1.4 billion people, 21% of the world's population, were connected to the Internet, with 37.6% of them in Asia, 27.1% in Europe, and 17.5% in North America. It's predicted that most people in the world will be connected to the Internet by 2022, making cyberspace an unprecedented medium for civilization.

A March-April 2008 survey by Frank N. Magid Associates reports that only 3% of Americans are not connected to the Internet. The average number of hours people who are connected spend online at home each week is as follows: 1-5 hours, 22%; 6-10 hours, 22%; 11-20 hours, 27%; 21-40 hours, 22%; and 41 or more hours, 5%. According to Neilsen ratings, the average American visits more than 2,000 website pages a month while at work.

Soulwise Conspirators have a tremendous opportunity to weave a worldwide web to communicate their message to the world effectively and rapidly and work together to make their dreams come true. People want to and are connecting around the world with a wide variety of cyber networking opportunities including e-mail, teleconferencing, video-conferencing, webinars, on-line learning, e-publishing, and social networking websites such as MySpace and Facebook. According to Blogherald.com, more than 60 million blogs flood the Internet, and the number keeps growing. In addition, 3.3 billion mobile phones now actively connect people and institutions around the world.

Activists are marching with their mouse on the Internet. For example, the giant Texas power company TXU announced plans to build 11 coal-fired, CO_2-belching power plants. Worried about the implications for climate change, Environmental Defense and the Natural Resources Defense Council used the Internet and shifted the local debate over generating electricity to a national debate over capping and reducing carbon emissions. As a result, TXU cut the number of coal plants to three, pledged its support to a U.S. cap on greenhouse gas emissions, and committed TXU to plowing $400 million into energy-efficiency programs and doubling the purchase of wind power.

The Internet also offers opportunity for global education. TV talk show host Oprah Winfrey jumped on the education bandwagon in a big way. Her weekly webcasts broke new ground with the world as her classroom. More than 700,000 people registered for a 10-week webinar (hosted at Winfrey.Oprah.com). Commonly her site attracts more than 6 million users and 80,000 e-mails a month!

A major part of the strategy for promoting my book *Soulwise: How to Create a Conspiracy of Hope, Health and Harmony* consists of weaving a worldwide web. Established international connections will continue to grow after this book is published. The book's website, www.livesoulwisenow.com, offers visitors opportunities to connect with other Soulwise Conspirators from around the globe, linking visitors to other sites and compassionate collaborators.

> *I hope you will feel at home on the book's website—www.livesoulwisenow.com—and will take ownership of the dream to ensure humanity thrives.*

I'll do the usual book tour, but put most of my publicity investment into creating, connecting, and shaping a digital community. To maximize the power of the Internet, I'll follow the 3M approach used by Mindy Finn, former director of e-strategy for Governor Mitt Romney's 2008 presidential campaign. Finn balanced messaging, mobilization, and money with the goal to turn out the vote. For my purposes, I want to get out the message that the world is choking, mobilize people from around the world to perform CPR to save our global family, and raise money to wisely and efficiently advance the movement.

Get your net working. Establish partnerships, weave a worldwide web, and also nurture sacred connections, to which we now turn our attention.

Nurture Sacred Connections

As a Christian minister for more than 40 years, I've witnessed people from all walks of life yearning for a connection with the divine. Moreover, the happiest people I know have a significant relationship with God, or whatever they wish to name a higher power.

People across the world crave to connect with the divine in order to make sense of their world and to seek assurance and hope for their future. Even nonreligious or secular people seek spiritual sustenance for daily living. Especially after 9/11 and with the threat of global terrorism, people are seeking answers to their questions about life and how they can be fully alive in the process of discovery and fulfillment.

From time to time, especially in difficult or painful circumstances, we all reach out for whatever support may be available in the universe. We are essentially spiritual beings, and our humanness prompts us to seek answers to our deepest questions.

Patricia Aburdene, co-author of *The New York Times* best-seller *Megatrends 2000*, affirmed our quest for spirituality in her book *Megatrends 2010: The Rise of Conscious Capitalism*. She contends that this spiritual quest is the "greatest megatrend of our era." One chapter titled "The Passion for Personal Spirituality" presents what Aburdene considers these five hallmarks of the era: meaning or purpose, compassion, consciousness, service, and well-being. Which of these draw *your* attention?

Many nurture sacred connections through a higher network commonly called prayer. Gallup polls in 2008 report that more Americans pray in one week than exercise, drive a car, have sex, or go to work. Nine out of ten Americans pray regularly, and three out of four pray every day. The International Communications Research for AARP found that nearly half of Americans 45 or older say they are somewhat religious and, of these, 20% indicated their most satisfying spiritual or religious experience is prayer.

Understood and accepted by many as a universal language, prayer connects our basic human needs with God's grace. "The reason why we pray," suggested American psychologist and philosopher William James, "is simply that we cannot help praying."

254

Prayer symbolizes our partnership with the Divine. A significant dimension of our trusting relationship consists of appreciating the often complex nature of our lives, including the tough questions about suffering in the world.

Mahatma Gandhi claimed to change the world through the power of prayer. He called it "soul force," an inspiring combination of integrity, service, forgiveness, prayer, self-reliance, self-purification, and love. He believed with absolute certainty that "Prayer from the heart can achieve what nothing else can in the world.... Properly understood and applied, it is the most potent instrument of action..."

I'm also a firm believer in the power of prayer. I must confess I don't understand prayer as much as I have experienced its influence on my own personal life and in the lives of thousands of others. To me, it acts as a catalyst of the soul that brings strength, comfort, and guidance to everyday matters. So I follow the biblical injunction to pray without ceasing.

One spring Saturday morning several years ago, the emergency department of the local hospital called me to come and pray for a little two-year-old girl who had fallen into a backyard swimming pool and had lost consciousness. The distraught parents, the medical staff, and I gathered around this still child whose body temperature had been substantially reduced. We joined hands and I began to pray. One of the physicians called out, "Her eyes are fibrillating!"

The medical team sprang into action and pushed me out of the way. Unfortunately, I fell backwards, hit my head on the floor and lost consciousness. The next thing I remember was the same physician's voice saying, "Good work, Reverend. One hell—sorry—heaven of a prayer." The hospital team resuscitated the child and she fully recovered to be a normal two-year-old.

To develop a genuine inner life, it helps to take time to be quiet and cultivate a spiritual discipline. Many find it essential to connect with the divine within other people in a spiritual or religious community that provides opportunities for involvement and support. This connection aligns with the Buddhist tradition, which respects the dignity of every human being with the ritual of bowing to the divinity in the other—also the meaning behind the greeting "Namaste." Religious or spiritual communities don't represent perfection by any means, but their company offers a spiritual connection of love and friendship to which I can personally and professionally attest.

John Wesley, founder of Methodism, called the gathering of the religious in community "holy conferencing," a key means of grace. Wesley believed that when people come together and see one another face to face, the Spirit of God through Christ also becomes present. In relationship, in coming together, in conferencing, we experience God's grace through one another. The United Methodist Church today maintains the practice of General Conference where clergy and lay delegates come together on a regular basis for worship, business, and fellowship.

We need a vital, honest community, not to judge but to help us test our own reality. The principle of relying on communities to guide introspective processes resonates with the religious and secular alike. Like personal prayer, the collective prayers of a religious or spiritual community can produce astounding results.

Shawn, a 17-year-old young man in my congregation, lay paralyzed in a coma from injuries sustained in a car accident. He had shown no movement for several weeks. At our Sunday worship, I left the chancel area and invited parishioners to join hands with me across the aisles and around the sanctuary to pray specifically for Shawn's recovery. We keenly felt the presence of God in the silence and in the simple words I spoke.

That afternoon, I visited Shawn at the hospital. His grandmother could hardly contain her excitement. When she saw me, she threw her arms around me and told me that Shawn had opened his eyes that morning at 11:22 a.m., the precise time the church community joined in prayer for him. Coincidence? I don't know. But I do know that today Shawn continues to make a remarkable recovery, and I keep on praying.

Remember, to develop your strategy as Soulwise Conspirators— think strategically, track the trends, and get your net working by establishing partnerships, weaving a worldwide web, and nurturing sacred connections. But also prepare for the worst.

PREPARE FOR THE WORST

Shift Happens

A flight attendant for a major airline prepared passengers for landing with these instructions: "We hope you've enjoyed giving us the business, because we sure have enjoyed taking you for a ride! Before opening the overhead bins, please be careful—because as we all know, shift happens."

Soulwise Conspirators acknowledge that shift does happen. I say "wise" especially because psychologists point out the tendency of most people to assume that current trends will continue forever. They call it "extrapolation bias." We can see the ramifications of this tendency in the housing crisis triggered in the United States beginning in 2007. Shattered were homeowners' beliefs that the value of their homes would continue to increase.

Moreover, many people suffer from "loss aversion." Surprisingly, numerous studies have shown that, in general, humans hate losses more than they like gains. For these people, losing $1,000 hurts twice as much as winning $1,000 feels good. We see the same behavior in the stock market when investors hold on to losers longer than winners, even though tax incentives encourage the opposite.

Sometimes a shift produces catastrophic results. In our memory banks, we have huge files of devastating images such as the flaming, crumbling Twin Towers on 9/11, genocide in Rwanda, hurricanes Charlie and Katrina, the Indian Ocean tsunami, earthquakes in China, floods in the Midwest United States, and wildfires in California. These shifts remind us of how fragile and precious life is. Perhaps that's why cartoon character Charlie Brown said, "I've developed a new philosophy—I only dread one day at a time."

> *It may raise considerable discomfort to imagine losing everything, but contemplating the worst scenario prompts us to reflect on what's really valuable and worth protecting.*

I can hardly imagine losing everything. Can you? It could happen. I'm not sure how I would respond. But if it did happen, I would hope

I could handle it like the Anderson family, whose house burned down the day they arrived home from vacation. I was unable to reach them to tell them the news until I picked them up at the airport. They were glad to be home and expressed how they were looking forward to sleeping in their own beds.

On the way to what was left of their home, I gently shared the sad news. Standing before the smoldering ruins, the family shared lots of tears, hugs, and expressions of disbelief. We all embraced, and Jim quietly said to his family, "We're blessed. We still have each other. That's what's most important. We have each other. Besides, we've been talking about moving for a couple of years. I guess it's time."

It's one thing to lose a house that can be replaced. But it's another to imagine losing civilization itself on a grand scale. The growing possibility of actually losing our civilization compelled me to write *Soulwise*. Just the thought of not having a human family to embrace was enough to put this humanitarian project in motion.

Vital signs indicate that civilization may be on the verge of collapse. Environmentalist and best-selling author Paul Hawken offered this unsettling description: "There is a real and increasing possibility that global warming, resource depletion, increasing world population, disease pandemics, technological anarchy, and the geopolitical tensions, economic instability, and social upheaval they generate will create a nightmare future for humanity this century."[83]

According to a World Bank study, a severe influenza pandemic would lead to worldwide economic losses of $1.5 trillion to $1.8 trillion. Developing countries would be the hardest hit because higher population densities and poverty would accentuate the economic impact in these countries. Health officials around the world have warned for years that a flu pandemic looms and the world needs to prepare. When it hits, it will have overwhelming consequences.

However, signs indicate that complacency has set in. "The risk of pandemic had its moment in the sun, where the public was interested and people were talking about it in the grocery lines," noted risk-communications expert Peter Sandman. "Then people got used to it, and interest settled into the new normal." Coincidentally, a spike in traffic to the Center for Disease Control and Prevention (CDC) occurred on January 24, 2006, between 4 and 5 p.m. EST, mystifying the communications office until the CDC identified the cause. On that day, Oprah Winfrey hosted a program on pandemic flu!

"The sky is falling." Chicken Little may have a point. Soulwise Conspirators prepare for the worst. Danger lies ahead for us, and if we don't act quickly and decisively, we may pay the ultimate price. The world is choking but it doesn't have to choke to death.

Formulate a Disaster Plan

Your Soulwise Conspiracy Dream Team will want to formulate a disaster plan to anticipate and respond to the shifts that may happen. A good strategic plan will go a long way to protect the investment in your dream and ensure your legacy for the causes you believe in.

A few years ago, a friend gave me a copy of *The Worst-Case Scenario Survival Handbook* by Joshua Piven and David Borgenicht. The book offers solutions for a wide variety of worst-case scenarios, including how to escape from a sinking car, wrestle an alligator, break down a door, land a plane, and perform a tracheotomy. The underlying message? "Better be safe than sorry." This approach agrees with the good advice of the Boy Scout motto, "Be prepared."

> *In formulating a disaster plan, ask these key questions: What do you want to protect? What's valuable to you? Red Cross staff, volunteers, and supporters ask and respond to these questions marvelously and generously around the world.*

Take the case of Ilja Gort, a winemaker, whose nose may be his most valuable asset. If Gort followed the old saying and cut off his nose to spite his face, Lloyd's of London would not be happy. The company agreed to insure Gort's nose. Gort said he can distinguish millions of different scents and he can't work without that ability, so he took out a policy on the loss of his nose and, more important, his sense of smell. Should anything happen to render his sense of smell useless, he'll be paid the equivalent of about $8 million. But the policy has restrictions—Gort can't be in a boxing match or be the target in a knife-throwing contest.

On a more globally significant note, ShelterBox, a project led by Rotary International, specializes in a ready-to-go response operation that provides emergency supplies for rapid distribution to disaster sites. Based in Cornwall, England, ShelterBox was conceived by Tom Henderson, a member of the Rotary Club of Helston-Lizard, England, as a millennium project. A ShelterBox includes bedding, cooking supplies, water purification tablets and containers, and custom tents modeled on an African bush hut.

Victims of the January 2001 earthquake in Gujarat, India, received the first delivery. As of 2009, the project had distributed 60,000 Shelter-Boxes, benefiting about 800,000 people in 57 countries. The aim is to get the ShelterBoxes to the scene of a disaster anywhere in the world within 48 hours. The international relief agency Feed the Children called the program "the best disaster-relief tool we have seen in 20 years of experience."

In the worst case scenarios of a planetary catastrophe, plant life would survive because of an extensive disaster plan instituted by Norway and supported by a wide variety of sources worldwide. The Svalbard Global Seed Vault, nicknamed by some the "Doomsday Vault," opened on March 7, 2008, on the remote Norwegian Island of Spitsbergen in the Arctic Ocean, 600 miles from the North Pole. Some describe it as a Noah's Ark for plant genetics at 4 degrees below zero F. It will preserve thousands of regional and local crop varieties that farmers worldwide have bred for thousands of years. At its opening, Norwegian Prime Minister Jens Stoltenberg announced, "Norway is proud to be playing a central role in creating a facility capable of protecting what are not just seeds but the fundamental building blocks of human civilization."

It's one thing to appreciate that shift happens. It's another thing to actually formulate a disaster plan to make it through the shift. As I wrote this chapter, safely in my home, I received word that a torrential storm, the worst storm in a hundred years, caused the river next to our cottage to rise and that it could potentially sweep the cottage off its foundations and hurl it into Lake Michigan. For years, I have intended to formulate a disaster plan and assemble a "disaster duffle bag" for my family's welfare in case of an emergency. The news about our cottage prompted me to take immediate action.

Gathering all the supplies for the basic emergency supply kit took less time than I thought. We now have peace of mind we never had before. As it turned out, our cottage remained standing, and now our family has a disaster plan in place and kits for our home and cottage. I hope we never have to use them, but we've got them just in case.

Sometimes, it takes a crisis to make us follow up on our good intentions. That time, it did for me.

Prepare for the worst, formulate a disaster plan, and if disaster hits, take a deep breath.

Take a Deep Breath

As exercise guru Richard Simmons constantly reminds his workout viewers, "Don't forget to breathe." That's good strategic advice not only when you exercise, but also when you face a disaster while on your way to make your dream for humanity's future come true.

Our family took a collective deep breath, actually three or four, when we got the news about the flooding near our cottage. Taking a deep breath slowed down the action so we could gain perspective on the situation and realize that we couldn't do anything at that point to change the outcome.

According to a baseball legend, the secret to success for major league baseball slugger Ted Williams involved being in the moment to such a degree that his mind could slow down the ball to where he could see the seams on it as the ball approached his poised bat.

In a similar vein, Rabbi Harold Kushner, in his book, *When Bad Things Happen to Good People,* encouraged people to slow down the action in their lives in order to deal with a tough situation or grieve a loss. Slowing down the action offers the opportunity to see things in a different light. In my role as pastor, a main task is to enable people to slow down in difficult circumstances: when a loved one dies, when they are diagnosed with cancer, when a spouse leaves the family, when they get negative test results.

Sometimes my encouragement takes strange forms. When a bright nursing student in my university oral communication course walked to the front of the classroom to present her five-minute prepared speech, she unfortunately was struck dumb by her nervousness. I encouraged her to take several deep breaths to calm herself so she could continue by reading from her notes, which she had given me earlier. She did take some breaths but still was unable to speak. So I walked over and stood beside her and said that, as a nurse, she would have to speak to doctors and patients, and that maybe it would help to imagine herself in her nursing role. That didn't work either. I took a risk. I lay down on the desk, propped up my head with a couple of books, and invited her to take a deep breath and speak to me as if I were her patient. She looked at me with two of the most relaxed, intense eyes, took a deep breath, and sang "There's a Place for Us" with the voice of an angel. After the song, she presented a memorable speech.

> *Many, many times, reframing the situation can*
> *facilitate the need to take a deep breath.*

When the MassMutual Insurance Company launched its ad campaign in August 2001, its theme "expect the unexpected" was quite effective. In a humorous way, the campaign warned consumers of how life's unpredictability calls for sound financial planning and service. One month later, however, the events of 9/11 took place. MassMutual had offices in one of the towers. The company executives practiced excellent crisis management by immediately coming together at the company's headquarters in Springfield, Massachusetts to primarily determine how to care for their employees in New York and then to consider how to deal with the advertising campaign.

In effect, the company took a deep breath and decided on September 11 to temporarily suspend their $10 million advertising campaign "You can't predict. You can prepare." In an understatement, MassMutual Senior Vice-President Victor Lipman explained, "The humorous tone was not particularly appropriate." The company's campaign was reinstated later.

Soulwise Conspirators should expect to have setbacks, and they can be extremely frustrating and heartbreaking. Rotary International, for example, experienced a big blow to its PolioPlus program. The northern Nigerian state of Kano, whose three million children under age five constitute one of the world's last reservoirs of the polio virus, refused to participate in a nationwide immunization campaign.

During 2007, the polio virus originating in northern Nigeria caused new polio outbreaks in nine African countries where the disease had earlier been eliminated. Kano's decision to continue its 12-month boycott of mass immunization threatens further spread of the virus, jeopardizing the 16-year $3 billion effort to eradicate the disease from the earth. Polio remains endemic, or freely circulating, in only six countries: Nigeria, Niger, India, Pakistan, Afghanistan, and Egypt. Kano stopped mass immunization because of rumors that the oral vaccine contained sterilizing drugs that comprised part of a global conspiracy against Islam.

When we consider the grave state of civilization today, let's take a deep breath, renew our resolve, and move on to breathe new life into humanity.

Move On

A wealthy man decided to go on a safari in Africa. He took along his faithful pet dachshund for company. One day, the dog started chasing butterflies, and before long he discovered he was lost. Wandering about, he noticed a leopard bounding rapidly in his direction with the obvious intention of having lunch. The dachshund thought, "I'm in deep trouble now!" Then he noticed some bones on the ground close by and immediately settled down to chew on the bones with his back to the approaching cat. Just as the leopard was about to leap, the dachshund exclaimed loudly, "Boy, that was one delicious leopard! I wonder if I can find any more around here."

Hearing this, a look of terror came over the leopard, and he halted his attack in mid-stride and slunk away into the trees. "Whew!" thought the leopard. "That was close. That dachshund nearly had me."

Meanwhile, a monkey who'd been watching the whole scene from a nearby tree figured he could put this knowledge to good use and trade it for protection from the leopard. So, off he scampered. But the dachshund saw him running after the leopard at top speed and figured something must be up.

The monkey soon caught up with the leopard, spilled the beans, and struck a deal for himself with the leopard. Furious that the dachshund had made a fool out of him, the leopard growled, "Here monkey, hop on my back and see what's going to happen to that conniving canine." Now the dachshund saw the leopard coming with the monkey on his back and thought, "What am I going to do now?" But instead of running, the dog sat down with his back to his attackers, pretending he hasn't seen them yet, and just when they get close enough to hear, the dachshund said, "Where's that monkey? I sent him off half an hour ago to bring me another leopard." When someone throws a monkey wrench into your plans, it's best to move on.

> *Soulwise Conspirators know that when adversity*
> *strikes a blow to the advancement of their dream,*
> *it's essential to take a deep breath, but that you can't*
> *stand there and hold your breath forever. You've got*
> *to exhale and move on.*

A few years ago, a widow in her early 60s in my congregation invited me to have lunch with her at her home. When we sat down at the beautifully decorated table, I noticed that the table was set for three. I asked if someone else would be joining us. "Oh," she responded, "that's where my husband Charlie sits." Taken a bit aback, I asked, "When did Charlie die?" "It will be twenty-seven years ago next month," replied the widow.

Unfortunately, some people become immobilized when faced with setbacks.

> *When the worst happens, and it can, take a deep*
> *breath and move on decisively and creatively in the*
> *direction of your dream. What happens after the deep*
> *breath will ultimately determine your success.*

Every sailor knows you can't control the winds, but you can adjust the sails. The American Red Cross followed that advice after a number of difficulties arose in the organization. Problems included a public outcry over its misuse of funds for victims of Hurricane Katrina, a $200 million deficit, mounting fines related to its blood collection and distribution, and low morale amid widespread staff cuts at the Washington headquarters. The organization's respected image became damaged, and many regular contributors withheld their financial support.

So the American Red Cross took a collective deep breath and then set a recovery plan in motion. In April, 2008, it appointed Harvard business professor Gail McGovern, a former senior executive at AT&T and Fidelity Investments, as its new president and chief executive officer. Including interim leaders, she was the seventh president and chief executive since 2002.

Attracted mainly by the Red Cross mission, McGovern aimed to jump-start the organization. "It's such a noble institution that helps people in times of need," she commented. "[It] helps educate them to be prepared in time of need, helps the armed services, gives the nation almost 50 percent of its blood supply." Undaunted by the problems that faced the organization, she chose instead to focus on the mission and help the Red Cross move on.

This chapter has focused on the need for Soulwise Conspirators to develop a strategy to fulfill their dreams for humanity. Effective results call for these four essential elements: think strategically, track the trends, get your net working, and prepare for the worst.

With a compelling dream, a committed dream team, and a solid strategy, you're ready to declare your dream to the world.

TAKE FIVE FOR REFLECTION

1. Why is strategic thinking so important and how does it differ from strategic planning?

2. Name two major trends in each of the categories that may affect the fulfillment of your vision.

   Social Trends

   -
   -

   Technological Trends

   -
   -

   Economic Trends

   -
   -

   Political Trends

   -
   -

   Spiritual Trends

   -
   -

3. How would planning backward apply in your situation?

4. Name three people in your network who can help you move your vision forward right now and in the future.

   •

   •

   •

5. Briefly describe a possible disaster in your life and your disaster response plan.

CHAPTER 12

DECLARE YOUR DREAM

Take the risk of telling others about your dream and inviting them to join you in performing CPR to save our global family. Declare your dream courageously: communicate with clarity, connect with confidence, and crackle with conviction. Let's begin by considering how to communicate with clarity.

COMMUNICATE WITH CLARITY

Communicate your dream with clarity of words, emotions, graphics, images, body language, setting, and appearance. Keep it plain, keep it simple, keep it precise, and keep it concise. As you communicate your dream, remember this poignant reminder to the monks: "Speak only if you can improve the silence."

Keep It Plain
Someone described the speeches of Warren Harding, the 29th president of the United States, as "an army of pompous phrases moving over the landscape in search of an idea." Soulwise Conspirators by contrast, communicate in plain, everyday language and images that are straightforward and without pretense.

"In books," advised 19th century novelist Samuel Butler, "it is the chief of all perfections to be plain and brief." So keep your communication plain to persuade, inform, and entertain your potential followers.

Persuade

No need to speak elaborately. If you plan to persuade someone to commit to your dream, tell them plainly about the need you've discovered, your vision that addresses that need, and how you intend to make your dream come true.

In its efforts to clarify language in government documents and "cease utilization" of jargon, the state of Washington initiated "Plain Talk," a program aimed at communicating with the public simply and in plain language. "Simple changes," said Janet Shimabukuro, manager of the Washington Department of Revenue's taxpayer services program, "can have profound results. Plain talk isn't only rewriting, it's rethinking your approach and really personalizing your message to the audience and to the reader." Governor Chris Gregoire said, "When we just talk in language everyone understands, we get a whole lot more done."

And maybe sell more. A local upscale restaurant carefully chose these descriptions of its wine selections for its customers:

- Chardonnay, Edna Valley Vineyard—Elegant and smooth
- Chardonnay, Morgan, Metallico—Rich and luscious
- Zinfandel, Kunde, Sonoma Valley—Velvety smooth and supple
- Merlot, Rutherford Ranch, Napa Valley—Yummy
- Cabernet Sauvignon, Hahn Estates—Friendly and attractive

Our group chose "Yummy"—and it was!

Plain talk works with kids, too. On an international flight, a child kept kicking the back of my seat. I tolerated it for a while hoping that the child's parents would come to my rescue. They didn't. So I got out of my seat and spoke plainly to the child. "Please don't kick my seat." To my amazement, the child stopped. At the end of the flight, I was curious about the child's change of behavior and asked why he had stopped kicking my seat. His response? "You said please."

When I talk to people about supporting Kibera Kids Kitchen, a program that feeds orphans in Kibera slum in Nairobi, I ask them plainly, "Will you help me feed hungry kids, many of whom haven't eaten in seven days?"

Because we learn from examples, I'm including three commercial and three organizational examples for each of the next three sections in Keep It Plain.

Three examples of commercial plain persuasive communication include:

- "Mucinex in. Mucus out." (Mucinex)
- "SHIFT_ the way you move." (Nissan)
- "Think Green." (Waste Management)

Three examples of organizational plain persuasive communication include:

- "Walk for the cure." (American Cancer Society)
- "Do what it takes." (UNICEF)
- "Together we can make a difference." (Festival of Children)

Inform

Malcolm Baldrige, former secretary of commerce, recalled how a high-ranking official once responded to a subordinate's request for a raise by saying, "Because of the fluctuational predisposition of your position's productive capacity as juxtaposed to governmental statistics, it would be momentarily injudicious to advocate an incremental increase." The staff person said, "I don't get it." The official said, "That's right."

Keep your communication plain to inform your potential followers about your dream and the role they might play in its fulfillment. When someone admires a sunset and says "Gorgeous," we know exactly what they mean. The "No Trespassing" sign on the fence gives a clear message. The Sa-Bai Restaurant in Madison, Wisconsin, informs customers plainly about the degrees of spiciness this way: "Tiny, Careful, Adventure, Fire."

The National Council of Teachers of English Committee on Public Doublespeak gave these five gems from their files:

- Entropy control engineer—Janitor
- Clothing refresher—Dry cleaner
- Career associate scanning professional—Checkout clerk
- Economically non-affluent—Poor
- Equity retreat—Stock market crash

Speak plainly and you'll definitely set yourself apart.

271

Three examples of commercial plain informative communication include:

- "Clearly different." (Pearle Vision)
- "We mean clean." (Bissell)
- "Trusted everywhere." (Duracell)

Three examples of organizational plain informative communication include:

- "1 in 3 will get cancer." (American Cancer Society)
- "United for a more equitable world." (Oxfam)
- "Prostate cancer strikes 218,000 men a year." (Prostate Cancer Foundation)

Entertain

Keep your communication plain to persuade, inform, and also to entertain. Your audience will appreciate your sense of humor, especially because your dream will probably involve dealing with life and death issues. The English proverb, "Garlic makes a man wink, drink, and stink," conveys a plain message that almost always gets a chuckle and a smile.

Last year, I attended a conference on climate change. The organizers creatively communicated the global warming theme in a playful way. The wilting flowers for centerpieces on "scorched" tablecloths, the half-full water glasses, and the PowerPoint slides with the sound of polar ice melting combined to drive home the message with a light touch.

Signs can be entertaining, too. A veterinarian's sign advised: "To find fleas, start from scratch." A semi-tractor trailer delivering pigs to the slaughterhouse defines its mission as The Last Ride. The website for Fruitbasket Flowerland plays on words to convey its message: thankyouverymulch.com.

Comedians know instinctively that they must speak plainly in performing their stand-up routines. Unless members of the audience understand the joke, they'll never get the punch line.

Every year, I receive for Christmas a "You Might Be a Redneck If..." calendar, the clever creation of comedian Jeff Foxworthy, one of the most respected and successful comedians in the country. I laugh every day at his redneck plain talk, a style that's been compared to Mark Twain's.

- "You might be a redneck if... you think a thesaurus is an extinct animal."
- "You might be a redneck if... you think 'megabytes' means a good day fishing."
- "You might be a redneck if... you think 'Microsoft Word' means whispering."

In the last few years, comedian Bill Cosby caused a stir with his plain-talk book *Come On People: On the Path from Victims to Victors*. Cosby addresses his concern about the loss of community in the world and the breakdown of parenting skills that puts young people, especially young black males, at risk. He communicates his discomforting message that the United States has lost its sense of community in an entertaining way.

Three examples of commercial plain entertaining communication include:

- "MMM... Toasty." (Quizno's)
- "Think about your drink." (America's Milk Processors)
- "Really good food for dogs." (Pedigree)

Three examples of organizational plain entertaining communication include:

- "Support Search and Rescue: Get Lost" (U.S. Coast Guard bumper sticker)
- "Peace. It's cheaper than war." (Better World Campaign)
- "Make a Hole in One." (Colon Cancer prevention poster)

Keep It Simple

"Right Achilles debridement with flexor hallucis longus transfer," my orthopedic surgeon recommended after a thorough diagnosis. "Would you please translate that for me?" I asked. "We're going to fix your Achilles tendon," he replied.

Soulwise Conspirators follow this advice from the great philosopher Aristotle: "Speak as the common people do." Their uncomplicated language is easily understood. They tell their story simply so others will receive it, recall it, and repeat it.

Receive It

I was fortunate to be a student in the 1960s when Marshall McLuhan taught at the University of Toronto. I personally heard this communications pioneer pronounce and explain that "the medium is the message," a phrase that made him famous around the world. Along with most of my fellow students, I listened with rapt attention to McLuhan but was clueless about the meaning of his message.

One day, McLuhan arrived at the university in downtown Toronto to find that someone, probably a student, had parked in his spot. McLuhan took one of his business cards and wrote on the back of it, "You're in my spot," and placed the card under the intruder's windshield wiper. The next day, McLuhan arrived to find the same car parked in his spot with the business card still on the windshield. He took the card and saw that the student had written this response: "Sir. This is first thing you've written that I've understood."

Soulwise Conspirators appreciate the complexity of communication. And yet some people increase the complication. Publisher Alfred A. Knopf once defined an economist as one who "states the obvious in terms of the incomprehensible."

Soulwise Conspirators are simple storytellers. They tell the story of what's happening now and offer their audiences a compelling picture of a desired future plus a strategy to get there so their message is received. In his book, *Changing Minds: The Art and Science of Changing Our Own and Other People's Minds*, Harvard psychologist Howard Gardner described the nature of storytelling this way: "Optimally, a new story has to have enough familiar elements so that it is not instantly rejected yet be distinctive enough that it compels attention and engages the mind. The audience has to be prepared, in one sense, and yet surprised, in another."[84]

Simple communication is, well, simple. "Take out the garbage." "I love you." "Damn, I'm good!" "Anybody seen the dog?" "No."

Communicating complex matters in a simple way can be difficult. When I teach communication to university students, I facilitate an exercise that challenges a student to give directions to two blindfolded students to put up a small tent. Students discover immediately that it's not as easy a task as it may seem at first. Over the years, I've witnessed students, usually avid campers, erecting the tent in record time, others ripping off their blindfolds in frustration, and still others proudly displaying their inside-out upside-down creation.

Effective communicators know that it's not what they say, it's what others hear them say that's important. They know that the plainer their message the more likely the message will be understood and acted on.

In spite of our limitations, we humans have an amazing capacity to receive messages. Consider "typoglycemia," where readers can understand the meaning of words in a sentence even when the letters of each word are scrambled. As long as all the necessary letters are present, and the first and last letters remain the same, readers turn out to have little trouble reading the text. See if you can read the following paragraph.

Aoccdrnig to a rscheearch at an Elingsh uinervtisy, it deosn't mttaer in what oredr the ltteers in a wrod are, the olny iprmoetnt tihng is taht the frist and lsat ltteer is at the rghit pclae. The rset can be a toatl mses and you can sitll raed it wouthit porbelm. Tihs is bcuseae we do not raed ervey lteter by it slef but the wrod as a wlohe.

> *"There is no agony," said writer and folklorist Zora Neale Hurston, "like bearing an untold story inside you." As a Soulwise Conspirator, you have a responsibility to tell your story simply so others will receive it.*

I'm privileged to tell my story about Little Joe. I met this bright seven-year-old boy on my first trip to Kenya. From the moment I set foot in his Maasai village on the mountain, he attached himself to my pant leg. We went everywhere together, and I got to know him quite well. His tribal chief, whose name coincidentally is also Joseph, told me Little Joe's parents had died and that because of malaria Little Joe himself knew he had five months to live. On the day I was leaving, he asked me whether I would come back to the mountain to see him. I replied that I'd be back the next summer. Little Joe looked at me with his big brown eyes and said, "I'll wait."

Unfortunately, Little Joe died three months later. When I saw Chief Joseph the following summer, he told me that before Little Joe died he asked him to give me this message: "Tell Ole Nadala (my Swahili name, which means 'the one who leaps for joy') I tried to wait. Tell him I'll see him in heaven."

You'll know if people receive your story. I know people receive my story about my young friend, Little Joe, because they come up to me after I finish speaking to a convention or association meeting and give me checks to protect kids from malaria. In the left-hand corner of the checks, you'll find tangible proof that they received my story: "For Little Joe."

Recall It

Soulwise Conspirators catch people's attention with memorable stories, recalled in large part because they contain meaning for listeners. Something in a story resonates with their experience, and they file the story away in their hearts like a precious jewel. An old Indian proverb echoes this reality: "Tell me a fact and I'll learn. Tell me a truth and I'll believe. But tell me a story and it will live in my heart forever." Good stories stick like glue.

We recall stories Soulwise Conspirators tell because they are genuine and authentic. While in Kenya, Little Joe and I spent time with Pastor Methuselah, a master storyteller. He truly lives his name; he was 71 years old in a country with a life expectancy of 45! We would walk for miles with this elder statesman known as "The Walking Library," and then sit under the welcomed shade of an 'acacia' tree and listen to him tell a thousand stories about the history of his tribe and the wonders of God's grace.

Corporations like 3M, Ford, and General Electric are using the Native American Indian art of storytelling to teach rising executives company values and help them appreciate and celebrate their distinctive corporate cultures. Stories that are handed down from one generation to the next play an important role in a company's overall success. In my leadership coaching practice, I've gleaned valuable insight from facilitating an oral tradition of corporate story time.

What's your story? Tell the story of how you plan to breathe new life into the global family so that people will receive your story and recall it. Most people have good memories. So make it easy for them to make it their own.

Repeat It

Soulwise Conspirators tell their stories so they're received and recalled, but most importantly so they can be repeated easily. There's no faster way of building "belief buzz" about your dream than to carefully craft your stories so that others can tell them. They personally share the news about the work you're doing and are going to do.

Soulwise Conspirators can learn a lot from advertising agencies. Their main aim in commercials is for us to receive their story so that we recall their story and then repeat their story as our story. It's an effective branding strategy that really works. Years ago, the Packard Motor Car Company used this method with the tagline "One man tells another." Today, social networking sites on the Internet, such as Facebook and MySpace, use the same principle.

You'll have to be creative. Present your dream in a way that begs to be repeated. Let your story stand out in the crowded marketplace where other dreamers are clamoring for attention. Differentiate your story so it can be heard above the noise. The producers of the hit musical *Mamma Mia* understand this principle of differentiation. People emerge from a live performance or from seeing the movie version of the musical singing the songs. Some are singing better than others, but they're singing. Many are not only singing, they're dancing to ABBA's timeless tunes.

The Monday morning after the National Football League's Super Bowl, people hang around the water cooler to talk not only about the game but the commercials. I've noticed in the past few years that people actually talk less about the game and more about their favorite ads. They repeat lines from the commercials word for word with the same inflections.

After the 2008 Super Bowl, one commercial in particular captured the attention of viewers. A friend asked, "Did you see that Budweiser commercial about Hank?" He was referring to the Budweiser commercial titled "Rocky," accompanied by the theme music from the movie of the same name.

The ad begins with this anticipated announcement from the Clydesdale team's trainer: "The final horse for this year's hitch team is Thunder. Thunder." The cameras turn to a horse that didn't make it. A somewhat hopeful voice says, "Maybe next year, Hank." A Dalmatian looks at Hank and then takes on the role of self-appointed coach. The beat of the *Rocky* music provides a rhythm for Hank's training. There's no time to lose. We see Hank, with the ever-present encouragement of the Dalmatian, running along the path, pulling weights on a pulley from the barn, training in the rain, running slalom among the trees in the snow, and pulling a train. One year later, after all the intense training, the hitch team's trainer says, "Welcome aboard, Hank." Hank and his Dalmatian coach high five it with hoof and paw.

I heard this same story from two friends. They obviously watched and listened intently because when I saw the actual commercial, it was as if I'd already seen it.

> *What stories do you repeat? Generally, we repeat the stories that are supported by images painted in our minds with indelible ink. Tell your story so your potential followers not only hear and see your dream but genuinely experience it. When people experience your message, they will remember and tell your story repeatedly.*

I recall seeing furniture designer Dana Magnuson's chair, "Life Support," for the first time. Her chair stands six feet tall and consists of stainless steel and 2,190 syringes. Dana's creation reflects her story as an insulin-dependent diabetic. Her engaging display represents the yearly average number of insulin injections given to an individual afflicted with juvenile diabetes. My friend Dana has given herself nearly 24,000 injections of insulin to maintain her life.

What stories does your family tell when members gather for a baptism, wedding, funeral, birthday, or holiday celebration? Cultures are particularly alive with stories. Soulwise Conspirators need to think "family" when they seek support for their dreams. Whether it's a dream to clean up the environment or increase literacy among children globally, we come together like a family to think and feel and plan and act out our stories.

One of my family's favorite stories is the time our 82-year-old grandma stood on the cottage dock on a beautiful sunny afternoon, and without any fanfare, took off her bra and threw it into the lake. Seven teenage boys and girls dove into the water to snag what grandma affectionately called her "over-the-shoulder-older-boulder-holder." Adults on the shore appeared shell-shocked, except her daughter who yelled,

"You go, girl!" One of her grandsons snagged the rare prize and draped the wet treasure over his head like a bonnet.

Several years ago, the president of an energy company invited me to address the banquet guests at the company's annual meeting. He asked me to use my skill as a hurdler to communicate that the company was working hard to clear its "high hurdle" challenges in the year ahead. After we enjoyed a delicious main course of cordon bleu, I got up to speak and knew instantly that I was in trouble. The cordon bleu had accomplished what it does so well—produce gas. I hoped that when the time came for me to actually hurdle down the ballroom's center aisle, the gas would have disappeared. Alas, it did not.

I asked the crowd of about 1,500 to be as quiet as possible so I could focus my attention. As I stood 15 yards away from the first of three 42-inch hurdles, I weighed these two choices: abandon my plan to hurdle, or take my chances and go for it. I decided on the latter choice and started to run. The moment of truth came when I lifted my lead leg to clear the hurdle. I realized there was no turning back. While sailing perfectly over the hurdle, I simultaneously emitted an audible, elongated trail of gas. The vice-president of operations leapt to his feet and cheered, "Let's hear it for the old fart!" Twenty years later, after a speech I gave in New York City, the new president of that company introduced himself and said, "It's good to finally meet the company's legendary 'old fart.'" The story is still being repeated.

Frame your dream in images and stories, and you will be well on your way to declaring your dream effectively. Communicate with clarity. Keep your message plain. Keep it simple so that others will receive it, recall it, and repeat it. Also keep it precise, to which we now turn our attention.

Keep It Precise

Declare your dream by communicating precisely about the problem you've uncovered, the promise you're making to address that need, and the program you're putting in place to fulfill your promise.

Problem

Define and describe the problem or need you've identified with accurate images and stories, as well as accurate facts and figures. Your potential followers deserve to have the benefit of your diligent research and firsthand knowledge. Beyond being appreciative of others' time, it will give you the credibility that's so important in gaining their trust and earning their long-term commitment.

To ensure that your presentation helps your audience understand and appreciate the precise picture of your dream, be specific. For example, Sister Kathy Avery informed students at St. Clare of Montefalco Catholic School near Detroit that they were not allowed to swear. To make sure they understood, she read a list of the forbidden words and phrases during morning mass. Sister Kathy reported, "It got a little quiet in church." Her specificity got attention.

It takes only a touch of inaccuracy to cause a dramatic ripple effect. A new young monk arrived at a monastery. As with all new monks, he was assigned to help the other monks copy the old canons and laws of the church by hand. He noticed, however, that all of the monks were copying from copies, not the original manuscript. So the new monk went to the head abbot to question this, pointing out that if someone made even a small error in the first copy, it would never be picked up. In fact, that error would be continued in all of the subsequent copies.

The head monk replied, "We have been copying from the copies for centuries, but you make a good point, my son." So he descended into the dark caves underneath the monastery where the original manuscript lay archived in a locked vault that hadn't been opened for hundreds of years. Hours go by and nobody saw the old abbot. So, the young monk became worried and went down into the caves to look for him. He found the abbot banging his head against the wall and wailing, "We forgot the 'R.' We forgot the 'R.' We forgot the 'R.'" His forehead bloody and bruised, he was crying uncontrollably. The concerned young monk inquired of the old abbot, "What's wrong, Father?" In a choked voice, the old abbot replied, "The word is *celebRate!*"

Precision can be relatively easy if you're working with facts and figures. For example, on June 17, 2008, the Boston Celtics won the final game of the National Basketball Association finals with the Los Angeles Lakers by a score of 131-92. A laser beam travels at exactly 299,792,458 meters per second. At three minutes and four seconds after 2:00 a.m. on June 5, 2007, the time and date will be 02:03:04 05/06/07. It will only happen once—at that precise moment!

> *Be as specific as you can. If you intend to provide fresh water to people in Nigeria, find out how many people don't have access to fresh water in various regions of the country. No vague guesstimates.*

If you want to reduce the mortality rate of children in Mozambique, do your homework and offer as accurate an estimate as you can of the mortality rate now and the percentage by which you hope to reduce it. If you want to address global warming, determine specific temperatures at the present time and provide your best estimate of temperatures based on scientific data if no one takes appropriate action.

Your audience will respect your precise documentation of the need you've identified. I did my research on the state of hunger in Kibera slum in Nairobi and made the sad discovery that tens of thousands of young children went to bed hungry every night. I realized I couldn't feed all these children, but I could feed 24 children I had met personally and knew by name, half of whom ate only one meal a week.

Promise

Express the promise you're making with precise, solid, colorful broad strokes. Promise only what you can reasonably achieve—no more, no less. Resist the temptation many humanitarians have to inflate their promises or offer vague suggestions that rarely secure support, such as the following statement:

Over the years, I have engaged in considerable deep thought about (among other things) our place in the universe, ancient civilizations, human migrations, international conflicts, local and world economics, ozone depletion, the human genome, cloning, pollution, racism, local and world politics, population growth, extinctions, natural disasters, the environment, health care, the Internet, human relations, the space-time continuum and other aspects of relativity, and other factors that affect mankind's struggle to exist.

After all of that deep thought, I have arrived at this conclusion: When all is said and done, in spite of or because of what we may or may not do or think, it is just as likely as not that, for better or for worse, everything will turn out one way or another, sooner or later.

Say what?

The eight Millennium Development Goals (MDGs) provide an excellent model for making promises. They range from halving extreme poverty to providing universal primary education, all by the target date of 2015. The MDGs form a blueprint agreed to by all the world's countries and all the world's leading development institutions. They have galvanized unprecedented efforts to meet the needs of the world's poorest.

These goals are to:

1. Eradicate extreme poverty and hunger
2. Achieve universal primary education
3. Promote gender equality and empower women
4. Reduce child mortality
5. Improve maternal health
6. Combat HIV/AIDS, malaria and other diseases
7. Ensure environmental sustainability
8. Develop a global partnership for development

As the MDGs model, carefully choose the words that best convey and zero in on your big promise, especially the key words that lift up its essence. You also need to frame your smaller promise within the larger context in the same way.

Soulwise Conspirators offer precise promises to their target audience like Rotary International's PolioPlus program that promises to "eradicate polio." The Juvenile Diabetes Research Foundation promises "to find a cure for diabetes and its complications through the support of research." The Pew Charitable Trusts describes its promise in this way: "To improve public policy, inform the public and stimulate civic life."

Here's my promise statement:

In the beginning, Kibera Kids Kitchen would feed 24 children by name, ages two to ten, one balanced, fortified, and protein-enhanced meal a day, seven days a week for nine months starting July 1, 2006.

Be precise in articulating your problem, your promise, and your program.

Program

Be precise in telling your audience about the program you've thought out to address the problem you've uncovered and the promise you're making to alleviate the problem. The specifics of the program you've developed to fulfill your promise will assure potential followers that you've drafted a responsible plan of action to achieve your purpose.

Most people are motivated by an inspiring vision of a preferred future. Increase their interest by giving them the major steps you expect to take to get the job done. It's imperative that people clearly understand your program. A precise expression of your program will prevent costly confusion and misunderstanding that can slow the process toward your vision.

Let me illustrate the precise information you need to share about your program to accomplish your dream by using Kibera Kids Kitchen, my feeding program in the slum. Indicate…

- What Soulwise Conspirators plan to do: Kibera Kids Kitchen will identify and feed 24 children in Kibera slum, Nairobi, Kenya.
- Which Soulwise Conspirators will do it: Pastors, members, and friends of Exodus Church in Kibera slum will prepare and deliver the daily meal for the children ages 2 to 10. Members and friends of New Day Church-On-The-Hill in Grand Rapids, Michigan will provide financial and prayer support, as will Dr. Johnson, who will also visit the site regularly.
- How Soulwise Conspirators will do it: Pastors will oversee, and members and friends of Exodus Church will coordinate serving the meals to the children.
- When and where Soulwise Conspirators will do it. Kibera Kids Kitchen will serve the children every morning at 8:00 a.m. at the church.
- What resources Soulwise Conspirators will need. Kibera Kids Kitchen will raise $200.00 a month for operating expenses.

Communicate with clarity about the problem you've uncovered, the promise you are making to address that need, and the program you are putting in place to fulfill your promise.

Keep it plain. Keep it simple. Keep it precise. And keep it concise.

Keep It Concise

A husband perusing the paper saw a study that reported women use more words than men. Excited to prove to his wife his long-held contention that women in general and his wife in particular talked too much, he showed her the study results. "Men use about 15,000 words per day," he pointed out, "but women use 30,000." His wife responded, "That's because we have to repeat everything we say." Her husband said, "What?"

A good speech or presentation generally has three concise parts: the introduction, which tells the audience what you're going to tell them; the body, in which you tell them what you want to tell them; and the conclusion, in which you tell them what you told them. Soulwise Conspirators need to be concise when inspiring others to join with them in their efforts to change the world. Here are my recommendations in a nutshell: begin, be brief, be gone.

Begin

Get straight to the point. Take the single most important point you want your audience to remember and state it right at the beginning of your presentation. Your beginning represents your headline, such as Rotary International's PolioPlus program goal to "eradicate polio."

Be Brief

Craft a concise presentation to communicate your dream and win support for it.

Publisher Prentice-Hall invited communication coach Richard Greene, called by *The Sunday Times* of London "The Master of Charisma," to write a book about the 20 greatest speeches of the 20th century. The speeches had to "shake the world." The result was *Words that Shook the World: 100 Hundred Years of Unforgettable Speeches and Events.* Green wrote that "All great speakers have a lasered, compelling message, not a bunch of facts or random points that they throw around like confetti."

Great presentations follow the "less is more" principle. Consider the number of words in the following documents:

- Pythagorean theorem: 24 words
- The Lord's Prayer: 66 words
- The 10 Commandments: 179 words
- The Gettysburg address: 286 words
- U.S. Declaration of Independence: 1,300 words
- U.S. Constitution: 4,440 words
- U.S. Government regulations on the sale of cabbage: 26,911

Here's a brief, content-rich invitation: "Walk for Water at Riverside

Park, New York City, on March 22, 2008, to celebrate United Nations World Water Day, a day to remember that 2.6 billion people worldwide live without proper sanitation facilities, and most of them are children dying of preventable diseases."

Choose the appropriate number of words to convey your message.

Be Gone

Begin. Be brief. Be gone.

As illustrated by this limerick, Soulwise Conspirators need to "be gone" so that their dream can live.

> There once was a couple distinct
> Who failed at being succinct.
> Long-winded and dry
> They made a valiant try
> But now their dream is extinct.
> *Philip E. Johnson*

CONNECT WITH CONFIDENCE

A professor stood before his class of 20 senior organic biology students about to hand out the final exam. "I want to say it's been a pleasure teaching you this semester. I know you've all worked extremely hard and many of you are off to medical school after the summer. So that no one gets their grade point average messed up because of celebrating a bit too much this week, anyone who would like to opt out of the final exam today will receive a 'B' for the course."

The classroom rang with rejoicing as students got up, passed by the professor to thank him, and signed out on his offer. As the last taker left the room, the professor looked out over the handful of remaining students and asked, "Anyone else? This is your last chance." One final student rose and took the offer. The professor closed the door and took attendance of the students remaining. "I'm glad to see you believe in yourselves. You all have an 'A' for the course!"

To effectively declare your dream, it's essential for you to connect with potential followers with confidence. You need to believe in yourself, live in synch with your dream, and believe that others will believe in your dream. Let's first consider the importance of believing in yourself.

Believe in Yourself

Believe in yourself because the success of your dream depends to a large extent on whether people perceive that you believe in yourself.

"You have to believe you are great. You have to have an air about you," said NFL quarterback Brett Favre. "Every time I step on that field, I want to prove I am the best player in the league. I want it more than anybody." Hall of Fame college football coach Joe Paterno encouraged his players by saying, "Act like you expect to get into the end zone."

> *Confidence lies at the heart of civilization.*
> *Everything about an economy, a society, an*
> *organization, or a team depends on it because every*
> *step taken and every investment made is based on*
> *whether we have confidence in*
> *others and ourselves.*

Harvard Business School professor Rosabeth Moss Kanter insightfully defined confidence as "the sweet spot between arrogance and despair." Arrogance, she explained, involves the failure to see any flaws, and despair results from the failure to acknowledge any strengths. In light of this definition, she contended that "the secret to winning is to try not to lose twice in a row. Confidence heads off losing streaks because it provides resilience to bounce back from defeat to victory."[85]

To be successful, foster confidence and humility. You may possess all the self-confidence in the world, but remember you're still human—so be careful what you think you can do. Don't overestimate your capacity like the fictitious Cyrano de Bergerac did when he declared, "I have decided to be excellent in all things."

Let your past successes remind you to believe in yourself. When I coach athletes and athletic teams in mental and attitudinal preparation, I start their training by asking them to identify their successful past performances. I encourage them to record their experiences on small cards and put the cards in a "memory jar," so that when their training is particularly challenging, they can retrieve the cards and recall how it felt to do well. Remembering positive successful experiences helps them recall what made them successful before. It also provides a foundation on which to build their self-confidence for immediate and future challenges.

Others often play a big role in boosting self-confidence, especially members of our family, teachers and coaches, and community leaders such as clergy. In particular, parents can influence the development of their children's self-confidence. I was blessed with a marvelous mother who told me repeatedly, "I believe in you. You can do anything you put your mind to." She would mail me "accomplishment cards" to affirm her belief in me when I accomplished something significant, and occasionally "just because, just because I love you."

Sometimes certain people will give you what I call negative encouragement. When I was a junior in high school, I had a teacher who was very skilled at this form of demotivation. For my personality, however, instead of feeling despondent or disheartened, I felt challenged by his demeaning judgments. Maybe because he was a vegetarian, his endearing name for me was "Meathead." He indicated that I probably didn't have the capacity to put a complete sentence together. Seizing every opportunity to reinforce his opinions, he made it clear I wouldn't graduate from high school and that college was out of the question.

His negative encouragement, however, strengthened my resolve. I did thank him for his help at the reception following our high school graduation. When I graduated with my bachelor's degree majoring in Greek and psychology, I sent him a copy of my diploma. Three years later, I sent him a copy of my master's degree diploma in communication and theology. And 10 years later, I sent him a copy of my doctoral degree diploma in leadership and liturgical theology.

When my first book was published, I sent him a complimentary copy. I did the same for my next four books. By the time my sixth book, *Time-Out! Restoring Your Passion for Life, Love and Work*, was released, I thought it was payback time. So I sent a copy of the new book with an invoice. To my astonishment, he sent me a kind congratulatory note and a check, and ordered 12 copies. I can hardly wait to send him a copy of *Soulwise: How to Create a Conspiracy of Hope, Health and Harmony.*

> *When you believe in yourself, you establish a firm foundation on which to build a life of significance, adventure, and surprise.*

Live in Synch with Your Dream

When you've found your dream, live in synch with it every day in every way. Consider belief in your dream as an extension of your belief in yourself. Present yourself and your dream as one, as synonymous. As Mahatma Gandhi counseled, "You must be the change you wish to see in the world."

Live in synch with your dream because even minimal inconsistency can undermine and negate the good you may do. Behavior inconsistent with your vision will stick out like a sore thumb. Don't be like a woman I saw a few months ago who was smoking while driving a van for "Visiting Physicians."

I conducted a seminar for 30 young insurance salespeople who were unsuccessful selling long-term care insurance. Their answer to my initial question of the day gave me the key reason why they couldn't present and sell this product. I asked how many of them personally had a long-term care insurance policy. Not one had a policy, even though they thought it should be part of everyone's basic financial portfolio.

The young can teach us about believing in our dreams. Emily has a dream and she definitely believes in it. She put a flyer with this message in our newspaper box: "SCARVES FOR YOU! Hi, My name is Emily. I am 9 years old and I love to knit! Could I knit a scarf for you? If you choose to buy your own yarn, I could knit the scarf for you, and would charge you just for the labor. If you are interested or need more information, please call me at 123-4567. Thank You."

> *Soulwise Conspirators believe fervently in their dreams. They're the designated cheerleaders who muster courage and declare their dreams confidently like world champions of change.*

Whether it's a dream to lose weight or a dream to eliminate poverty, it takes courage to declare your dream publicly. Who can forget the image of a Chinese university student defiantly facing off a tank in Tiananmen Square on June 4, 1989? Declaring your dream publicly takes so much courage in part because it invites others to hold you accountable as you pursue your dream.

As Soulwise Conspirators, we're called to live a vision that some may view as a voice of protest. Whenever we take on the responsibility of changing the status quo, we run the risk of offending those who've worked so hard to preserve it. Civil rights leader Dr. Martin Luther King Jr. knew only too well about the consequences of living his vision—even the possibility of assassination.

Like Christopher Columbus, the Italian navigator who in 1492 launched four voyages to discover the New World, Soulwise Conspirators refuse to cling to the shoreline for safety and launch their dreams into the deep. George and Ira Gershwin reminded us in their 1937 musical, *Shall We Dance*, that everyone laughed at Christopher Columbus when he said the world was round.

Believe in and take responsibility for your dream. I personally believe in my dream to transform Kibera slum, and I've taken the risk to publicly declare my vision of KaraKibera, a community radically transformed for a future of promise. In addition, I believe in and take responsibility for the success of this book, *Soulwise: How to Create a Conspiracy of Hope, Health and Harmony*.

Believe in yourself, live in synch with your dream, and then you are ready to believe others will believe in your dream.

Believe Others Will Believe

When Ben Franklin first proposed his idea of streetlights to the Philadelphia City Council, the idea was voted down as ludicrous. Rather than being discouraged, he decided to install a lantern on the street near his house. Others liked walking in the warm glow by his home and decided to place lanterns close to their homes as well. Before long, the streets of Philadelphia were lit with Franklin's idea.

Believe in yourself. Live in synch with your dream and believe others will believe in you and your dream. I'm writing *Soulwise* believing that readers will recognize the dangers the global family faces and be inspired to perform CPR with compassion so humanity will survive and thrive.

To accomplish this, Soulwise Conspirators adopt the mindset and spirit of social entrepreneurs, who are society's change agents. They comprise the pioneers who innovate to benefit humanity. They combine the heart of business with the heart of the community through the creativity of individuals working together. They are what Bob Danzig, former

CEO of Hearst Newspapers, called "destiny architects."

Jeff Skoll believed in his dream. In 1999, he established the Skoll Foundation to pursue his vision of a world where all people, regardless of geography, background, or economic status, could enjoy and employ the full range of their talents and abilities. Skoll, who was the first president of eBay, believes that strategic investments in the right people can lead to lasting social change. He is using his business acumen to support his foundation's mission to advance systemic change to benefit communities around the world by investing in, connecting and celebrating social entrepreneurs.

Human rights activist John Pendergrast, senior advisor to the International Crisis Group, and actor Don Cheadle believe in their dream. They collaborated on a book, *Not On Our Watch: The Mission to End Genocide in Darfur and Beyond,* describing what they learned by visiting the region. In it, they have offered recommendations on how to end the mass atrocities in Darfur.

"Social entrepreneurs are not content just to give a fish or teach how to fish. They will not rest until they have revolutionized the fishing industry," said Bill Drayton, CEO, chairman, and founder of Ashoka, a global nonprofit organization devoted to developing social entrepreneurship.

Teenager Zach Hunter is a 21st century abolitionist who wants to empower young people to believe in this mission: to abolish slavery and liberate the millions of men, women, and children forced to work uncompensated or indentured. Hunter first learned about slavery at age 12 from his mother, Penny Hunter. In response, he initiated a campaign, Loose Change to Loosen Chains, a student-run fundraiser to help free modern-day slaves. He has estimated that Americans have roughly $10 billion in loose change. In two weeks of fundraising at his high school, he raised $6,000. Zach has also written a book, *Be the Change,* which encourages kids to get involved, using lots of examples of what he calls "world-changers"—people who have made a difference.

I believe in myself. I live in synch with my dream. And I believe others will believe in my dream. It's already happening. Even before the publication of *Soulwise,* hundreds of people from all walks of life have committed themselves to my—now our—dream to breathe new life into the human family. The release of this how-to book for social entrepreneurs, together with speeches and seminars on The Soulwise Conspiracy, will expand our reach around the world.

Take in these leadership thoughts of sixth-century
philosopher Lao Tsu.

Go to the people
Live with them
Learn from them
Love them
Start with what they know
Build with what they have
But with the best leaders
When the work is done
The task accomplished
The people will say
'We have done this ourselves!'

CRACKLE WITH CONVICTION

Soulwise Conspirators communicate with clarity, connect with confidence, and crackle with conviction. These skills are essential to convince others to share your dream of leading the global family to sustained vitality.

"One who attempts to move people to thought or action must concern himself with their emotions," the Greek philosopher Aristotle believed. "If he touches only their minds, he is unlikely to move them to action or to a change of mind—the motivations of which lie deep in the realms of the passions."

If someone asked me to name a person who epitomizes "crackle with conviction," my immediate answer would be my friend Dr. Nido Qubein. He personifies the spirit of conviction—a word from the Latin *convincere*, which means to persuade with certainty born of argument or evidence for a course of action.

The son of a Lebanese mother and a Jordanian father, Nido came to the United States as an 18 year old with no contacts, little knowledge of English, and only $50 in his pocket. He mastered the language by learning 10 words each day using small note cards.

He worked hard so he could attend High Point University in North

Carolina, where now, as president of the institution, he inspires a dramatic renovation and revitalization program. "My first goal," he pointed out unapologetically, "was to raise $10 million in 60 days to get us started on what I deemed our most basic, desperate needs. We actually raised $20 million in 29 days and have since raised more than $50 million in one year. At this institution, we focus on the art of the possible."

Also chairman of an international consulting firm, Nido addresses more than 100 business and professional groups around the world each year. An entrepreneur, he has active interests in real estate, advertising, and banking. His foundation provides scholarships to 48 deserving young people each year. To the end of 2008, the Qubein Foundation has granted more than 600 scholarships worth over $3 million. He lives by William Barclay's mantra, "Always give without remembering; always receive without forgetting."

I've known Nido for more than 25 years. I got to know him personally as part of his IQ group, an invitation-only think tank dedicated to personal and professional transformation. Nido possesses a rich combination of an astute mind and a generous heart. A gifted, irresistible communicator, he fuses substance and style in his speeches and the 15 books he's written. He crackles with conviction in every fiber of his being.

This section will show Soulwise Conspirators how to crackle with conviction to:

- Ignite the apathetic,
- Incite the dead-to-the-world,
- Intoxicate the hopeless,
- Indict the skeptics, and
- Induce the pregnant.

When you can do these things, you can persuade just about anyone! First, let's consider how to ignite the apathetic.

Ignite the Apathetic

Soulwise Conspirators encounter apathy up close and personal. It comes with the territory. Apathy abounds today, and it's contagious. Apathy intensifies the challenge to ignite hearts and minds, to set them ablaze with your compassionate dream.

I'm familiar with this challenge because my life and leadership coaching business deals with apathy on a daily basis. I'm in the igniting business and have branded myself as "Dr. Phil Johnson, The FireStarter: Igniting People's Passion to Do the Impossible."

Remember that it only takes one spark to start a fire. Just one single spark at the right time and place can create a firestorm for your dream. Put passion in your presentation and watch sparks fly.

Ray Esquith, teacher at Hobart Elementary School in Los Angeles and author of *Teach Like Your Hair's on Fire*, lights a fire under his fifth graders. I observed Esquith direct his students, dubbed the "Hobart Shakespeareans," in a live performance of a Shakespearean play. "The key to classroom management," he said, "is to make the work so interesting and relevant that the ultimate punishment is the missing of the activity itself."

Ignite the apathetic like Sam Kenny, a 26-year-old comedian who happens to be a cashier at a D&W Food Center, a grocery store chain in Michigan. He offers the usual paper or plastic—plus a punch line. That's the redheaded bachelor's shtick. Kenny, who has an English degree, openly admits to his patron audience that "I'm insanely enthusiastic about groceries!" If you pay with a credit card, his line is "Can I ask you to sign the treaty right here? May the peace last a thousand years. And here's a copy to show to your people." If you take your receipt, Kenny might say, "Here's something to remember our time together." Or "Here's a short story for you that I wrote about groceries."

Some people summarily dismiss the apathetic. That's a mistake. In my experience, the apathetic are tremendous supporters once they escape their apathetic funk. "The only reason some people get lost in thought," said actor Paul Fox, "is because it's unfamiliar territory." When Soulwise Conspirators take the time to familiarize those who are apathetic with a need to address, even the apathetic respond with support.

For example, on an international flight to Africa, I met a man in his mid-50s who suffered from advanced apathy. "You do-gooders amaze me," he told me before we even got off the ground. "Why do you keep on disappointing yourselves?" he asked. I took out a photo of Nicodemus, an eight-year-old boy with HIV, and showed it to my new acquaintance. "That's why," I said. Three weeks later, when I returned home, I received a check in the mail from him with this message: "For Nicodemus. Let me know how he's doing."

Incite the Dead-to-the-World

In my backyard, I set a "live trap" to catch a raccoon that I suspected might be rabid.

A couple of days later, I looked out the window and saw a large ball of fur in the trap, but I couldn't tell if it was the raccoon. I went outside and approached the trap carefully. To my surprise, I'd snagged a possum, admittedly one of God's least attractive creations. Well, I half-snagged a possum. The trap's door remained open. I tried everything I could think of to get the possum out of the trap. Finally, I put on my gloves, picked up the trap at the closed end, and swung the trap like a discus. The possum didn't budge. He did what he's named to do—play possum. He might as well have been dead.

Soulwise Conspirators encounter people who, for a variety of reasons, play possum. Note the use of the word "play." One chooses to play possum, or appear dead. People deliberately choose to act in a dead role on life's stage. They want others to think they're dead, even though they're alive. In the 1987 movie, *The Princess Bride*, the Miracle Worker played by Billy Crystal asked if the subject brought to him is "mostly dead or completely dead." I know people who play dead with one eye still open so they don't miss anything.

Incite the dead-to-the-world by making some noise. The dead-to-the-world won't listen if you gently hint. Beat the drums. Sound the sirens. Ring the bells. Blast the trumpets. Rouse the dead-to-the-world with a stimulating speech. Let the power of love fill your words with passion. Speak so they wake up and remember what you said. Remember what Tim Sanders, Yahoo's leadership coach and former chief solutions officer, said, "The only reason to give a speech is to change the world."

> *Many people who are dead-to-the-world don't see the plight of the global family because they can't bear to acknowledge its pain. Encountering the seven inconvenient truths in Chapter 3 can be overwhelming. And if you're at a loss about how to deal with poverty and injustice and war and disease, then playing dead may seem like a realistic alternative. However, if everybody plays dead, then our civilization's as good as dead.*

I received my wakeup call to incite the dead-to-the-world when I contracted malaria and typhoid fever—and survived. Today, I have the privilege and responsibility to wake the dead and mobilize them to rescue the global family that's choking to death. I will do whatever it takes to fulfill my calling to rouse people from their state of sleepwalking.

You need courage to wake the dead-to-the-world. Some people and institutions don't wake up well, especially sleeping giants that possess lots of power and play possum. If you even nudge them, they'll claim that you're disturbing their sleep and tell you to get lost or worse. You have to *believe* you can wake them up. "Courage," observed Oscar Arias Sanchez, former president of Costa Rica who won the Nobel Prize in 1987 for developing a Central American peace plan, "... begins with one voice."

Intoxicate the Hopeless

You can understand why some people throw up their hands in frustration and shake their heads in disbelief and dismay. Sometimes life seems hopeless with one thing after another. As a dieter told her friend, "I've tried every diet under the sun. It's no use. Pass the Twinkies."

Under the constant unrelenting pressures of life, some people resign themselves to a hopeless future. They give up on what might have been a desire to get ahead and limit their lives to mere existence. Over time, they get hooked on hopelessness in every aspect of their lives. They count on hopelessness as their means of gaining the attention of others and ironically thrive on their hopeless status. Such people become disappointment-dependent and are satisfied to be losers in the human race.

Soulwise Conspirators treat those who feel hopeless with sensitivity. People who want to escape from the world usually don't have much interest in being fully alive, nor do they welcome the messengers of hope. But they do respond positively when others genuinely care about their hopelessness.

I feel hopeless about my lawn. I've tried many "guaranteed" products to get rid of the moles, but without success. When I saw the sign at a local nursery announcing a Mole Seminar, I made plans to attend. I thought that on a Saturday morning in June, maybe 15 or 20 mole-molested gardeners would show up.

When I arrived at the seminar, to my surprise I found 150 potential mole-busters with great expectations crowded into a small room. Chuck Meehan, the mole guru who conducted the seminar, didn't disappoint us. Like an evangelist, he gave us hope that we could eliminate moles with his foolproof strategies. "The best mole," he declared, "is a dead mole!" Chuck's enthusiasm gave us hope. Chuck would rev us up saying, "The best mole ..." and the crowd would shout out together with conviction, "is a dead mole!" We left his seminar with hope and his death-to-the-moles package. Best of all, his recommendations worked!

Like Chuck, intoxicate the hopeless with your message of hope and your dream for humanity.

Indict the Skeptics

An association of national newspaper reporters invited me to give a motivational speech at its annual conference. In preparation, I interviewed five reporters from across the country and shadowed another for 24 consecutive hours. One of my insights into their demanding profession revealed that their skepticism derives from interacting with people who don't always tell them the truth.

I recognized that my main challenge consisted of earning the trust of these skeptics. The fact that like a good reporter I had done my homework was a plus and signaled that I wanted to engage them. I also introduced a sense of play into my presentation by wearing a pair of deely-boppers on my head. Unfortunately, or fortunately, one of the red sparkly balls fell off and rolled precariously down the aisle next to a crusty old police reporter. He picked up the ball and handed it to me, wryly remarking, "Doctor, you just lost one of your balls." I quipped, "Don't you hate when that happens?" That incident broke the ice, opening up the energy for a successful speech. Trust lies at the very heart of indicting the skeptics.

No doubt all of us harbor a little bit of skepticism because, like the reporters, we've encountered people who have not told us the truth or people who've made promises they haven't kept. But discerning reality and making good decisions requires a healthy degree of skepticism. It's difficult to relate to someone who displays a bumper sticker that reads "I believe that for every drop of rain that falls, a flower grows. And a foundation leaks and a ball game gets rained out and a car rusts and..."

Soulwise Conspirators sometimes get derogatorily defined as bleeding-heart liberals who fall for every sad, tear jerker. But Conspirators don't need to overreact. Rather, they need to surprise skeptics by building trust so that genuine dialogue can result. Abraham Lincoln, after he took office as president of the United States, surprised his opponents with a stroke of genius and political magic by appointing them as his cabinet ministers.

Soulwise Conspirators run into people who've adopted skepticism as their standard operating procedure and try to monopolize the pessimism zone. In Barry Levinson's 1998 movie *Wag the Dog*, a scandal erupts less than two weeks before Election Day that threatens to cripple the United States president's bid for a second term. Before the incident can cause irreparable damage, a mysterious "fixer" is summoned to the White House. The ultimate spin doctor, Conrad Brean, played by Robert DeNiro, has the uncanny ability to manipulate politics, the press, and the American people. Anticipating the reaction of a frenzied press corps, Brean deftly deflects attention from the president by creating a bigger and better story—a war. With the help of Stanley Motss (Dustin Hoffman), a famed Hollywood producer, and his irreverent entourage, Brean assembles an unlikely crisis team that orchestrates a global conflict. Although fictional, the movie has historical overtones truer than many would care to admit. Skepticism of politicians from the local to the international level has increased dramatically in the last few years especially in the light of scandals of global proportions.

Soulwise Conspirators need to work openly with skeptics because we need each other to change the world. As journalist Sydney J. Harris stated, "A cynic is not merely one who reads bitter lessons from the past; he is one who is prematurely disappointed in the future." I'm facing skeptics even before the publication of this book. When I tell people what I'm writing about, some claim to my face that I'm wasting my time and that my efforts will have little or no impact on the world. "Keep dreaming, Johnson," they chide. Although I'm saddened by their skepticism, I appreciate that maybe comedian George Carlin was right when he observed, "Scratch any cynic, and you'll find a disappointed idealist."

So I press on, recalling the story of a little girl in a Sunday school class. The teacher asked the little girl to tell her about the picture she'd drawn. "It's God," she said confidently. The teacher then replied, "But nobody really knows what God looks like." The little girl responded, "They will now."

Induce the Expectant

When I was a newly ordained minister of 11 churches headquartered in the small town of St. Anthony in northern Newfoundland, a man in my congregation phoned late at night during a blizzard. He asked me to come immediately to take Marjorie, his wife and mother of 10 children, to the hospital to deliver her baby. I hopped on my snowmobile and traveled the nine miles to her home in Great Brehat, an outport community, and then started my return trip to the hospital in St. Anthony.

Unfortunately, on the way back, my engine cut out. I re-gapped the spark plugs but above the roar of the wind and blowing snow, I heard Marjorie moan as she lay under several quilts on the comitic, a sled drawn behind the snowmobile. I went over and lifted up the quilts. "Comin'! Comin'!" she cried out. "Catch him!" So I did. Marjorie was expectant and ready for delivery. All I did was catch "the little rat" as she affectionately called him, and then delivered mother and child to the hospital.

Unlike the skeptics considered in the previous section, the expectant comprise people pregnant with possibility, ready to give birth to their purpose, and open to seizing an opportunity to activate their compassionate vision. Soulwise Conspirators induce the expectant and gently help them bring their new visions to life.

> *Soulwise Conspirators include people of various ages—young people 18 to 35, seeking their place to serve in the world; mid-lifers, 36 to 59, examining how they can impact the future of humanity; and second-lifers, 60 and older, searching how to leave a lasting legacy.*

You'll find the 18-to-35 group ready to be induced. They're eager to take on life anywhere in the world a need calls out to be filled. They possess a global perspective that maintains we have a responsibility to take care of each other as members of the global family. These folks just need a hint at a direction they might travel, and they're on their way to a compassionate adventure.

They're not reluctant to get their hands dirty. Most often, they receive minimal financial rewards, but their lives are changed forever. You'll find them serving with the Peace Corps, Teach America, Rotary International Student Exchange, and a host of other civic or religious organizations that need their fresh insight and youthful enthusiasm.

People in mid-life, 36 to 59 years of age, are critically evaluating where they've been and examining how they can impact their own future and the future of our global family. For many at this age, mid-life crisis and mid-life opportunity combine to help them create a significant contribution to the world with their lives.

Tom and Lori Wheeler saw it that way when they accepted the challenge to help Rwanda continue its journey to peace and prosperity. Tom, a civil engineer, quit his job as public works director of Santa Margarita, California, to spend a year working for the city of Kigali. Lori, who has a background in teaching, and their two children, Hannah, 12, and Zack, 10, will be in Rwanda for at least a year. "We wanted to serve God and we wanted to be part of something big," explained Tom.

Second-lifers, 60 and older, are searching for a way to leave a lasting legacy. This is potentially the largest group to be induced. Millions of them who possess an invincible spirit already engage themselves as Soulwise Conspirators all over the world.

What will 78 million baby boomers do as they continue to work into traditional retirement age? That's the question the 2008 MetLife Foundation/Civic Ventures Encore Career Study conducted by Peter D. Hart Research Associates explored with more than 3,500 people between the ages of 44 and 70. The study estimates that between 5.3 and 8.4 million Americans have already launched encore careers: positions that combine income and personal meaning with social issues.

In this chapter, Declare Your Dream, you've considered how to communicate with clarity, connect with confidence, and crackle with conviction. Now you're ready to take a bold, giant leap in the conspiratorial process. The next and final chapter of Part IV, A Guide to Becoming a Soulwise Conspirator, will explore how to deliver your dream.

TAKE FIVE FOR REFLECTION

1. When you communicate, do you predominantly persuade, inform, or entertain?

2. What favorite story do you like to tell others, and why? How is this story a good model for storytelling in general?

3. Tell a story about how you came to believe in yourself.

4. How have you been able to touch the hearts *and* minds of people about your dream? Be specific.

5. Describe your audience of potential followers and determine in what ways they are pregnant with anticipation.

CHAPTER 13

DELIVER YOUR DREAM

This final chapter shows you how to make your dream for humanity come true. You're ready to move from imagination to reality to secure a better future for our global family.

To deliver your dream as a Soulwise Conspirator, you need to secure commitment, mobilize your mission, direct the flow, and maintain momentum.

SECURE COMMITMENT

Soulwise Conspirators know they can't deliver their dreams alone. They need others who are committed to making the dream come true. To secure commitment, strike while the iron's hot, ask for the order, welcome resistance, and seal the deal.

Strike While the Iron's Hot

When I was a kid, we spent our summers at our cottage on Notawasaga Bay in northern Ontario, Canada. Every Monday morning, we'd go to the horse stable to watch 6'2" Horseshoe Lou shoe his horses, Big Ben and Tess, who drew the ice wagon that delivered big blocks of ice for cottage iceboxes. The highlight of the visit was the moment when Lou, after waiting patiently for the shoe to get red hot, struck the molten shoe on the anvil, and then carefully dipped it in the pail of water with an unforgettable hissssssing sound.

Soulwise Conspirators follow the edict to strike while the iron's hot. When telling and selling their dream, they determine if their potential supporters are ready, willing, and able to commit to their dream.

Ready

Soulwise Conspirators are change agents. By definition, they're in the business of transformative, systemic change—not simply altering, adjusting, or fine-tuning the current system. Without systemic change, long-term success will falter.

These major change agents require a balanced combination of heart and mind with a reverence for all life. Michael Novak, in his book, *Ascent of the Mountain, Flight of the Dove,* noted that these change agents have undergone a "conversion to the standpoint of the sacred" and therefore see all life through sacred eyes.

Heart-ready and mind-ready themselves, Soulwise Conspirators are better prepared to assess the change-readiness of others. Conspirators need to present their dreams heart to heart, and mind to mind for them to genuinely take hold. When the heart is ready, the heart will hear. As Episcopalian priest Barbara Brown Taylor submitted, "What you long to hear is already in your heart ready to be spoken."

Substantial change always requires heart- and mind-readiness. Soulwise Conspirators assess the readiness of their audience and discern the best time and place to present their dreams. Although probably no perfect time exists to present their dreams, the context of their presentations remains paramount. Ice cream sells well on hot and sticky days on the National Mall in Washington. Street vendors in New York City always have umbrellas ready for sale when it rains.

While I was considering the timing of my proposal to the senate of Daystar University to establish the Daystar University Global Leadership Center, events in the country provided a golden opportunity. I responded to the apparent lack of leadership in Kenya after the December 27, 2007, elections. One of the main areas of violent conflict was Kibera slum, just three blocks from the University's downtown campus. So I intuitively presented my proposal when the senate could actually smell the burning tires in the slum.

Willing

One Sunday morning during my message at our church in Grand Rapids, I reported on my work with our sister congregation, Exodus Church, in Kibera Slum. Spontaneously, one of our members, Mark Carpenter, shouted, "Pastor Phil, I'm coming with you next summer!" Mark is obviously ready and willing.

Soulwise Conspirators check to see if members of their audience are ready and willing to dedicate their time, energy, and resources. Do they have the desire to say yes to your dream and move forward? Are they willing to walk the talk?

To my knowledge, the Senate at Daystar University has never approved a resolution on first reading. Like most boards, it carefully considers every nuance before it puts its stamp of approval on anything, especially if it involves financial implications.

However, the Senate unanimously approved the proposal to establish the Daystar University Global Leadership Center—obviously ready and willing to support what had now become *our* dream with staff, property, and financial support.

"A leader takes people where they want to go," reflected former U.S. First Lady Rosalynn Carter. "A great leader takes people where they don't necessarily want to go, but ought to be."

> *Soulwise Conspirators inspire people with a vision of a preferred future, a readiness of heart and mind to move forward, and a willingness to commit to breathing life into the global family.*

Able

Soulwise Conspirators check to see if members of their audience are ready, willing, and able to do what it takes to put their full weight behind the dream. Potential Conspirators must be capable of complementing their readiness and willingness with their talent, energy, and resources.

Are they able to make a responsible decision? New studies suggest that we're not as proficient at making decisions as we may think. Dan

Ariely, a behavioral economist on the faculty of the Massachusetts Institute of Technology, has studied the way people make economic decisions. In his book, *Predictably Irrational: The Hidden Forces that Shape Our Decisions*, Ariely contended that humans are predictably irrational. He revealed the "underlying logic of our illogic" so that readers will make better decisions about their time and money.[86]

Are potential supporters actually able to find and use the skills and resources they possess?

Soulwise Conspirators need to address this issue openly and realistically. It's noble to have a dream to change the world, but only the combined currency of the people, including their money, skills, expertise, and connections, will make the dream come true. The ability to actually perform closes the gap between readiness, willingness, and reality. I call it realistic optimism.

I believe it's morally wrong and irresponsible to persuade someone to do something he or she cannot possibly accomplish. Soulwise Conspirators need to be constructively doubtful when assessing a potential follower's ability to actually contribute, even if he or she may be ready and willing. I'm particularly careful in choosing people to help in the Kibera Kids Kitchen feeding program. It takes more than a willingness to go and serve.

I'm happy to report that Daystar University is not only ready and willing, but able. Under the visionary leadership of Dr. Godfrey Nguru, the spirited vice-chancellor of the university, and the solid commitment of the senate, faculty, staff, and students, Daystar is putting its resources into action.

Are your potential followers ready, willing, and able? If they are, ask for the order.

Ask for the Order

Henry Ford's neighbor, a life insurance executive, read in a Detroit newspaper that Ford had purchased a huge life insurance policy, so the neighbor went next door to find out why Ford bought his insurance from someone else. Ford's response? "You never asked."

> *Declare your dream with the sole purpose of getting the order. Be resolute in asking. Ask for the order to secure commitment to your dream. Otherwise, your dream will remain only a dream.*

Soulwise Conspirators must have a clear, compelling vision plus the capacity to convey their vision verbally. In a speech delivered to the Public Relations Society of America at the Cleveland Forum in Cleveland, Ohio, in 1997, communications expert James E. Lukaszewski said that in order to communicate dreams effectively, one must become "a verbal visionary in a world that moves at verbal speed." He said that the dominant force in decision-making is verbal power—talking.

In asking for the order, Soulwise Conspirators follow this ABCDE method: Ask for the order Boldly, Candidly, Directly, and Eagerly.

Boldly

I learned a valuable lesson about accountability from Rev. Dr. Norman Vincent Peale, senior minister at Marble Collegiate Church in New York City. In the early '80s, I took on the pastoral responsibilities of a growing church that needed to raise a significant amount of money. I phoned Peale, the positive-thinking wizard, and asked if he could provide some time-tested strategies. He told me bluntly that he was too busy to address my situation. I countered by telling him that I had read his book, *The Power of Positive Thinking*, and that I would follow his advice in Chapter 3 and call him every Tuesday at two o'clock until he agreed to see me. With that, he agreed to meet me at a pastor's retreat in Poughkeepsie, New York.

Gracious when we met, the best piece of advice Dr. Peale gave me was this: "Know what you want and ask for it." So I went home and followed his counsel. I called seven faithful persons with resources in my congregation and invited them to meet me for breakfast the following Tuesday morning. Boldly, I asked them to bring their checkbooks. We had a wonderful breakfast. All the guests brought their checkbooks and gave generously. As British Prime Minister Winston Churchill once remarked, "If you have an important point to make, don't try to be subtle or clever. Use a pile driver. Hit the point once. Then come back and hit it again. Then hit it a third time, a tremendous whack."

> *Soulwise Conspirators adopt the social entrepreneurial mindset and spirit—with no reason or room for timidity. Confidently, definitively, explicitly, and specifically ask for the order. Sales people know this reality: If you don't ask boldly, you don't eat!*

Candidly

I read an article in *The Grand Rapids Press* written by Tommy Brann, whose family owns and operates several restaurants in our area. The article recommended that we do more for people who are less fortunate than we are, and specifically, feed hungry children in Africa. I made an appointment to see Tommy and candidly shared my efforts to feed hungry children through Kibera Kids Kitchen. Tommy approached his family's foundation, which continues to enthusiastically and generously support the project.

I didn't have to persuade Tommy to contribute to my project. He was already committed.

He only needed me, the vehicle, to make his contribution. Be careful not to make a redundant request.

Candidly invite others to be part of your dream. Make your approach to potential followers open and sincere in expression, straightforward, unprejudiced, and impartial. Make it easy for them to seriously consider your dream and follow.

My dear friend Tom Stoyan, known as "Canada's Sales Coach," put "selling" your dream in perspective by saying, "The simple truth is we buy people, ideas and services in that order. And it's up to you to demonstrate the competence and compatibility your future clients are looking for." Present yourself as candidly as you can. You and your vision must be, and be perceived as, one.

Directly

Bob Lee, a faithful member of my congregation, dropped in to see me at my church office. He told me he wanted to make a contribution to the church, and asked me if there was anything in particular that the money could be put toward.

I asked Bob, "How much were you thinking of contributing?" Bob replied, "Five thousand." I continued, "We do need new musical instruments like drums for the contemporary service band. We estimate the investment to be $10,000." Without blinking an eye, Bob got out his checkbook and said, "Ten thousand it is." I wondered later what the result might have been if my estimate for the instruments had been higher.

I dealt directly with Bob because we had a trusting relationship. The fact that we both sincerely cared for each other and the work of our church made it possible to engage him in an honest and upfront way. I asked for the order directly: frankly, honestly, respectfully, and politely, with no dancing around the issues or beating around the bush.

Soulwise Conspirators don't just present their dreams. They reveal them. They show the needs, the action that must be taken with specific, measurable action steps, and express a sense of urgency to take action now. To outsiders, the approach may seem blunt and even aggressive, but with a trusting relationship as the foundation, it's an efficient and effective way to interact.

Eagerly

> Present your dream with the upbeat presence of a visionary missionary. Convey your vision as if it has already happened in your mind and heart. Make it known that, for you, it's not a matter of if, but how, your dream will be fulfilled. Ask for the order eagerly.

Psychologist William James summed up the confident attitude of Soulwise Conspirators with these words: "I will act as if what I do makes a difference." When your audience senses your resolute approach, they may feel like they're a part of the movement already. Enthusiasm, like laughter and confidence, is contagious.

Let me offer a word of caution. Sometimes Soulwise Conspirators come across as too eager, giving others the impression that they're imbalanced or desperate. Melodramatic presentations, while somewhat entertaining, usually don't result in long-term commitments.

Whenever you Ask Boldly, Candidly, Directly, and Eagerly, be prepared for people to express their resistance. The next section will enable you to openly welcome this resistance.

Welcome Resistance

Soulwise Conspirators welcome resistance because they know it indicates their potential followers are seriously considering the dream they're presenting and deciding their response to it. Resistance demonstrates a willingness to consider the possibility of commitment. Usually more positive than negative, it can spark meaningful conversations. In this section, we'll explore how to welcome resistance—how to expect it, embrace it, and enlist it.

Expect It

A couple of hunters hired an Alaskan bush pilot to drop them in a remote location then return in seven days to pick them up. At the appointed time, the pilot arrived and loaded the hunters and their gear in the plane.

"Wait a minute," said the first hunter. "What about our moose?" "Sorry," said the pilot. "We're at maximum weight already." "But our pilot last year loaded our moose and he had the same size plane as this one." "Really?" asked the pilot. "Well, I guess we could give it a try."

With that he strapped a moose carcass on each pontoon. They sputtered to the end of the lake to get the longest possible takeoff. He shoved the throttle forward; the plane began to move, and finally, it lifted off the lake, just skimming the trees. But the pilot was right. The plane was seriously overloaded and crashed just minutes into the flight. Both hunters were knocked unconscious and came to at about the same time. The first hunter looked around at the mess— moose meat and plane parts everywhere. "Where are we?" he asked his partner. His partner responded, "About fifty yards from where we crashed last year."

Like the Alaskan hunters who stubbornly stuck to their pattern of behavior no matter how wrong and in spite of the devastating consequences of their earlier behavior, we like to keep the same routines. To some degree, we're all creatures of habit. Doing what we've always done may appear on the surface to be safe, but in reality it may prove to be dangerous, life-threatening or even fatal.

Howard Gardner, in his book *Changing Minds,* wrote that seven factors could be at work in all cases of a change of mind: reason, research, resonance, redescriptions, resources, and rewards, real world events, and resistances.[87] We lose our capacity to change our minds as we get older because we develop strong views and perspectives that are resistant to change. Gardner pointed out that a mind change most likely comes about when the first six factors operate in consort and resistances remain relatively weak. Conversely, mind changing is unlikely to come about when resistances are strong and other factors don't point in one direction.

Whenever you endeavor to make a change, especially a major change, expect resistance. It comes with the territory so get used to it.

The Roman Catholic Church is experiencing liturgical resistance. In June 2006, Roman Catholic Bishops in the United States voted to change the wording of many of the prayers and blessings that Catholics have recited at daily Mass for more than 35 years. It's the latest volley in what many English-speaking Catholics have dubbed "the liturgy wars."

Two predictable responses have been noted: traditionalists who longed for an English version more faithful to the Latin in use before the Second Vatican Council in the 1960s welcomed the change, but many Catholics who had committed the current prayer book to heart and to memory and who take comfort in its more conversational cadences were upset.

Expect resistance to change. It lets you know you're on to something worth exploring and talking about.

Embrace It

On June 17, 2008, a Romanian village re-elected 57-year-old Mayor Neculai Ivascu, although he died of liver disease shortly before the election. Ivascu had been mayor for nearly 20 years. He won the election over his living opponent, Gheorghe Dobrescu, by a margin of

23 votes. One pro-Ivascu voter admitted, "I know he died, but I don't want to change."

Welcome the resistance to change by your potential supporters as a conversation starter. Studies show that people who complain at a store about its service or the quality of its merchandise are expressing a sincere desire to do business with that company. More businesses need to wake up to this reality. If customers didn't want to do business with a particular store or restaurant, they'd simply walk away and tell others about their bad experience. Complaining directly to the source may be, ironically, the ultimate expression of loyalty.

Rather than fight resistance, embrace it. If I worked for United Airlines, I'd try to find the person who wrote a note on a poster in their gate area at O'Hare Airport in Chicago. The poster asked, "Is loyalty to an airline worth it? Stretch out, relax and think it over." A passenger took the time to write, "Not this one."

Embrace people and their resistance to show them respect. If they see you taking their concerns seriously, they'll be more likely to take you seriously and perhaps support your dream. As a rule, pay attention to resistors because they're looking for someone to listen to their story. Then the conversation has begun. "Honest differences," observed Mahatma Gandhi, "are often a healthy sign of progress."

> *Embrace people's resistance as normal.*
> *Legitimize the act of resistance, not necessarily*
> *the content of the resistance. Connecting with others*
> *with respect opens up the possibility of dialogue.*
> *As poet T. S. Eliot wrote, "Humankind cannot*
> *bear very much reality."*

Risk that accompanies change is real. Living is risky; purposeful living is *really* risky. If your dream invites people to play in the deep end, be prepared for resistance that might indicate their fear of drowning. Openly welcome their concerns about your dream and its ramifications. People don't care how much you know until they know how much you care for them.

It takes courage to risk on purpose, so help others consider the risk, especially when inspiring long-term commitment. Risk is real even for Spiderman, who has to choose between superhuman powers or the earthly powers of Kirsten Dunst.

An important insight regarding change comes from Dr. Ronald A. Heifetz, director of the Leadership Education Project at the John F. Kennedy School of Government at Harvard University. A psychiatrist, professional cellist, and author of *Leadership without Easy Answers*, Heifetz submitted, "We don't fear change. We fear loss."

When I understand resistance from this point of view, I go beyond a fear of change to assess what loss someone may encounter with change. It's a valuable distinction, especially in my work with individuals and with organizations. When people strenuously resist change, I ask what they're afraid of losing and gain a much better appreciation of their concerns.

"At every crossing on the road that leads to the future," observed Belgian playwright and Nobel Prize-winning author Maurice Maeterlinck, "each progressive spirit is opposed by a thousand appointed to guard the past." John Arnold, executive director of Harvest Gleaners, knows how local food bank boards guard their turf, protecting it from his innovative program to expand the work of food banks. Arnold wisely listens to their leaders who maintain that the tradition of contributing cans and the benefit of participation must be preserved.

Enlist It

English writer Hilaire Belloc decided in 1906 to follow his passionate convictions and seek election as a member of Parliament. He knew that, as a Roman Catholic, he would have a struggle to overcome the voters' religious prejudices.

At his first campaign speech at Salford, he appeared on the rostrum with a rosary in his hand and made the following declaration: "I am a Catholic. As far as possible I go to Mass every day. As far as possible I kneel down and tell these beads every day. If you reject me on account of my religion, I shall thank God that he has spared me the indignity of being your representative." He was elected.

Belloc embraced the public's expected resistance and then effectively enlisted it to win the election. We often underestimate the breadth and power of resistance. Belloc was elected because he converted the voters' resistance into commitment.

Psychologists point out that we have three options when it comes to dealing with stress: endure it, escape it, or enlist it. Soulwise Conspirators choose to enlist resistance to engage people to commit to their dream. They agree with this analysis from Frances Hodgson Burnett: "At first people refuse to believe that a strange new thing can be done, and then they begin to hope it can be done, then they see it can be done, then it is done and all the world wonders why it was not done centuries ago."[88]

I believe resistance can be enlisted because of my own experience of resisting and then committing to God's call to transform Kibera Slum. I wasn't happy with God's choice, and I used every opportunity to share my strong feelings with the Creator. Perhaps the divine muses got the wrong apartment at the university where I was staying. Didn't God know I had personal and professional responsibilities at home?

Late one afternoon, I stood in the middle of a muddy street in the pouring rain and shouted angrily at God, "Why did you have to choose me?" I waited but I didn't hear God answer. And then, without warning or fanfare, like the prophet Nehemiah in the Old Testament, I accepted the dream I'd been given. My resistance to lead the movement to transform Kibera was miraculously converted into commitment

Some people laugh at my commitment to transform a slum. I sometimes wonder what God has gotten me into. But I press on, hoping that someday I may be able to convert those who declare "that's impossible!" into committed supporters.

We've addressed how to strike while the iron's hot, ask for the order, and welcome resistance. We're almost there. What's remaining? To seal the deal. It's time to close the sale.

Seal the Deal

To move forward with your dream, you must seal the deal—inspire your potential followers to commit themselves wholeheartedly to your dream and become co-conspirators.

Some may hear about your dream and sign up immediately. Others may take more time to consider various aspects and implications of your dream before they pledge their commitment. Whether commitment comes swiftly or slowly, the process of getting people to say yes involves moving them through three distinct transitions: from attention to intention, from intention to resolution, and from resolution to action. Let's consider the first transition, moving potential followers from attention to intention.

From Attention to Intention
By now, you probably have your potential followers' attention. But it's a good thing to check and see if you still have their *undivided* attention. Getting attention may be the initial phase of the commitment process but it doesn't guarantee action. Here's an example. A few months ago in a large American city, a car hit an 80-year-old man on a busy street. Video cameras recorded the crowd's attention to the accident plus their unwillingness to leave the curb to help the victim.

My wife, Melody, got my attention one morning at breakfast when she said, "Don't die!" I asked her what prompted her statement and she responded, "Have you seen the basement? If you die, I'll have to deal with all your valuable stuff you've been collecting over the years." Melody got my attention—and subsequently my intention to clean the basement.

As we all know, intentions are philosophically slippery. Sometimes I'm guilty of what psychologists call "structured procrastination." I gave no indication of when I would tackle the basement. I only promised to get to it sometime. Quite frankly, cleaning the basement wasn't high on my priority list.

Several months ago, I saw on television California wildfires engulf a home and reduce it to a heap of smoldering ashes in a matter of minutes. That frightening scene certainly got my attention—and my intention to prepare for a disaster.

From Intention to Resolution
The transition from intention to resolution represents a significant shift. Proverbial wisdom warns us about intentions:
- If wishes were horses then beggars would ride.
- The road to hell is paved with good intentions.
- If we were paid for our good intentions, we'd all be millionaires.

To *resolve* means to make a firm decision to follow a particular course of action with determination. A resolution formalizes intentions. How did I formalize my intention to deal with my stuff in the basement? By telling Melody that I would clean the basement the next Saturday morning at nine o'clock. By stating my resolution publicly, I expressed my willingness to be accountable to her and to myself.

Soulwise Conspirators invite people to formalize their intentions by persuading them to make a resolution to help a dream come true in specific, measurable ways. Conspirators recognize that unless people make this important mental and emotional shift, their commitment will be, at best, tentative and produce mediocre results.

After seeing the California wildfires destroy a house, I honestly intended to get ready for a disaster, but I did not resolve to actually make preparations. About a month later, however, this scene got my attention: homes were being flooded in the Midwest United States. That day, I resolved to put together the "disaster duffel" in case of emergency. (Occasionally we need reminders.)

From Resolution to Action

I actually cleaned the basement on that Saturday morning, an action that surprised even me. And my disaster duffel lies ready for an emergency. Apparently, I may be part of a small percentage of people who follow their resolutions with action. I've been in hundreds of meetings in which people resolve to perform certain tasks, yet the assignments never get done.

Fitness magazine reports that 80% of people don't keep their New Year's resolutions. Research shows that 4 in 10 of us make resolutions—some business-related, most individual. Three quarters of the resolutions last a week, two-thirds of the remaining last a full month, and a little less than half (46%) of the rest last until the middle of the year or beyond. In other words, only 20% of those who say they'll make an adjustment of some kind actually follow through.

> *Soulwise Conspirators must make this critical leap from resolution to action and ensure that their supporters do also. Visionary missionaries need to press people to act so their collective dreams become reality.*

Let's take a look at examples of making the transition from attention to intention to resolution to action.

Attention →	Intention →	Resolution →	Action →
State of the basement	clean basement	clean Saturday	cleaned
California wildfires	prepare for disaster	put on calendar	get materials
Fall in love	marry	get engaged	have wedding
Read about death tax	prepare a will	meet attorney	sign document
Meet hungry children	feed children	provide food	write a check
Overweight/ out of breath	get in shape	diet & exercise	hire a coach
Ice cap melting	reduce CO_2	research hybrids	buy hybrid
Widening rich/poor gap	eliminate poverty	micro-finance	lend money

MOBILIZE YOUR MISSION

You have a dream to bring hope to the world. You're committed to doing whatever it takes to make your dream come true. Now it's time to deliver your dream.

Jennifer Granholm, governor of Michigan, passionately addressed the citizens of her state this way: "I urge you to be bold. Life isn't changed from the balcony. Get onto the floor and dance, dance, dance."

Almost everybody has a dream to make things better in the world. But only a few actually mobilize their mission. Until you thoughtfully and convincingly declare and deliver your dream, it's as if the dream never existed. So come down from the balcony, put on your dancing shoes, find some partners, get out on the floor, and dance!

Come Down from the Balcony

To mobilize means to get things moving purposefully. Some people are immobilized on life's balcony. They see the action below, including the misfortunes of members of the global family, but are reluctant to move

315

from their surveillance position. They feel sorry in a sort of condescending compassionate way for the people struggling on the floor and praise the work of those dancing to help those in desperate need. You can hear them cheer the good deeds of the "floor people" feeding the hungry, housing the homeless, and comforting the dispossessed.

Yet the "balcony people" are isolated from the real action. They're spectators of the global games. They watch, like birds lined up on a wire with birds that share similar views, and survey all. Birds of a feather do flock together and rarely stray. They experience the world's agony and ecstasy from a safe distance, and like reporters, describe world events from their perspective on high and offer their commentary. They may speak with assumed authority on what is, what should have been, and what probably will be.

The "balcony people" encourage but rarely empower. They choose to observe rather than dance. They are the dance critics who dissect the movement but lack the courage to take a single step.

I know how it feels to be stuck in the balcony. When I was a freshman in high school, I played in a Friday night basketball game and then went to a dance that followed. I did well in the game but had considerable difficulty summoning the courage to get on the same floor and dance. I went up to the gymnasium balcony and watched others enjoying themselves on the floor, but I couldn't bring myself to ask Penny, a beautiful girl in my English class, to dance. I watched for what seemed forever. Then, to my surprise and delight, Penny tapped me on the shoulder and asked me if I'd like to dance.

Soulwise Conspirators often play the role of a "tapper-on-the-shoulder," inviting others to join in the dance to breathe life into the global family. One of these "tappers" is Lester Brown, president of the Earth Policy Institute. *The Washington Post* called Brown "one of the world's most influential thinkers." His book, *PLAN B 3.0: Mobilizing to Save Civilization*, invites world citizens to come down from the balcony and adopt his comprehensive plan for reversing the trends that are undermining civilization. His plan includes these four overarching goals: climate stabilization, population stabilization, poverty eradication, and restoration of the earth's ecosystems. Brown challenges his readers to be the generation that mobilizes to save civilization.

> *Although Soulwise Conspirators may occasionally start in the balcony, they see what's happening down below and quickly come down and become the "floor people." They know instinctively that if they want their dreams to come true, they must come down from the balcony.*

In the 2004 movie *Shall We Dance,* John Clark, a stuck-in-his-job attorney played by Richard Gere passes a dance studio on his way home from work on the commuter train. Day after day, he sees the sign. But one day, he decides to get off the train and check out the studio, where he meets Paulina, a ballroom dance instructor played by Jennifer Lopez. Before he knows it, he's on the floor and becomes a decent dancer. Committing to action has its bonuses.

Before Christmas, my wife asked me if I wanted anything special, and I answered, "I'd like a pair of tap shoes." I explained that a couple of nights before, I'd had a dream where I was tap dancing on the marble in Vatican Square before the pope. She acknowledged my dream by saying, "Right. You were dreaming." On Christmas morning, our family gathered around the tree, and I was handed a parcel the size of a shoebox addressed to me from Santa. I thought it would be slippers, which were also on my list. To my surprise, the box contained a pair of Capezio black patent leather tap shoes with jingle taps and a voucher for 10 lessons.

Come down from the balcony, and...

Put on Your Dancing Shoes

What kind of "dancing" shoes will you don to fulfill your dream? Perhaps, like me, your footwear indicates where you've been and what you've done in your life. Chances are that a quick listing of the footwear you've worn (or are still wearing) will also give you clues about where you might be going. Here's my short list, along with a brief description of the purpose/use of my adult footwear.

Footwear	Purpose/Use
• Paratrooper boots	Canadian military officer training
• Ski-Doo boots	Traveling as a pastor in northern Newfoundland
• Rockport Chukkas	Guiding tours in Israel, Egypt, and Jordan
• Nike track shoes	Running sprint and hurdle track events
• Wolverine work boots	Building a cottage & chain sawing (Husqvarna)
• Bjorn red shoes	Promoting my business as The FireStarter
• Kenneth Cole shoes	Attending formal occasions
• Cole Haan burgundy loafers	Going anywhere anytime shoes

Consider matching the main thrust of your dreams with the appropriate "dance" footwear. I matched my dream—Kibera Kids Kitchen, my feeding program for children in Kenya—with colorful sneakers. If you're going to stomp out poverty, you might want to wear combat boots.

Here are seven more possible pairings to help you identify your best footwear match.

• Prevent youth drug abuse	running shoes
• Construct a medical clinic	work boots
• Care for the homeless	slippers
• Fight the spread of AIDS	soccer cleats
• Conserve the environment	ballet point shoes
• Resolve cultural conflict	moccasins
• Lead a parade for justice	marching boots

It's hard for me to describe how exhilarated I felt when I put on my brand new tap shoes. Although the shoes had to be broken in, just standing in them brought a smile to my face. I danced around our Christmas tree with sheer joy to the cheers and jeers of my family. That day I gave birth to my "new shoe dance," which has become a tradition in our family when anyone buys a new pair of shoes.

Just putting on my dancing shoes brought me closer to my goal of tap dancing. Swiss physician and author Dr. Paul Tournier summarized the transition that took place in my mind and heart this way: "There is an astonishing contrast between the heavy perplexity that inhibits before the adventure has begun and the excitement that grips us as soon as it begins. As soon as a person makes up his or her mind to take the plunge into adventure, they are aware of a new strength they did not think they had, which rescues them from all their perplexities."

At my first lesson, I discovered that tap dancing isn't as easy as I had imagined. I recognized that I had to close the big gap between dancing in my dream and dancing in reality. My tap teacher patiently encouraged me and 15 female novices to learn the steps, including the "shuffle ball change," the "shuffle hop step," and my favorite, the "shuffle off to Buffalo." Believe me, there was a whole lot of shuffling going on! Some steps, like the "shim sham shimmy," I never quite mastered. I found learning the steps hard but pleasurable work that demanded concentration, a keen sense of rhythm, and a willingness to make mistakes and try again.

> *"We're fools whether we dance or not," as the Japanese proverb states, "so we might as well dance."*

Come down from the balcony, put on your dancing shoes, and then...

Get Out on the Floor

Mobilize your mission by putting on your dancing shoes and getting out on the floor. No excuses. Once you've got the shoes on and have the steps mastered, take your dream to the floor. Or, as Caribbean Cruise Line encourages in its commercial, "Get out there."

At some point, if you're really serious about your dream to change the world, you'll have to fish or cut bait, or face the distinct possibility of becoming a "someday" person—"someday" I'll get on the floor. Or "someday" when things get settled, I'll get out there. Someday.

Tragically, phenomenal dreams that could save civilization and enhance life on earth lie piled up beside the dance floor because "someday" never came. As Jesuit priest and psychotherapist Anthony de Mello observed, "People who deliberate too long before they take a step may spend their lives on one leg."

I can appreciate why so many dreams remain beside the dance

floor. Putting on your dancing shoes is a small step compared to getting out on the floor, which is a giant leap that requires a refusal to put life on hold coupled with a willingness to live without a map. It takes tremendous courage to throw your hat over the hedge, as the British commonly say, because you don't know for sure what you might encounter on the other side. Nobody knows for sure. Nobody. That's what makes it exciting. Rather than being afraid of what's ahead, Soulwise Conspirators welcome the adventure with anticipation.

My opportunity to publicly get out on the floor and dance consisted of playing a leading role in *Singing in the Rain,* performed by our tap-dance class. None of my female classmates wanted the male role, so I got to dance the role made famous by legendary dancer Fred Astaire. I don't get anxious speaking before large audiences, but on opening night, I was operating outside my personal comfort zone. I felt anxious and vulnerable. But I knew my part, and after I settled my stomach butterflies into formation, I took a deep breath and got out on the dance floor. Oh what a liberating feeling!

You can wish upon a star all you want, but you'll still have to put on your dancing shoes and get out on the floor to put your dream in motion. Wishing is not acting! The peril of waiting presents the possibility of contracting an occasionally fatal disease: analysis paralysis.

"Words are so easy, action is so difficult," commented Adlai Stevenson, United States presidential candidate and former ambassador to the United Nations. "To proclaim one's beliefs, to profess one's convictions is one thing; to enact them, to face the hard ugly realities is quite another."

> *Singer Lee Ann Womack encouraged us by singing, "And when you get the choice to sit it out or dance, I hope you dance... I hope you dance." So don't miss the chance to dance. The music is playing and calling you to mobilize your mission.*

Dance Like Nobody's Watching

You've come a long way from your discovery of a need and how you imagined that need could be fulfilled. Take that first step knowing that without it, there can never be a second or third. Take that first small step and your dream can be fulfilled not just in your mind but also on the global dance floor.

"When you pray," advises my favorite African proverb, "move your feet."

Take that critical first step, and then dance like nobody's watching! Dance like race car driver Helio Castrovenes, who with his professional dance partner, Julianne Hough, won the 2007 *Dancing With the Stars* competition on ABC television. They danced with abandon, oblivious to the glare of bright stage lights and the eyes of millions of viewers glued to their television sets in rapt attention.

Once the production of *Singing in the Rain* got underway, I felt exhilarated being on stage with my colleagues. I forgot about the audience and experienced an uncanny freedom that comes from being intentionally unconscious to what anyone else thought.

To dance your dance and make your mark, you need to take the first step. What you do will have an effect far beyond what you can see and realize.

Meteorologist Edward Lorenz stumbled on chaos theory while studying models of weather patterns. Lorenz's discovery showed that even small changes in a system could have extensive and unexpected consequences. He presented his findings in 1972 in a paper titled "Predictability: Does the Flap of a Butterfly's Wings in Brazil Set Off a Tornado in Texas?" His work soon became known as the "butterfly effect." "When a butterfly flutters its wings in one part of the world," Lorenz discovered, "it can eventually cause a hurricane in another." When Soulwise Conspirators take even a small step to breathe life into one part of the global family, the effect may be felt by the whole of humanity.

> *Mother Teresa explained that she attended*
> *the needs of only one destitute person in*
> *Calcutta at a time. "I never look at the masses as my*
> *responsibility; I look at the individual. I can only love*
> *one person at a time just one, one, one.*
> *So you begin. I began. I picked up one person. Maybe*
> *if I didn't pick up that one person, I wouldn't have*
> *picked up forty-two thousand. The whole work is only*
> *a drop in the ocean. But if I didn't put the drop in, the*
> *ocean would be one drop less. The same goes for you,*
> *the same thing in your family, the same thing in your*
> *church, your community. Just begin one, one, one."*

I follow Mother Teresa's philosophy and theology, especially in my ministry in Kibera Slum. I focus on the needs of one person at a time, even though I'm often frustrated because the world has far too many "ones" to love and care for. There's only one of me. But I keep on dancing, knowing that my small steps will result in a musical of hope, health and harmony.

To deliver your dream, first mobilize your mission. Then direct the flow toward your vision.

DIRECT THE FLOW

To efficiently direct the flow of your mission, you've got to know where you're headed. To direct the flow, fast-forward to the future, fix your eyes on the prize, fixate on one thing at a time, flex your focus, and do first things first.

Fast-forward to the Future

Make the preferred future you've imagined the singular focus of your attention and take up permanent residence there. As a Soulwise Conspirator, you owe it yourself, your co-conspirators—as well as those you're serving—to spend most of your time in the future. Familiarize yourself with every dynamic dimension of life in the new world.

Superlative leaders I coach devote as much as 90% of their time and energy experiencing, thinking about, and planning for the future. They're obsessed with creating the future rather than merely responding to whatever is happening in the present. They instinctively entrust and delegate others to deal with the myriad of day-to-day concerns so they can be fully attentive to the big picture.

I have observed many otherwise responsible leaders who are unable to resist the strong seduction of the present. They end up consumed with putting out fires instead of increasing the creative temperature of their organizations to stoke the fires of their business.

By modeling an orientation to the future, you give a clear signal to the "missionaries" that the future is ultimately the only thing that matters. You'll encourage them to foster a future-focus climate in which they can take initiative and responsibility for their own journey on the way to the vision. You affirm for them that life is a journey, not a guided tour.

Acclaimed chef Steve Badt dreamed that one day he'd run his own restaurant. He fast-forwarded to the future and could taste ownership. Badt used to cook in trendy restaurants in Washington and New York City that got great reviews in *The New York Times* and *The Washington Post*. But then he had a change of heart. Instead of pursuing the dream where he might have become a TV personality, he quit. Badt fast-forwarded to a different view when his future wife gave him this ultimatum: the restaurant business or her. It was difficult thinking about having a family while working restaurant hours, so he had to come up with a way to merge his culinary experience with his desire to help people. In July 2001, he started a new mission—running a soup kitchen.

Fix Your Eyes on the Prize

Maintain a sharp focus on your future and never lose sight of it. This becomes the reference point for your perspective on matters in the future, as well as the past and the present. With your eyes fixed on the prize, you can concentrate on relevant, pertinent issues, block out the extraneous, and silence the noise of inevitable criticism. Like a hurdler in the blocks on the starting line, focus on the finish line and consider the hurdles as temporary challenges on the way.

Gary Zukav, in his book *Thoughts from the Seat of the Soul*, described the personal power you release when you fix your eyes on the prize. "Before it incarnates, each soul enters into a sacred contract with the universe to accomplish certain things. It enters into this commitment in the fullness of its being. Whatever the task that your soul has agreed to, all the experiences of your life serve to awaken within you the memory of that contract, and to prepare you to fulfill it."[89] Your investment in a single-minded focus will pay big dividends in the long run.

We seem to be losing the art and discipline of focusing, especially among the young.

A 2007 report by the National Endowment for the Arts found that 15 to 24 year olds spend an average of just seven minutes a day on voluntary reading. Two-thirds of all college freshmen indicated they almost never read a book or article outside their schoolwork. On the Internet, these students engage in a world of fragmented attention and immediate gratification that doesn't value, encourage, or reward focus. Moreover, national tests have found that the ability to read and write complex materials is withering, even among graduate students.

Beware of weapons of mass distraction that can range from internal negative thinking to subtle external stimuli.

Twenty-five years ago, I lost my focus while preaching about the intriguing encounter of Jesus with a Samaritan woman at a well (John 4:7-9). In my congregation, a gorgeous woman sat at the end of a pew next to the center aisle about half way down, so I could not avoid seeing her. Occasionally, she would cross her legs and gently bounce one leg on the other. On that Sunday morning, she crossed her legs and I tried not to look but it was virtually impossible not to admire God's exquisite creation. A battle ensued. Part of my mind said, "Look, appreciate the beauty of God's creation," and another part warned, "Look away. Don't look." "Look." "Don't look." "Look." "Don't look."

Unfortunately, I lost my focus and said, "And Jesus said to the woman at the well, 'What great legs you have!'" The congregation appreciated my 'Freudian slip" smiled and laughed. Most of the men cheered! After the service, a parishioner in her mid-eighties whispered in my ear, "I used to have great legs." Then she paused and added, "Sexy, too."

Fortunately for Chef Steve Badt and his patrons at the soup kitchen, he kept his eyes fixed on the prize. He knew that once you're on the street, it's hard to get back on your feet. "So my energy," he explained, "comes from the fact that if I can start these guys off with a beautiful nutritious meal, that will increase the odds that maybe they'll get housing, that maybe they'll get off drugs, that maybe they'll have a good day."

Fixate on One Thing at a Time

I once saw over a little store an extremely large sign in the shape of a donut. At the top of the donut in big letters were the words "RANDY'S DONUTS," and at the bottom of the donut, "AND LEGAL SERVICES." A much smaller sign in one of the store's windows informed customers that the businesses remain open 24 hours a day. I could imagine a Monday morning special that offered a dozen donuts and coffee with every last will and testament purchased. Aside from the interest that such an unlikely combination of two businesses engenders, the enterprise offers a reminder that it's best to do one thing at a time. Focus.

Discipline yourself and concentrate. Don't be seduced into multitasking—the attempt by human beings to operate like computers doing two or more things at the same time. We're simply not wired for multitasking. Neurologist Richard Restak said the brain works best "on a single task and for sustained rather than intermittent or alternating periods of time."[90]

Multitasking becomes dangerous when it morphs into standard operating procedure and can result in stress, mediocre work, and limited concentration. Multiple studies show that multitasking slows thinking. Because of the back-and-forth stress, a brain attempting to perform two tasks simultaneously will experience a substantial lag in information processing. In his book *Brain Rules: 12 Principles for Surviving and Thriving at Work, Home, and School*, molecular biologist John Medina applied brain science to the workplace, pointing out that the brain's attentional spotlight can focus on only one thing at a time.

Steve Badt fixates on one thing at a time; he is committed to achieving his mission. Badt oversees the menu at Miriam's Kitchen in Washington, D.C., which is located in the basement of a church a mile away from the White House. On an average morning, he coordinates a group of dedicated volunteers to prepare and serve more than 200 homeless people a six-course breakfast. He fixates on this one thing: treating his guests as he would paying customers.

Flex Your Focus

"A rattlesnake loose in the living room," observed essayist Lance Morrow, "tends to end all discussion of animal rights."

I live in Michigan and I can tell you that if you want to see the weather change, wait five minutes. Loose rattlesnakes, weather, and life in general bring constant changes, and as Soulwise Conspirators, you need to respond to those changes appropriately. From time to time you must flex your focus, or bend your attentional focus to match changing needs you identify.

Badt, for example, floats from one quadrant to another of his kitchen as he coordinates his volunteer staff to prepare and serve breakfast. He knows that his calling requires agility to move from preventing the eggs from being overcooked to listening to the needs of his guests. He plans his work, then works his plan, and is always prepared to alter his plan if necessary. Badt admits that what makes his job so interesting is that no two mornings are alike.

When you've got a resolute focus on the future, what do you do first?

Do First Things First

Look through the lens of compassion and fix your eyes on the prize, the future you've imagined. Your present context will help you discern what to do first to fulfill your dream. Do first things first, everything else second.

> "Whenever anything is being accomplished," observed Peter Drucker, the father of modern management theory, "it is being done... by a monomaniac with a mission." Soulwise Conspirators keep a maniacal focus on high potentials, which guides their decision about what to do first.

Analyze the context of the starting point of your mission by immersing yourself in its real life conditions, circumstances, and constraints. Because it may have been some time since your initial observations of the need and your subsequent dream, it's wise to update your knowledge about what's actually happening on the ground. In 2008, 2.1 million American youth went on mission trips to immerse themselves in the conditions of the world with its needs and opportunities. They saw for themselves the needs that otherwise may have gone unnoticed.

Let me illustrate by sharing my immersion in the African context to establish the Daystar University Global Leadership Center in Nairobi with the mission of inspiring servant leaders to transform Africa for a future of promise.

As part of my research, I studied The Worldwide Governance Indicators project reports, which show indicators for 212 countries and territories over the period 1996–2007 for these six dimensions of governance: voice and accountability, political stability and absence of violence, government effectiveness, regulatory quality, rule of law, and control of corruption.

I discovered a continent crying out for effective leaders. Over and over, I heard citizens express their deep desire for leaders who would deal openly, honestly, and creatively with the current state of affairs. They yearn for leaders who will address immediate issues, including regional instability, armed conflict, ethnic/tribal/religious clashes, indebtedness, hunger, poverty, diseases, and environmental degradation.

In early 2008, I traveled to Kenya to sharpen my perspective on a country recovering from the violence that erupted after the presidential and parliamentary elections in December 27, 2007. The violence, which appeared to be ethnically and politically based, was concentrated in Nyanza, Rift Valley, and Western provinces, as well as the slums in Nairobi. At least 1,000 people died as a result of the post-electoral civil unrest. More than 300,000 were internally displaced. Moreover, disruptions in public transportation services occurred as a result of political violence, strikes, or work stoppages.

The temperature on the continent continues to rise, especially in hot spots including Zimbabwe, the Democratic Republic of Congo, Sudan, Darfur, Rwanda, Somalia, and Ethiopia.

In the light of the articulated context of your mission, discern what action is critical. For the purpose of deciding what to do first, "critical" means essential for survival from danger or death, or essential for progress.

The answers to two interrelated questions will determine if an action you're considering is critical. First, is it imperative? (Is the action absolutely necessary for survival or progress?) Second, is it immediate? (Does it have to be done now?) Critical windows of opportunity are always narrow and accompanied by a sense of urgency.

In establishing The Daystar University Global Leadership Center, the critical action I took was to appoint an associate director and a lean and meaningful leadership team that models the tenets of the Center.

MAINTAIN MOMENTUM

Once you've got the ball rolling toward fulfilling your dream, maintain momentum. Take small steady steps, take a giant leap, keep on keeping on, and sustain your passion.

Take Small Steady Steps

Most of the time Soulwise Conspirators practice the discipline of taking small steady steps.

Like a turtle crossing a busy highway, the challenge becomes to keep on taking those seemingly inconsequential steps and dodging the obstacles. Robert Maurer's book, *One Small Step Can Change Your Life: The Kaizen Way*, affirmed this discipline, noting that *kaizen* is the Japanese technique of achieving great and lasting success through small, steady steps. Toyota, the Japanese car company, followed this principle. Its success started with small steps more than 30 years before it became a formidable competitor in the global marketplace.

Ram Charan, one of the world's most renowned management consultants and authors, used a baseball metaphor to illustrate this principle in *Profitable Growth Is Everyone's Business: 10 Tools You Can Use Monday Morning*. He pointed out that to sustain growth, corporations must hit singles and doubles rather than home runs.

The Plant for the Planet Project: Billion Tree Campaign sponsored by the United Nations Environment Program (UNEP) started with one small step by Nobel Prize Laureate Professor Wangari Maathai. She and Prince Albert II of Monaco are co-patrons of the campaign that invited individuals, community groups, businesses, and governments to help UNEP reach its goal of planting 1 billion trees in the year 2007.

Soulwise Conspirators benefit from maintaining a marathon attitude and spirit. Compassionate work can be unbelievably slow, but that's what people who are changing the world should expect. Pressing toward your dream requires embracing a marathoner's mindset from start to finish. For me, writing a book is like a marathon. I take on the mindset of a marathoner and write one page at a time.

Most of the time, Soulwise Conspirators need to take small steps toward their goal. From time to time, however, small steps alone won't get you to your destination when a giant leap is needed.

Take a Giant Leap

Occasionally, in delivering your dream, you may want to consider taking a giant leap to propel you toward your vision. Soulwise Conspirators sense when they have to take a giant leap. With Helen Keller, they believe that "Security is only a superstition. It does not exist in nature, nor do the children of humans as a whole experience it. Avoiding danger is no safer in the long run than outright exposure. Life is either a daring adventure or it is nothing."

> *Take a giant leap into the unknown to accelerate the movement toward your dream's fulfillment. To be sure, your leap needs to be well conceived and produce anticipated results worth the risk. Your investment of time, energy, money, and other resources must generate a significant return.*

Some people are risk-averse while others have a much greater risk tolerance. Proverbial wisdom says that fortune favors the bold. I agree. If you don't have to be bold about taking a risk, it's probably not a very big risk.

Thirty years ago, I observed the full range of risk tolerance at the church where I was serving as pastor. I had just preached a sermon at a Sunday morning service on Jesus's parable of the talent, challenging the members to use their talents wisely. Unannounced, I went among the congregation and gave away $25,000 in cash. People were free to take as much cash as they wanted until the money was gone. The risk-averse congregants visibly shook in shock. The risk-embracing members smiled, rubbed their hands together, and took the bills. The result turned out to be worth the risk. In three weeks time, we more than doubled this initial investment!

Here's another example. For a long time, my son Tim didn't feel ready to water ski. I invited him repeatedly to ski, but every time he responded, "Maybe tomorrow, Dad." I noticed, however, that Tim intently watched every move of his uncle, a terrific skier. One morning, I walked down to our dock to go for a swim. When I got there, Tim was already in the water with his water skis on. I drove the boat around and handed Tim the ski rope. Tim shouted, "Hit it!" I did, and he got up the first time and stayed up to ski twice around the lake. His mental preparation had enabled him to "take the leap" successfully.

William Wilberforce, a British politician, took a giant leap. His conversion to evangelical Christianity in 1785 influenced him to change his lifestyle and set him on a lifelong journey to combat injustice and abolish slavery. He took on the cause of abolition and headed the parliamentary campaign against the British slave trade until the passage of the Slave Trade Act of 1807.

Nicholas Negroponte, on leave from MIT where he co-founded and became director of the MIT Media Laboratory and the Jerome B. Wiesner Professor of Media Technology, also took a giant leap. Negroponte recognized that most of the nearly two billion children in the developing world are inadequately educated, or receive no education at all. One in three does not complete the fifth grade. Along with a core of Media Lab veterans, he founded One Laptop Per Child, a nonprofit organization with the mission to create educational opportunities for the world's poorest children by providing each child with a rugged, low-cost, low-power laptop with content and software designed for collaborative, joyful, self-empowered learning.

To maintain momentum, take small steady steps and occasionally take a giant leap. But the biggest challenge of maintaining momentum might be to simply keep on keeping on.

Keep On Keeping On

Soulwise Conspirators must keep moving in the direction of their dreams no matter what. In spite of difficulties and obstacles that prevent them from doing what they're called to do, they must face the many twists and turns along the way.

Everybody doing something worthwhile faces disappointment. You may be tempted to throw in the towel, but resist the urge to call it quits. Remember Winston Churchill's words: "When you're going through hell, keep going."

Another example. While on a solo outing in Utah's Canyonlands National Park in April 2003, Aron Ralston accidentally set loose an

800-pound boulder that crushed his right hand and pinned him inside a narrow slot canyon. He described how he coped with the ordeal in his book, *Between a Rock and a Hard Place*.

A mechanical engineer with years of backcountry experience, Ralston survived five nights at the mercy of the boulder. He tried chipping away at the stone and lifting it with a series of pulleys but without luck. He smelled infection consuming his hand and knew it would spread to the rest of his body. So he severed his right forearm with a dull Leatherman pocketknife. He then rappelled down a 65-foot cliff and hiked seven miles before being rescued by helicopter.

"Motivation overcomes hardship," Ralston said. "I'd never even broken a bone before, but I had to break two in my forearm before I could amputate. You just do it. The pain was significant but not important. It was a gateway to getting back my life." Today he has special attachments to his prosthesis that allow him to keep climbing.[91]

> *If you're not moving forward, you're probably moving backward because people and organizations rarely remain in one spot. Stopping your work completely may give you breathing space, but it may make it hard to re-energize yourself and your team.*

Twenty-six publishers rejected *A Wrinkle in Time*, Madeline L'Engle's classic children's book, before the editors at Farrar, Straus & Giroux read it and enthusiastically accepted it. It proved to be her masterpiece, winning the John Newbery Medal as the best children's book of 1963 and selling, so far, eight million copies. It's now in its 69th printing.

I can identify with L'Engle. I failed to get my second book, *Goodbye Mom, Goodbye*, published until the 27th publisher accepted my work. However, I must admit that my rejection rate pales when compared to mystery writer John Creasey, who holds the world record of 743 rejections before going on to publish 564 books.

Soulwise Conspirators, as wonderful as they are, present their own challenges to keep on keeping on. Soulwise Conspirators can drive you crazy. Several years ago, a television interviewer asked me if I had ever had the urge to kill one of my congregants. I answered truthfully that I hadn't, but that I was looking forward to burying a couple of them. Even the saints can test the limits.

Sustain Your Passion

In my conversations with Soulwise Conspirators, their recognition of and acceptance of a calling to change the world in some way creates the colorful common thread woven through their stories. They respond to an internal urge that captures their attention they can't ignore and to which they devote their passion. In my life, I have responded to a call to serve humanity in the church as a pastor, in the business community as a leadership coach, and in Africa as a social entrepreneur.

One of the best resources to appreciate the concept of calling is Robert Coles's book *The Call of Service: A Witness to Idealism*. His depth of understanding comes not only from his psychiatric education, but from his personal experience devoting most of his life to community service, working for desegregation in the southern United States, tutoring the ghetto areas in the Northeast, and advocating for human rights.

For Coles, idealism embodies a deeply human impulse that enlightens an urge toward action. In his book, he examined what inspires and sustains calling, how it's expressed, and why it's so necessary to each of us and to society. He indicated the complicated nature of motivation behind serving an idealistic cause.

> *Setting out to fulfill our calling to change the world makes us vulnerable to danger, depression, and despair—the three D hazards of service to others. As a Soulwise Conspirator, you run the risk of being in dangerous situations. The very nature of attempting to change the status quo means running into opposition.*

At the far end of the vulnerability spectrum, you may face danger so fierce that you could be killed in the process of fulfilling your calling. On August 19, 2003, a suicide bomb targeted the United Nations headquarters in Baghdad that killed Vieira de Mello of Brazil, a veteran UN troubleshooter, and 21 other staffers. Another 150 people were injured. Since 1948, when the world body established its first peacekeeping operation in the Middle East, the United Nations Truce Supervision Organization, 709 peacekeepers have been killed in the line of duty.

In November 2004, Margaret Hassan, who spent decades bringing food and medicine to Iraqis as the head of CARE International operations, was kidnapped and slain. I don't point this out to scare you but to indicate that caring for the human family can be risky.

Soulwise Conspirators may also encounter depression. German philosopher Friedrich Nietzsche summarized the difficulty of sustaining passion when he said, "Life always gets harder toward the summit—the cold increases, the responsibility increases." Depression constitutes exaggerated despair that expresses a general sense of futility and hopelessness. The individual loses perspective and just goes through the motions. Energy drains away and fun disappears. Depression is accompanied by exhaustion that takes over the spirit. Fears and anxieties converge to immobilize an individual or an organization.

Soulwise Conspirators are vulnerable to danger and depression, but particularly prone to despair. This often comes when they reflect on the minimal progress of their work. They wonder if what they're doing will amount to much in the end, even though they may have learned valuable lessons from their experiences in the process.

In 2005, journalist Donna Foote visited a friend's classroom at Locke High School in Los Angeles and was shocked to discover that ninth graders couldn't read. A former *Newsweek* writer, Foote had been following Teach for America (TFA), the elite teacher preparation program since its founding in 1990. She soon learned that Locke was home to the largest cluster of TFA recruits in Los Angeles.

Foote decided to write about how we teach our most impoverished students through the eyes and the experiences of our most privileged. Her book, *Relentless Pursuit: A Year in the Trenches with Teach for America*, chronicled her adventure following four corps members during their first year at Locke High. At one point or another, each one of them experienced moments of self-doubt and feelings of futility. TFA reports that 12% of corps members fail to complete their two-year assignment. By comparison, in the regular school system, 14% of all new teachers quit after their first year and almost 50% are gone within five years.

I experienced despair, or what some call compassion fatigue, in the summer of 2007 while working in Kibera slum. It hit me like a ton of bricks. I felt the heavy weight of my calling and perceived that my contribution to humanity was merely a tiny drop in the bucket. What would hardly satisfy any of the overwhelming needs of my new friends in the slum? In the big scheme of things, what difference would my efforts make? I quietly walked from the slum to my apartment at Daystar University and sat, dejected, on the edge of my bed. I didn't know whether to laugh or cry.

Then I looked down at my shoes and started to laugh uncontrollably. I could see and smell fresh shit on my shoes! Kibera has no toilets. The excrement reminded me that if I was really serious about changing the world, I'd certainly get dirty. Changing of systems and power structures and cultural habits can be messy. I also appreciated that my tiny "drop in the bucket" was still good—the very best drop I could offer.

In the light of these three vulnerabilities of danger, depression, and despair, here are four strategies that will help sustain the passion: retreat, reflect, recall, and restore. Let's begin with the strategy of retreat.

Retreat

Take a break to take care of yourself. Stepping back from your work renews your energy and nurtures traits of emotional resilience so you can deal with life's roller coaster stresses and strains. It will help you to be aware of yourself so you can take a break before you're forced to take a break. You'll also be refreshed to tackle even the biggest problems with confidence and hope. When flying, the instructions of the flight crew have implications for taking timeouts: "If you are traveling with small children, put your oxygen mask on first, then help your child." You've got to take care of yourself if you want to do your best to help others.

Reflect

Take time to reflect on the progress of the work you've already accomplished and the difference, however minimal it may seem, you've made in the lives of others. Maya Angelou, a great voice of contemporary literature, put caring for others in perspective this way: "If you find it in your heart to care for somebody else, you will have succeeded." Don't get unreasonably emotional or sentimental. Just tell it like it is with all its ups and downs. "If something comes to life in others because of you," reflected Norman Cousins, "then you have made an approach to immortality."

Recall

Remember why you got involved in your mission in the first place. Recall what initially sparked your attention to dream of how you could fulfill the need you identified. Recollect why you generously devoted your time and energy in pursuing your dream.

Going back to your dream's beginnings will enable you to have a perspective on the good work you've done already and remember why you're committed to your vision. It will also show you how you've grown personally and professionally since you took on your adventure. My Kenyan friends gave me a Swahili name, Ole Nadala, which means the one who jumps for joy. Every morning, I look in the mirror and say my name out loud. I recall my honor to be part of the Kenyan family.

Restore

The underlying purpose to retreat, reflect, and recall is to restore your dream. That way, with new eyes and a renewed spirit, you can attend to your mission with vigor and enthusiasm.

So you can rekindle your passion for your dream and become positively dangerous in making it happen. Erik Erikson, known for his psychosocial theory on social development, said, "Be careful when we try to understand the thoughts and actions of people who are going about the business of changing the world."

> *Be sure you know specifically why you are engaged in changing the world, and with passion rekindled, make sparks fly for the benefit of humankind. Remember when you once sang, "Nothing's going to stop us now," and then sing it again with unbridled determination.*

To sustain my passion for my calling in the world, I turn to this poem by Yehudi Menuhin, an American-born violinist and conductor.

We are granted the greatest gifts of all:
our life
our soul
our mind
and the capacity of wonder.

Nothing is expected in return, save to give
our blessing
our affection
our protection
as would satisfy a thousand lives.

Let us turn again, it's not too late,
and start at the beginning:
honor all life in its variety.
Honor the soul in all its mystery...
Let us give
our blessing
our affection
our protection
as would satisfy a thousand lives.[92]

To deliver your dream—secure commitment, mobilize your mission, direct the flow, and maintain momentum.

You now have a working knowledge of the seven essential steps to becoming a Soulwise Conspirator:

- Discover Your Passion
- Define the Need
- Dream the Need Fulfilled
- Draft Your Dream Team
- Develop Your Strategy
- Declare Your Dream
- Deliver Your Dream

Join with Soulwise Conspirators everywhere and accept the challenge to breathe hope into humanity.

TAKE FIVE FOR REFLECTION

1. Articulate your dream in one simple sentence.

2. What kind of dancing shoes will you wear as you pursue your dream? Are you already wearing them? What do they look like?

3. List three people you'll invite to commit to your dream.

    •

    •

    •

4. What are the top five things you must do in delivering your dream?

    •

    •

    •

    •

    •

5. Describe a situation in which you have sustained your passion for a project. What exactly did you do to keep on keeping on? Be specific.

CONCLUSION

"Mankind faces a crossroads," commented Academy Award-winning American film director, writer, and actor, Woody Allen. "One path leads to despair and utter hopelessness. The other to total extinction."

I agree with the first part of Allen's statement, but I think we have more choices than the two he presents. Certainly, we're at a crossroads. The important thing is that we read the signs to understand where we are and how we can progress as a civilization.

It appears that as a global family we've lost our way. "Half the world," reported the *2008 State of the Future*, "is vulnerable to social instability and violence due to rising food and energy prices, failing states, falling water tables, climate change, decreasing water-food-energy supply per person, desertification, and increasing migrations due to political, environmental, and economic conditions."

We're standing at a crossroads not sure which path to follow. So which road do we take in an environment of unprecedented complexity? How will our story turn out? Will we choose to survive and thrive, or spiral to extinction?

I passionately believe we will not only survive but thrive as a civilization. My singular purpose in writing *Soulwise: How to Create a Conspiracy of Hope, Health and Harmony* is to spark a movement to achieve that compelling vision.

At the beginning of the 21st century, I believe we have the wealth, the wisdom, and the will to breathe hope into the global family.

We have the *wealth* of human and natural resources to rise to our common global challenges. We are at our core inherently good, compassionate, and generous.

We have the *wisdom* of the ages to inspire, inform, guide, and sustain us on our journey into the future. We have the capacity to learn from the past, anticipate the future, and live fully in the present.

We have the *will* to fulfill the dream of One World One Family in which hope, health and harmony are nurtured and celebrated. We have the drive to thrive interdependently so we can be good ancestors.

As I pursue my dreams for The Soulwise Conspiracy, Kibera Kids Kitchen, KaraKibera, and the Daystar University Global Leadership Center, I trust that you will pursue your dreams, too. I trust that they reflect your unique perspective and your loving gifts for humanity.

The Greeks appreciated the distinction between two kinds of time. *Chronos*, from which we get the word chronology, signifies ordinary measured time on a watch. *Kairos* means opportunity time, the right season, the right time for action, the critical moment. As a civilization, we are facing a *kairos*.

> *I encourage you to become a Soulwise Conspirator. Don't delay. Go to the book's website (www.livesoulwisenow.com) and join the movement to breathe hope into humanity. Accept your responsibility as a world citizen. Be a significant part of a global life-saving enterprise.*

Let's stay in touch. Together, we can save our global family.

NOTES

1 M. Scott Peck, *A World Waiting to Be Born: Civility Rediscovered* (New York: Bantam, 1994).

2 John Dewey, "Morals Are Human." *Middle Works.* Vol. 14, p. 207.

3 Allen Tough, *Crucial Questions About the Future* (New York: University Press of America, 1991), p. 1.

4 Martin Luther King Jr. Papers Project, from a letter addressed to "My Dear Fellow Clergymen" by Martin Luther King Jr. from a Birmingham jail on April 16, 1963.

5 From a speech titled "Our Country is in Trouble" delivered by Al Gore to the Democratic National Convention, New York City, July 16, 1992.

6 Anil Hira, "Time for a Global Welfare System." *The Futurist.* May-June, 2007, p. 28.

7 Tough, *Crucial Questions*, p. 123.

8 Mahatma Gandhi, the journal *Young India.* March 21, 1929, p. 93.

9 Statistics derived from Donella H. Meadows in a "State of the Village Report" first published in 1990. See www.odt.org/Pictures/popvillage.pdf.

10 The World Bank, *Atlas of Global Development: A Visual Guide to the World's Greatest Challenges* (Washington: Collins, 2007), p. 95.

[11] Oxfam International, *Fifteen years of conflicts have cost Africa around $300bn.* (www.oxfam.org/en/node/209)

[12] The World Bank, *Atlas of Global Development*, p. 46.

[13] Crossette, Barbara. "Why Children Go Hungry." *The Interdependent.* November 2006. (http://www.unusa.org)

[14] "War" written by Barrett Strong and Norman Whitfield and performed by Bruce Springsteen on album *Live/1975-85* released on November 11, 1986.

[15] P. W. Singer, *Children at War* (Los Angeles: University of California Press, 2006).

[16] James Glanz, "The Economic Cost of War." *The New York Times.* March 1, 2009.

[17] Linda J. Bilmes and Joseph E. Stiglitz, "The Iraq War Will Cost Us $3 Trillion, and Much More." *The Washington Post*, March 9, 2008.

[18] Eric Hoffer, *The Passionate State of Mind: And Other Aphorisms* (New York: Harper, 1955).

[19] Ambrose Bierce, *The Devil's Dictionary* (New York: Oxford University Press, 1999).

[20] "Airline Security a Waste of Cash". *Wired.* 1 Dec. 2005. http://www.wired.com/politics/security/commentary/securitymatters/2005/12/69712

[21] Stephen Prothero, *Religious Literacy: What Every American Needs to Know—and Doesn't* (New York: HarperOne, 2008).

[22] Sir Jonathan Sacks, from his speech "The Dignity of Difference: Avoiding the Clash of Civilizations," 2002 Templeton Lecture on Religion and World Affairs, May 21, 2002.

[23] Bill Clinton, *Giving: How Each of Us Can Change the World* (New York: Knopf, 2007).

[24] "Q&A with Susan Arnold." *The Interdependent.* Fall 2007, pp. 12–13.

[25] www.whitmanarchive.org/published/LG/index.html

26 Marlo Thomas, *The Right Words at the Right Time* (New York: Atria Books, 2002), p. 16.

27 James Surowiecki, *The Wisdom of Crowds: Why the Masses Are Smarter Than the Few and How Collective Wisdom Shapes Business, Economies, Societies, and Nations* (New York: Anchor, 2005).

28 Ibid, p. xix.

29 Dan Buettner, "New Wrinkles on Aging." *National Geographic.* November 2005. Vol. 208, Iss. 5, pp. 2–19.

30 Jim Collins, *Good to Great: Why Some Companies Make the Leap... and Others Don't* (New York: HarperCollins, 2001), pp.17–40.

31 Timothy Johnson, *Finding God in the Questions: A Personal Journey* (Downers Grove, Ill.: InterVarsity Press, 2004), p. 51.

32 Edie Weiner and Arnold Brown, *FutureThink: How to Think Clearly in a Time of Change* (New York: Prentice Hall, 2006).

33 Malcolm Gladwell, *Blink: The Power of Thinking without Thinking* (New York: Little, Brown and Company, 2005).

34 Andrew Strickler, "Subway hero plays it down." *Grand Rapids Press.* January 3, 2007.

35 James Newton, *Uncommon Friends: Life with Thomas Edison, Henry Ford, Harvey Firestone, Alexis Carrel, and Charles Lindbergh* (Boston: Mariner Books, 1989).

36 Maggie Riechers, "A Life in Letters: The Story of John and Abigail Adams." *Humanities.* January/February 2006. Vol. 27/No. 1.

37 Po Bronson, *What Should I Do With My Life? The True Story of People Who Answered the Ultimate Question* (New York: Random House, 2002).

38 Jean Vanier, *Community and Growth: Our Pilgrimage Together* (Toronto: Griffin House, 1979).

39 Eduardo Galeano quoted by Frederic and Mary Ann Brussat in *Spiritual Literacy: Reading the Sacred in Everyday Life* (New York: Simon & Schuster, 1996), p. 369.

[40] George Sheehan, *Personal Best: The Foremost Philosopher of Fitness Shares Techniques and Tactics for Success and Self-Liberation* (Emmaus, Penn.: Rodale Press, 1992), p. 79.

[41] Taleb Nassim, "Learning to Expect the Unexpected." *The New York Times.* April 8, 2004.

[42] Trudy Lieberman, "Fatal Mistakes." *AARP Bulletin.* November 2004.

[43] "Tired interns make more medical errors." *USA Today.* October 28, 2004.

[44] Sternberg, Robert and Lubart, Todd, *Defying the Crowd: Cultivating Creativity in a Culture of Conformity* (New York: Free Press, 1999), p. 283.

[45] Maria Tippett, "Reason over passion?" *Times Online.* April 24, 1998.

[46] Evan Simpson, *Reason over Passion: The Social Basis of Evaluation and Appraisal* (Waterloo, Ontario: Wilfrid Laurier University Press, 1979).

[47] Odelia Englander, Jake Hyman, and Nelly Soudah, youth leaders of the joint Israeli-Palestinian peace movement OneVoice in an audio lecture, "Reason Over Passion: A Partnership for Peace in the Middle East." http://frontrow.bc.edu/program/soudah

[48] Carl Hammerschlag, *Professional Speaker.* July/August, 2001, p. 29.

[49] Stephen Brookfield, *Developing Critical Thinkers: Challenging Adults to Explore Alternative Ways of Thinking and Acting* (San Francisco: Jossey-Bass, 1991).

[50] Beth Adler, "Obama Shines Spotlight on Agriculture." April 3, 2009. www.one.org/blog

[51] Howard Gardner, *Frames of Mind: The Theory of Multiple Intelligences* (New York: Basic Books, 1983).

[52] Gardner, Howard. *Changing Minds: The Art and Science of Changing Our Own and Other People's Minds* (Boston: Harvard Business School Press, 2004), pp. 31–42.

[53] Arnold Bennett quoted by Lea Brovedani in "Mastering Emotional Intelligence to Accelerate Your Career." *Professional Speaker.* July/August 2004, p. 13.

54 Lea Brovedani, "Mastering Emotional Intelligence," p. 11.

55 Joan Chittister, *Called to Question: A Spiritual Memoir* (Lanham, Maryland: Sheed & Ward, 2009).

56 Cathy Lynn Grossman, "Sister Joan's arc of activism travels true: Committed to Catholicism, yet ready to change it." *USA Today*. July 21, 2004.

57 Ronald Gross, *Socrates' Way: Seven Master Keys to Using Your Mind to the Utmost* (New York: Jeremy P. Tarcher/Putnam, 2002), pp. 64–6.

58 Peter Block, *The Answer to How Is Yes: Acting on What Matters* (San Francisco: Barrett-Koehler, 2003).

59 Seth Godin, "If It's Urgent, Ignore It." *Fast Company*. April 2004, p. 101.

60 Bruce Springsteen, "Chords for Change." *The New York Times*. Aug. 5, 2004.

61 Eric Hoffer, *Reflections on the Human Condition* (Titusville, N.J.: Hopewell Publications, 2006).

62 Alvin Tofler, *Future Shock* (New York: Bantam, 1984).

63 Joe Califano, *High Society* (New York: Public Affairs, 2007).

64 Gladwell, *Blink.*

65 Jack Cornfield, *After the Ecstasy, the Laundry: How the Heart Grows Wise on the Spiritual Path* (New York: Bantam Books, 2000), p. 272.

66 T.E. Lawrence, *Seven Pillars of Wisdom: A Triumph (New York: Anchor, 1991),* p. 7.

67 Christopher Reeve, *Nothing Is Impossible: Reflections on a New Life* (New York: Random House, 2002).

68 Michael J. Fox, *Lucky Man: A Memoir* (New York: Hyperion, 2002).

69 Peter Senge, *The Fifth Discipline: The Art and Practice of the Learning Organization* (New York: Currency Doubleday, 1990), p. 340.

70 Mike Krzyzewski and Jamie K. Spatola, *Beyond Basketball: Coach K's Keywords for Success* (New York: Warner Business, 2006).

[71] Ann Roulac, *Power, Passion and Purpose: 7 Steps to Energizing Your Life* (Green Island Publishing, 2006).

[72] "Colorectal Cancer Facts and Figures 2008-2010." American Cancer Society. 2008.

[73] Larry Weber, *The Provocateur: How a New Generation of Leaders Are Building Communities, Not Just Companies* (New York: Crown Business, 2001), p.14.

[74] Chip Heath and Dan Heap, *Made to Stick: Why Some Ideas Survive and Others Die* (New York: Random House, 2007), pp. 14–18.

[75] Allison Glock, "Ashley Judd's Love Trip." *Redbook*. November, 2007.

[76] David Meyer, *The Pursuit of Happiness: Who is Happy and Why* (New York: Harper, 1993).

[77] Chris Knape, "Bono takes GR pulpit: Rock star returns, preaching and pleading for Africa aid." *Grand Rapids Press*. May 5, 2006.

[78] Joe Klein, *The Natural: The Misunderstood Presidency of Bill Clinton* (New York: Broadway, 2003), p. 79.

[79] James E. Lukaszewski, "Becoming a Verbal Visionary." *Vital Speeches of the Day*. Vol. 63 (July 15, 1997), p. 600.

[80] Daniel Pink, *A Whole New Mind: Why Right-Brainers Will Rule the Future* (New York: Riverhead Books, 2006).

[81] Henry Mintzberg, "The Fall and Rise of Strategic Planning" published in this book: Joel Kurtzman with Glenn Rifkin and Victoria Griffith, *MBA in a Box: Practical Ideas from the Best Brains in Business* (New York: Crown Business, 2004), pp. 119–133.

[82] Jack Kornfield, *After the Ecstasy the Laundry: How the Heart Grows Wise on the Spiritual Path* (New York: Bantam, 2000), p. 268-9.

[83] Paul Hawken quoted by Richard Eckersley in "Nihilism, Fundamentalism, or Activism: Three Responses to Fears of the Apocalypse." *The Futurist*. Vol. 42. January-February 2008.

[84] Howard Gardner, *Changing Minds: The Art and Science of Changing Our Own and Other People's Minds.* (Boston: Harvard Business School Press, 2006), p. 74.

[85] Rosabeth Moss Kanter, *Confidence: How Winning Streaks and Losing Streaks Begin and End* (New York: Three Rivers Press, 2006).

[86] Dan Ariely, *Predictably Irrational: The Hidden Forces that Shape Our Decisions* (New York: HarperCollins, 2008).

[87] Gardner, *Changing Minds.*

[88] Frances Hodgson Burnett, *The Secret Garden* (New York: Signet Classics, 2003), p. 1.

[89] Gary Zukav, *Thoughts from the Seat of the Soul* (New York: Fireside, 2001), p. 252.

[90] Richard Restak, *The New Brain: How the Modern Age Is Rewiring Your Mind* (New York: Rodale Books, 2004).

[91] Marco R. della Cava, "One hand gone, but not his spirit: Brush with lonely death lays the path for new life." *USA Today.* September 7, 2004.

[92] Frederick Franck, Richard Connolly, and Janis Roze, *What Does It Mean to Be Human? Reverence for Life Reaffirmed by Responses from Around the World* (New York: St. Martin's Griffin, 2001), pp. 22–23.

INDEX

ABOUT THE AUTHOR

Dr. Phil Johnson, founder of Soulwise International, is an inspirational speaker and life and leadership coach to senior corporate and non-profit executives worldwide. An ordained minister in the United Church of Christ, Dr. Johnson is fulfilling the African proverb, "When you pray, move your feet" as coordinator of Kibera Kids Kitchen, a feeding program in the Kibera slum in Nairobi, Kenya. He lives in Grand Rapids, Michigan. Contact him at drphil@drphiljohnson.com.

VISIT THE SOULWISE WEBSITE
www.livesoulwisenow.com

When he was a child, Dr. Phil Johnson's mother told him the world needs people who are soulful and wise. Her words resonate today as worldwide poverty, hunger, illiteracy, disease and suffering have created an environment of unprecedented complexity and need.

As the world around us gasps for breath, we find ourselves overwhelmed and asking *is there anything I can do to make a difference?*

Soulwise: How to Create a Conspiracy of Hope, Health and Harmony answers with a resounding *Yes!* and serves as your guide to discovering your passion and developing your personal plan to make a world of difference.

Dr. Johnson sees our 21st Century civilization equipped, as none before, to make a change. We stand at what the Greeks called a *kairos*—the opportune moment for action—with a *wealth* of human and natural resources, the *wisdom* of the ages to guide our journey and the *will* to breathe hope into the global family.

Soulwise aims to spark a movement that challenges and inspires conspirators to embrace the dream of *One World One Family* and unleash their collective capacity to care for a world in need. Whether you take action in your neighborhood or across the globe, *Soulwise* invites you to seize this opportunity, engage in an urgent dialogue to shape the future, and discover how you can:

- Be a Soulwise Conspirator—a radical global servant leader.
- Become a catalyst for change in your organization, congregation, corporation or community.
- Make a significant impact on the future and leave a lasting legacy.

As a citizen of vision and courage, *Soulwise* calls on *you* to help breathe life into our suffocating world and satisfy humanity's hunger for hope.

Let's continue the conversation at the book's website
livesoulwisenow.com.